Design'd & etch'd by Theodore Lane.

*The celebrated Dog BILLY killing 100 Rats at the Westminster Pit*

London Published by Knight & Lacey July 1 1825.

# OLD ENGLISH SPORTS

BY FREDERICK W. HACKWOOD

"Sport that wrinkled care derides"
MILTON

WITH SIX COLOURED AND THIRTY-TWO HALF-TONE PLATES
FROM OLD PRINTS

**The Naval & Military Press Ltd**

published in association with

Published by
**The Naval & Military Press Ltd**
Unit 10 Ridgewood Industrial Park,
Uckfield, East Sussex,
TN22 5QE England
Tel: +44 (0) 1825 749494
Fax: +44 (0) 1825 765701
www.naval-military-press.com

*in association with*

*In reprinting in facsimile from the original, any imperfections are inevitably reproduced and the quality may fall short of modern type and cartographic standards.*

# Analytical Table of Contents

Game-cocks naturally pugnacious—The points by which to judge a good one—The age for pitting—The dieting and training of the birds—The rules for matching them—Girth indicative of strength—A contrivance for gauging the size of a game-cock—Fighting weights—Scaling for matches.

Preparation for the cock-pit—Trimming a game-cock for the fight—The cruelty of the practice—How the operation is performed—The spurs—The trainer—His duties after the battle—The treatment of wounded birds—How competitors were named—Favourite strains—The "Hen-cock," the "Wednesbury Gray," and the "Duck-wing."

The cocker's kit—The bird bag—The Cock-fighting Code—The setters-on permitted to handle to prevent ogling too long—And to carry a craven bird ten times to the scratch—"Dying game" though vanquished.

The Main—"Catch weights"—The Welsh main—The "battle royal"—Only one battle for each bird—The bye-battle.

The cock-pit—Indoor and outdoor pits—Tavern cockings—The arena—The "Welsher's" cage.

Popular meetings—Newmarket, Bath, Nottingham, Walsall, Lichfield, Newcastle, Birmingham—Duddeston Hall—Sunday cockings—The "Paradise of Cockers"—A cocking described in detail.

Feeding and "walking" cocks—The Gillivers of Polesworth, the last of the great cock-masters—"Cockspur" village—Some of the Gilliver records—Breeders—The mysteries of the cocking cult.

The patrons of the sport—Schoolmasters and clerics—A Tipton clergyman reproved—Willenhall's Cock-fighting Parson—Noble patrons—The mixed company at a cock-pit—Rowdyism rampant among cockers—Cockers *v.* "Methodys"—Some Bilston records of the sport—Magisterial cautions issued—A barbarous cock-fight at Shrewsbury—West Country depravity (1703)—The "judgment of God" on a cocker—A fatal quarrel over a cock-fight.

Prohibition of Cock-fighting—*The Field* denies that it is extinct now—How the Act is evaded—Police-court prosecutions.

The folk-lore of Cock-fighting—St. Peter and the cock—The weathercock—Charming a fighting cock—How to gain a turn of fortune—Consulting the oracle to spot a winner—Casting spells over a competitor's bird—Sacrilegious rites to secure victory in the arena.

The literature of the sport—Place-names derived from it—The gambling element—Words and phrases coined from the sport—"That beats cock-fighting"—"Cock-pit" a figurative battle-ground—The terms "cock-master," "cocker," "cocking"—"No cock's eyes out yet"—"Cock-stride"—"Cock-eyed."

# OLD ENGLISH SPORTS

## I

### INTRODUCTORY—A GENERAL SURVEY

Sports an index to the national character—The dulness of Saxon pastimes—The privileged sports of the Normans—Mediæval festivals and processions—London's playing-fields—Henry VIII. an all-round sportsman—Church influences on the amusements of the people—Church ales—Sunday churchyard sports—"Lying the Whetstone"—James I.'s declaration concerning lawful sports—Puritan restrictions—"Merrie England"—"The Cotswold games"—Angling—The Restoration recovery—"The Lord of Misrule"—Rustic games—Wenlock Olympian Society—Skating—The Englishman's love of sport—Spurious sports.

THE Sports of the people afford an index to the character of the nation. They show how the people have met the stress and the exigencies of life by varying their pursuits during those hours of leisure stolen from the more serious efforts of bread-winning; how they have taken advantage of their climatic and other physical environment for the purposes of recreation; what progress they have made along the paths of civilisation towards culture and moral refinement; and, generally, it may be accepted that the temperamental qualities of a people not infrequently manifest themselves in the outlets they seek for their superabundant energies.

In early Saxon and Norman times the sports of the common people were few and cheerless. Those most in favour were Bowling, Cudgel-playing, Fencing with Sword and Buckler, the Sword Dance, Wrestling, and a now-forgotten game called Kayle-pins. At a little later period came Animal Baiting and the Quintain.

In Castle hall dances and music whiled away the long winter nights. On summer evenings the Castle courtyards resounded with the noise of Football, Nine-pins, Wrestling, and Leaping.

These were for the retainers—the common people. As to the Norman baron himself and his friends, there was the mimic fight, there was the pursuit of game with hawk and hound.

Rousing the forest game with dogs, they shot at it with arrows. The details of "woodcraft," therefore, became an important part of every noble youth's education; he had to learn the signification of a number of bugle-calls, and how to use his hunting-knife in the precise, formal, and proper cutting up of a slaughtered stag. After the Conquest, to kill a deer or own a hawk came to be regarded as the exclusive privilege of the upper class.

As yet England was scarcely the "Merrie England" of tradition. With the emancipation of the serf, however, the horizon of the peasantry began to brighten, and in the later Plantagenet times the village greens and the open spaces on the outskirts of the towns were the regular rendezvous of the inhabitants for the pursuit of popular games and diversions on all "high days and holy days," saints' days and festivals, which in pre-Reformation times were so frequent, and which did much to break the monotony of a villein's life.

As the Middle Ages advanced, increased intercourse with other nationalities did much to remove the Englishman's churlish reserve, till the London of the thirteenth and fourteenth centuries came to be by no means a dull place to live in. Its streets were narrow, but they were brightened by the dresses of the people—the distinctive tinted liveries of the City Companies — the badgebedizened liveries worn by the retainers of the great nobles — the splendid costumes of the knights and the richer classes. And although the craftsman worked from daylight till curfew in winter, and from five or six in the summer, he had his evenings, his Sundays, and the greater festivals of the Church in which to disport himself.

There were not only taverns with their music and singing to frequent; there were pageants, wonderful processions through the streets representing all kinds of marvels, devised by the citizens to pleasure the King or please themselves; there were plays and mysteries enacting episodes in the Bible or scenes from the Lives of the Saints; there were exciting tournaments and knightly displays to look at.

On the great festivals of the Church feasting and merriment were looked upon as bounden duties. They were Christmas-day, Twelfth-day, Shrove Tuesday, Easter, May-day, and St. John the Baptist's-day (June 24th). Besides Cock-fighting, Boar-fights, and the Baiting of Bulls and Bears, the recognised winter games were Football, Hockey, Quarter-staff, and Singlestick; while in summer Wrestling, Foot-racing, Shooting with Long-bow and with the Cross-bow for prizes, were all largely indulged in, the Eve of St. John the Baptist marking the great Midsummer holiday. On May-day a Maypole was erected in every parish, a May Queen was chosen, and the season of flowers was welcomed with dancing. At Whitsuntide it was all Hobby Horse and Morrice-dancing, with youths dressed up to represent Robin Hood and his boon companions, Will Scarlet, Little John, Friar Tuck, Tom the Piper, Maid Marion, the Dragon, Bavian the Fool, and other famous characters of legend and ballad lore.

> "The Hobby Horse doth hither prance,
> Maid Marion and the Morrice-dance."

The Midsummer-eve festival was celebrated with bonfires, in country places lit on the hill-tops, around which people danced with Bacchanalian mirth and abandonment. In the towns the "setting of the watch," performed under the eye of the aldermen, was accompanied with much parade of fire, and the whole of the proceedings on this day of the year betray some long-forgotten connection with the faded-out superstitions of ancient Fire Worship. A procession of hundreds of Watchmen, carrying lighted cressets, was accompanied by bowmen and pikemen, fifers and drummers, minstrels and morrice-dancers, their armour polished bright and even gilded, making this annual event one of the most beautiful and picturesque scenes of mediæval life. Lighted lamps hung over every good citizen's door, the doors being wreathed in garlands and left invitingly open for easier hospitality; while the songs of prentice lads and dancing girls resounded through the streets almost throughout the whole of the Midsummer night.

"The goodly buildings that till then did hide
Their rich array, open'd their windows wide,
Where kings, great peers, and many a noble dame,
Whose bright pearl-glistening robes did mock the flame
Of the night's burning lights, did sit to see
How every senator in high degree,
Adorned with shining gold and purple weeds,
And stately mounted on rich-trapped steeds,
Their guard attending, through the streets did ride,
Before their footbands, graced with glittering pride
Of rich-gilt arms, whose glory did present
A sunshine to the eye, as if it meant,
Among the cresset lights shot up on high,
To chase dark night for ever from the sky;
While in the streets, the sticklers to and fro,
To keep decorum, still did come and go,
Where tables set, were plentifully spread,
And at each door neighbour with neighbour fed."

Yet another great holiday in the citizens' calendar was Company's day, that is, the day of the saint who happened to be regarded as the patron of the Trade Guild to which a man belonged; for each trade and craft was organised into a separate company for the protection of its own particular industrial interests. On that day the members of a Guild assembled in their own Hall in the morning, every man clad in a new livery, and proceeded in a body to church; the procession was headed by priests and singing boys, chaplains and clerks, after whom came the Court of Master and Wardens, followed by the "Livery"—otherwise the members.

Though these be "amusements" rather than "sports," they indicate the tone of the social life of the period, the atmosphere in which the people lived, and the opportunities afforded them of disporting themselves in the hours of leisure. By such forms of ritual attaching to all the public corporate bodies colour was introduced into the life of the people in mediæval times; something of the kind nowadays would do much to relieve the drab aspect of modern town life.

Towards the close of the fourteenth century Londoners resorted, some to "merry Islington," some to the playing-fields of Finsbury, and some to the wide, unenclosed plains of vast Mile End. Sir Edward Bulwer Lytton, in his opening chapter of "The Last of the Barons," gives an animated description of a holiday scene in the year 1467 on the then newest playground of Old Cockaigne, a green stretch of land lying westward of the pleasant little village of Charing, and recently acquired for the use of the citizens of Westminster.

Although feudalism was slowly dying, both the yeomanry and the squirearchy were still trained during childhood for the soldier's career; and all exercises calculated to make them strong and agile, as Running,

Leaping, Swimming, and Wrestling were regularly practised.

In the cities to wrestle, to cudgel, to pitch the bar or the quoit, as well as to draw the bow and wield the sword and buckler, were among the manly sports and feats of dexterity popular with the youth and manhood of the country generally, but more particularly with what may be termed the commercial element, that newer factor in the social life of England, the bold and boisterous apprentices of the towns. Perhaps the rollicking exuberance of life which characterised the apprentices as a class was attributable more or less directly to their commercialism and their town environment; anyway, it is certain they were regarded as adepts at Cudgel-playing, and the cry of "Clubs" would quickly bring an army of them in the streets for the preservation of their privileges and the determined defence of their common rights.

Had the spirit of the people always reflected the personal character of their ruler, the days of bluff King Hal should have been the age of "sportiveness." For truly of all our kings, Henry VIII. was the most gamesome.

The youthful Henry of eighteen, at the beginning of his reign, brilliantly matched with Catherine of Aragon, was a high-spirited and gallant young Englishman. He was not only handsome and learned, but was vigorous of body and strong of limb; not only a patron of the Arts, but an expert hunter; "a marvellous good archer and strong," a jumper who could clear a ditch with the stoutest yeoman in England, and an athlete who could give points to some of the famous wrestlers of Cornwall. Fond of a horse, a hound, and a hawk, he was at home in all outdoor exercises; and once when he wished to entertain the envoys of Venice, he overthrew in their presence a jouster and his horse, and then taking off his helmet he "came under the window where they were," talking and laughing with them in the most nonchalant manner. Such a kingly example ought to have produced a nation of sportsmen.

But it was doubtless the Church which had the greatest influence over the amusements of the people in olden times. For centuries in pre-Reformation times the parish churchyard was regarded as the public playground on Sundays and Holy-days; and after Matins and Mass in the morning the rest of the day was spent in games and revels which were not always of too refined a character.

Also on the eves of the Feasts of the Saints, Combats, Dances, and Stage Plays were often held within the sacred precincts. Morrice-dancing was almost invariably associated with such religious celebrations; while at Church Ales, Bowls, Dice, Card-playing, and merrymaking of all descriptions were indulged in almost without reserve or restriction.

Church Ales, it may be explained, were generally held in the parish churchyard at Whitsuntide, and were instituted for obtaining money for repairing the church, for helping the poor, and various other charitable purposes; and this was effected somewhat on the same principle as the modern Church Bazaar. The churchwardens begged as much malt as they could, and with it brewed a quantity of strong ale, which they sold at these churchyard festivals, not only to their own parishioners, but to visitors from all the countryside; these Church Ales being extremely popular.

By the thirteenth century it was found necessary to forbid Wrestling matches, and all such games, sports, and dances as engendered lasciviousness, to be holden in the churches and churchyards at these customary festivals. At Salton, in Yorkshire, in the year 1472, Wrestling, Football, and Handball were specially forbidden under a penalty of twopence forfeit.

In 1542 Bonner, Bishop of London, issued to his clergy a proclamation prohibiting all games, plays, and interludes which irreverent custom had hitherto allowed within the churches and chapels.

Even in post-Reformation times—to be explicit, in the year of grace 1570—we read that at Church Ales held on a Sunday there were still practised Bull-baiting, Bear-baiting, Bowls, Dice, Card-playing, Dancing, and other diversions of a less exciting nature, including the "Singing of Songs." In *Pericles*, does not Shakespeare thus refer to a song—

> "It hath been sung at festivals,
> On Ember eves and holy ales."

Little wonder, then, that in 1572 the Protestant clergy of the reformed Church of England were severely censured for neglecting their obvious duties, while thus encouraging all kinds of amusements within their churches.

In the following century the Puritan clergy of the Commonwealth period took up a severer attitude towards Sunday sports; as witness an inscription on a stone forming part of a stile entering the churchyard at Llanfihangel Discoed, in Monmouthshire:—

> "Ye that come here on Sunday
> To practise playing ball,
> Take care that before Monday
> The devil won't have you all."

The Puritan, stern and sour-visaged, found plenty of scope for his censorious invective, and railed at such worldling shepherds as would allow "games to be played in the afternoon, as lying the whetstone, heathenish dancing in the ring, a beare or bull to be baited, or else jack-an-apes to ryde on horseback, or an interlude to be played; and if no place else can be gotten it must be done in the church."

The allusion to "lying the whetstone" in this passage calls for some explanation, for it was one of those diverting practical jokes in which our ancestors delighted. Thus if a person were known to be a confirmed liar or an offensive and unscrupulous boaster, he was presented with a whetstone, jocularly to infer that his inventiveness if he continued to use it so freely would need sharpening.

From this method of curbing the propensity to gross exaggeration "hurling the whetstone" became a phrase equivalent to that better known one, "throwing the hatchet," in the old tale of the man who was so incredibly skilful that he could throw his hatchet at any distant object and never fail to sever it.

Says the old rhyme:—

> "The Whettstone is a knave that all men know,
> Yet many on him doe much cost bestowe;
> Hee's us'd almost in every shoppe, but why?
> An edge must needs be set on every lye!"

Shakespeare makes allusions illustrative of this old jest. In *As You Like It* the appearance on the scene of the fool Touchstone is greeted by Celia as a lucky event, "Fortune's work . . . who perceiving our natural wits too dull . . . hath sent this natural for our Whetstone; for always the dulness of the fool is the Whetstone of the wits." Touchstone was a veritable Whetstone.

Again, in *Troilus and Cressida*, Thersites satirically alludes to the duplicity of Cressida in these words:—

> "Now she sharpens; . . . well said, Whetstone."

Ben Jonson makes a more direct allusion where one of his characters declares to another, "He will lie cheaper than any beggar, and louder than most clockes; for which he is right properly accommodated to the whetstone, his page!"—thus branding both master and man as liars by collusion.

All this by the way. Now to proceed.

Not the least remarkable document which has appeared in the history of English sport was the Declaration of James I., in 1618, concerning what sports might be permitted to law-abiding Englishmen.

James I., though he delighted to be thought a "Second Solomon," was dubbed by his enemies "the wisest fool in Christendom"; for in trying to play the *rôle* of "the father of his people" he often interfered unduly in matters which did not concern him, or (not unlike a modern Kaiser) in a way which the world in general thought more fussy than politic.

The document in question illustrates once more the close connection which always existed between Sport and the Church in those times. For the causes which drew forth this royal pronouncement were as deeply concerned in the upholding of the new Protestant religion as in any anxiety for maintaining the purity of English sport.

We are given to understand that the King on his "returne from Scotland, coming through Lancashire, found that his subiects were debarred Lawfull Recreation vpon Sundays after Evening Prayers ended, and vpon Holy Days. And Hee prudently considered that if these times were taken from them, the meaner sort who laboured hard all the weeke should have no Recreation at all to refresh their spirits."

Here we recognise the old theory that "all work and no play makes Jack a dull boy"; but the King's solicitude for the welfare of his people in this instance will be better understood when it is mentioned that at that time Lancashire "abounded more in Popish Recusants than any County of England," and that their conversion to the reformed faith was believed and declared by James I. to be hindered by "their priests persuading them that no honest mirth or recreation is lawful or tolerable to our religion—which cannot but breed a great discontentment in our Peoples hearts. . . . Also such prohibition debarreth people from using such exercises as may make their bodies more able for Warre; and in place thereof sets up filthy tipplings and drunkennesse, and breeds a number of idle and discontented speeches in the Alehouses."

The argument is a plausible one—from the monarchical point of view. The King therefore benignantly permits Sunday indulgence in lawful sports such as "Dauncing either of men or women, Archery for men, Leaping, Vaulting, and other such blameless Recreation; nor from having of May-Games, Whitson Ales, and Morris-dances."

At the same time were prohibited "on Sundays, as unlawful, Beare and Bullbaitings, and Interludes," and "at all times in the meaner sort of people by law prohibited, Bowling." It was a remarkable manifesto, rebuking the Puritans and Precisians for their intolerance. Strangely enough in this cause there were leagued with the Puritan party, who naturally considered all such practices profane, the Papists whose motives seem to have been mere jealousy that the reformed religion should presume to possess the same privileges as their own.

These fatherly concessions, however, were sternly "debarred to Recusants, and prohibited to all not present at the church at the service of God." To clench the matter, disobedience was made punishable by expatriation, as in the case of recusants generally.

Such was the remarkable edict of 1618. To this Charles I. appended another declaration in 1633, "because in some counties, under pretence of clearing away abuses, the Feasts of Dedication of Churches, commonly called Wakes, have been forbidden."

King Charles therefore promulgated his "pleasure they all be observed, and that Justices of the Peace shall look to it to prevent and punish disorders, but allow freedom to all manlike and lawfull exercises. And also Justices of Assize on their several circuits to see that no loyal and dutiful subject is molested in lawful recreation."

And in these set terms the two kingly "commands" were then ordered to be published by the Bishops of the Church of England through all the parish churches in the land.

It only remains to be added that "The Book of Sports" met with great opposition from the Puritans, and in 1644 the Long Parliament ordered all copies of it to be collected and publicly burnt.

Yet, notwithstanding a declaration so authoritative, objectionable and cruel pastimes, such as Cock-fighting and the baiting of animals, were not discontinued for more than two centuries afterwards; as a matter of historic fact, these degrading pastimes were recognised items in the celebrations of Eccles wake as late as the year 1834.

In tracing the history of our subject we cannot fail to notice that the seventeenth century was remarkable for the decline of the ancient and noble sport of Hawking, and the rise of the newer pastime of Horse-racing—the supersession of an innocent and healthful recreation by a fleeting and feverish pastime, which from the first induced all who took part in it, whether of the aristocracy or of the democracy, to indulge in the unhealthy excitement of gaming—a change in the national habit which, it is contended, has contributed something towards the moral degeneracy of the nation.

But when existed the "Merrie England" of the poet and the idealist? that golden age described in the lines—

> "When Tom came home from labour
> And Cis from milking rose,
> Merrily went the tabor
> And nimbly went their toes"?

Was it in the peaceful days of great Elizabeth? or was it after the "glorious restoration" of the urbane and charming Charles II.? On behalf of the claim for Good Queen Bess's beneficent sway, have we not the testimony of Shakespeare:—

> "In her days every man doth eat in safety
> Under his own vine what he plants, and sings
> The merry songs of peace to all his neighbours"?

For support of the other contention there can be no denial that with the restoration of the "merrie monarch" to the throne of his fathers, there were not wanting at that period certain outward evidences of an exuberant national merriment. But this came of the great reaction after the restrictions and austerities of the Commonwealth, during which the extreme views of Puritan rulers had classed many innocent games and sober forms of recreation with drinking and brawling, with profanity and licentiousness.

The country was heartily tired of the gloom which had accompanied the Commonwealth rule—for unmistakably that was the period when Englishmen began to "take their pleasures sadly"—and the temper of the public mind opened the way for the reactionary tide which then set in, washing the Puritan party aside, and for a time placing supreme power in the hands of libertine courtiers and immoral legislators.

With the removal of all the absurd restrictions upon the ancient amusements of the people, with the setting up again of the Maypoles in the villages, and the reopening of the theatres in the towns, the pendulum perhaps swung too far to the opposite side, and reprehensible excesses of pleasure were indulged in. And there was little to choose between the Carding and the Dicing and other dissolute pursuits of the upper classes, and the Cock-fighting, Animal Baiting, and other brutalities of the common people. This cannot be accepted as the real "Merrie England"—the pleasures of the people lacked in innocent Arcadian simplicity, and the vine-leaf was too much in evidence.

The "Merrie England" of tradition, when our rustics danced hand-in-hand to the music of pipe and tabor, must therefore be referred to that halcyon period of our history when the country—its peasants no longer feudal serfs, but freeborn Englishmen—enjoyed a long unclouded prosperity as the result of the pacific policy pursued by Elizabeth and continued by James I., and which only came to an end by an internal collision, the disastrous outbreak of Civil War.

This was the period when the Cotswold Games were established—an epoch in the history of English Sports. One Robert Dover, living at Barton-on-the-Heath, in South-west Warwickshire, an attorney with strong views of the menacing character of the growing Puritanism, which he considered to be a possible public danger in the future, conceived the idea of organising a national annual festival for the holding of English Sports—for a sort of English Olympia which was to form a counter-

THE COTSWOLD GAMES.

*To face page 14*

check to the spirit of religious austerity then spreading abroad.

We have evidence on the subject at first-hand. Dover states his case for outdoor sport in this strain :—

"I've heard our fine refined clergy teach
Of the Commandments, that it is a breach
To play at any game for gain or coin ;
'Tis theft, they say—men's goods you do purloin ;
For beasts or birds in combat for to fight,
Oh, 'tis not lawful, but a cruel sight.
One silly beast another to pursue
'Gainst nature is, and fearful to the view ;
And man with man their activeness to try
Forbidden is—much harm doth come thereby ;
Had we their faith to credit what they say,
We must believe all sports are ta'en away ;
Whereby I see, instead of active things,
What harm the same unto our nation brings ;
The pipe and pot are made the only prize
Which all our spriteful youth do exercise."

The same arguments against sotting in taverns and public-houses have been raised in recent days, on behalf of Cricket and Football, as were thus pointed out by Dover three centuries ago in his published apologia, from which the above lines are taken.

The formal assent of James I. was obtained to this scheme, and an extensive natural amphitheatre banked up by the ranges of the Cotswold Hills was selected by Dover as the most suitable spot for holding these annual festive assemblages. The arrangements were systematic and excellent in every respect ; all ranks of people were brought together, Coursing and Horse-racing being provided for the upper classes, Leaping and Wrestling for the men, Dancing for the maids, and everything else of a like nature which could command the approbation of the competitors and the applause of the multitude.

Dover never failed to appear upon the ground himself each year, well-mounted, and accoutred to act as Master of the Ceremonies.

And so things went merrily on for nearly forty years, "till the rascally war broke out"; and though the Cotswold Games were revived after the Restoration, they do not seem to have flourished in their later as in their pristine days.

The true-born Englishman can feast his mind on no greater "pleasure of the imagination" than the conjuring up and contemplation of this Arcadian scene in the midst of pastoral England, where—

> ". . . whilst the bag-pipe plays, each lusty jocund swain
> Quaffs sillibubs in cans to all upon the plain,
> And to their country girls, whose nosegays they do wear,
> Some roundelays do sing; the rest the burthen bear."

In 1636 was published "Annalia Dubrensia"—a collection of poems composed in praise of the Cotswold celebrations, to which there were upwards of thirty contributors, including some of the leading poets of the day.

Michael Drayton, in his topographical poem, Poly-Olbion, is responsible for the quotation just made; it occurs in his description of the beautiful and fertile Vale of Evesham, where these jovial festivities were always held around a signal flagstaff erected on the highest hill, the flag inscribed with the terse rallying cry, "Heigh for Cotswold!" Here he pictures in glowing words a pleasant scene of peace and plenty, the country folks sporting and contending, and exhibiting their best bred cattle; the winners of prizes feasting their friends and neighbours on the grass, to the accompaniment of music, song, and dance.

Continuing our quotation, Drayton is found to be most complimentary to Dover :—

"We'll have thy statue in some rock cut out,
With brave inscriptions garnished about;
And under written—'Lo! this is the man
Dover, that first these noble sports began.'
Lads of the hill and lasses of the vale,
In many a song and many a merry tale
Shall mention thee; and having leave to play,
Unto thy name shall make a holiday."

And yet, notwithstanding all this laudation by the poet, how few at the present day know even the name of Robert Dover. The thought occurs—Will the name "St. Lubbock," founder of the modern Bank Holidays, sink in like manner into comparative oblivion? However, to conclude this poetic picture of an Arcadian England, not forgetting that the Cotswold country in olden times was the typical centre of pastoral England—

"The Cotswold Shepherds, as their flocks they keep
To put off lazy drowsiness and sleep,
Shall sit to tell, and hear, thy story told,
That night shall come ere they their flocks can fold."

Then we have "an epigram to my jovial good friend, Mr. Robert Dover, on his great instauration of hunting and dancing at Cotswold," contributed by rare Ben Jonson:—

"I cannot bring my Muse to drop vies
'Twixt Cotswold and the Olympic exercise;
But I can tell thee, Dover, how thy games
Renew the glories of our blessed James;
How they do keep alive his memory
With the glad country and posterity;
How they advance true love, and neighbourhood,
And do both church and commonwealth the good—
In spite of hypocrites who are the worst
Of subjects. Let such envy till they burst!"

It might be said, if only the references were more generally "understanded of the common people" that these renowned sports have been immortalised by at least two allusions in Shakespeare's works. In the *Merry Wives of Windsor*, Justice Shallow, enumerating the bravest roysterers of his own youthful days, names among them "Will Squell, a Cotswold man"; and elsewhere it is mentioned as a mishap to Master Page's fallow greyhound that it was "outrun on Cotsall."

In the accompanying illustration Dover is seen on horseback, carrying his wand as master of the revels, and drawn three times the size of life (in accordance with the antique heroic in art) to give him due prominence as founder of the institution delineated. The upper centre of the picture is occupied by a building (which was a temporary affair, constructed every year, of woodwork, like stage scenery), from which gun-fire salutes were made from time to time during the sports; it was called Dover Castle. Of this redoubtable edifice one poetical panegyrist assures the founder—

"... thy castle shall exceed as far
The other Dover, as sweet peace doth war."

The tents were erected for the accommodation of the gentry, who came in large numbers and from all quarters and distances; the tables spread in the open air were for the regaling of the commonalty.

"None ever hungry from these games come home,
Or e'er make plaint of viands or of room;
He all the rank at night so brave dismisses,
With ribands of his favours, and with blisses."

Ribbons of Dover's colour—yellow—were abundantly used to decorate all the successful competitors, men or animals; for in the Horse-racing only honorary prizes of the most trivial value were given, though in the Hunting and the Coursing the best dog was rewarded with a silver collar. Besides which sports, as the picture shows, there was Dancing for the maidens, Wrestling, Leaping, Tumbling, Cudgel-play, Quarter-staff, Throwing the Hammer, and various other feats of strength and dexterity for men.

The celebration was held at Whitsuntide, and the name of the founder is still preserved locally in the name Dover's Hill, applied to one of the Cotswold eminences about a mile from the village of Camden.

The gentle art of Angling had reached a high pitch of perfection in England at this period, if we are to judge it by a book upon the subject, published in 1653, which has become a classic.

Angling, or the use of an angle made by a rod and a line for the allurement of fish to a baited hook at the end of the latter, is probably older than civilisation. Mention is made of the practice in the Bible. In Isaiah xix. 8 the Revised Version reads—

"The fishers also shall lament, and all they that cast angle into the Nile shall mourn, and they that spread nets upon the waters shall languish."

There was published in 1486 a celebrated book, supposed to have been written by Dame Juliana Berners, sister to Lord Berners, and prioress of the nunnery of Sopewell, dealing with the subjects of Hunting, Hawking, and Heraldry. It is called the "Book of St. Albans," because it was printed there in the year named. The subjects were dealt with most exhaustively, and the work has been reprinted several times and under different titles; and what is directly to the point under review is the fact that the second edition had an additional "Treatyse of Fysshynge with an Angle." But the work which attained to the dignity of a classic is "The Compleat Angler; or, the Contemplative Man's Recreation," of Izaak Walton, which since 1653 has gone through nearly a hundred editions. In reading its breezy pages one scarcely knows which most to admire, its literary excellence or the depth of knowledge of his subject disclosed by the author. No more fascinating treatise has ever been penned on this or any other branch of sport; and to its delightful chapters the reader is referred for further enlightenment on the gentle art of fishing with an angle.

With the Restoration of 1660, not only did the theatre and the cock-pit come in for a renewal of popular favour, but the revels of old-time May-day, Whitsuntide, and Christmas were revived with fresh zest. At the last-named season it was customary for some gay young fellow to be chosen master of the sports, and, as the Lord of Misrule, to be invested with an authority which lasted from Christmas-day to Twelfth Night.

The Lord of Misrule's Court consisted of the usual Hobby-Horse characters, all masked or fantastically dressed, Maid Marion generally being represented by some lanky fellow dressed up in female attire. This band of merry-makers went about committing the maddest pranks imaginable, some conception of which may be gathered from a passage by a contemporary writer :—

"They bedeck themselves with scarves, ribbons, and laces, hanged all over with gold rings, precious stones, and other jewels; this done, they tie about either leg twenty or forty bells, with handkerchiefs in their hands. Thus things set in order, they have their hobby horses, dragons and other antiques, together with their pipers and drummers.

"Then march the Company towards the Church and churchyard, their pipers piping, drummers thundering, their legs dancing, their bells jingling, their handkerchiefs swinging, their hobby horses and other monsters skirmishing amongst the throng.

"And in this sort they go to the church (though the minister be at prayer or preaching) dancing and swinging their handkerchiefs, with such a confused noise that no man can hear his own voice. Then the foolish people, they look, they stare, they laugh, they jeer, they mount upon forms and pews to see this pageant."

It will be observed that the licence these mummers took, and the wild tricks they played, reflected little credit upon themselves or those who foolishly encouraged them with largess.

Of sports proper, Quoits, Wrestling, Cudgel-playing, and Quarter-staff still found favour, though now becoming more popular were the matches fought with Broadsword and Singlestick. And while Archery was still practised at the butts, it was now regarded as a mere pastime, the musket having replaced the long-bow as a weapon of warfare, and shooting with the firearm at the popinjay—a mark in the form of a bird—being considered the more correct sport for marksmen.

The village life of England in the earlier half of the eighteenth century doubtless found its reflection in that of the sister isle, and such has been painted for us in Goldsmith's well-known lines—

> "When toil remitting lent its turn to play,
> And all the village train, from labour free,
> Led up their sports beneath the spreading tree;
> While many a pastime circled in the shade,
> The young contending as the old surveyed;
> And many a gambol frolicked o'er the ground,
> And sleights of art and feats of strength went round."

If these pleasant lines can be applied to this country, surely the golden age of English country life had not as yet passed away.

About this time, however, as may be read in another part of this volume, Pugilism was rapidly rising into popularity among English sportsmen; and this, together with what may be termed the blood sports of Cock-fighting and Bull-baiting, congenial associations, continued to hold popular favour till within the memory of many still living.

In the last quarter of the nineteenth century the Much Wenlock Olympian Society was a very flourishing institution. Its founder and main support was Dr. W. P. Brookes, a Shropshire gentleman animated by a profound desire to prevent that race deterioration with which the neglect of physical training seems to threaten the English people. His fears for the maintenance of British stamina have been certainly justified since his death, which happened some dozen years ago. Every Whit Tuesday a high Athletic Festival was held in the little town, when prizes consisting of medals, silver cups, books, works of art, &c., were given for literary, artistic, and industrial attainments, though the interest of this annual meeting always centred in its athletic competitions which thousands of visitors from all parts assembled to witness. The most attractive contests were the Wenlock Pentathlon, or Five-fold Competition, and the Tilting at the Ring. The latter item was the most popular. Horsemen, after leaping two flights of hurdles, tilted with ten-foot spears, full speed, at a ring one inch in diameter, suspended from a cross-bar. And some of the Shropshire yeomen (who were attired in variously coloured tunics for this contest) were very clever at this pastime; the one who first succeeded in carrying off the ring three times being acclaimed the victor, and with much ceremony crowned with an olive wreath and invested with the champion's scarf. Since the death of their public-spirited promoter these Olympian Games have languished very much.

That SKATING cannot be reckoned among the characteristically English sports only the vagaries of our climate can be held accountable. As early as 1180 it was chronicled that Londoners did "tye bones to their feete under their heeles," and shoved themselves along the ice of the "fennes" (the chains of moat and ditch outside the city walls) by the aid of a spiked staff. Bone runners

Pub^d by Sherwood, Jones & C^o. March 1. 1823.

SKAITING MATCH AT S^T. IVES.

thus preceded steel skate-blades; and the term "skate" is said to be derived from a Low-German word for "shank-bone," introduced into East Anglia by Flemish refugees.

Skating is always bracing and exhilarating; to some the rapidity of the motion through the keen frosty air which it affords is almost ecstatic. Speed Skating, which doubtless came before Figure Skating, requires a combination of skill, strength, and endurance. It is a sport most popular where exist the best facilities for it; particularly among the lakes, on the Norfolk Broads, and on slow rivers and artificial waterways. No better opportunities are afforded than on the Great Level of the Fens, which is traversed by four considerable rivers, intersected by drainage canals, and presents an area of 1,200 square miles easily frozen, with possibilities of continuous runs of thirty or forty miles. Here Skating is very popular, and nowhere is there a prettier winter scene to be found than on the frozen Ouse at St. Ives.

To an Englishman sport is as the salt of life—particularly the field sports of country life. He does not consider any game or pastime a true sport unless the playing of it calls for considerable bodily exertion, and some amount of endurance; and if there is also a spice of danger in it so much the more he likes it.

It is to the manly exercises, particularly to the field sports of Old England, that so much of the national vigour and hardihood are due. Wherever the Englishman makes his home he fails not to indulge his sporting instincts—he plays Cricket on the plains of Australia with the zest of a Cambridge undergraduate, or Football on the veldt of Africa with the enthusiasm of a Rugby schoolboy—and it is honestly believed that he will maintain his dominant position among the nations of the earth only so long as that instinct is unimpaired, so long as the founts of his athleticism are left unsapped.

The modern American citizen, true to the old stock, when returned to his home in the States after a visit to the motherland, cannot recall his reminiscences of the old country without his thoughts reverting to the pleasures of its sports :—

"On a cloudy morn I hear the horn,
  The fox steals from his lair,
The baying sound of eager hound
  Comes echoing through the air.
From find to kill, o'er vale and hill,
  I watch the red-coats fly;
All unsuppressed my 'View Halloo!'
  When hounds are scampering by.

And now I seem to see the stream
  Where trout were wont to rise;
Disciples of 'Old Izaak,'
  Their hats bedecked with flies.
A little splash, a sudden dash,
  I see a silvery gleam;
Five minutes' play, and a lusty trout
  No longer swims the stream."

In conclusion, let it be observed that Sportsmanship, if true, remains untainted by inhumanity, and is never brutalised by callousness. The latest movement is to promote a Bill in Parliament to put down the pursuit of animals under unnatural conditions. The proposed Spurious Sports Bill would prohibit such pastimes as the hunting of carted deer, the coursing of bagged rabbits, and the shooting of birds from traps. Every true English Sportsman will agree that this is a consummation devoutly to be wished.

*The Accomplished Sportswoman.*

## II

## HUNTING

The oldest sport in the world—Ancient British hunting-dogs—The Chase under Saxons, Danes, and Normans—The severe Forest Laws—A royal forest, a baronial chase, and an enclosed park—Free warren—Forest terms—Vert and covert—Restrictions within forest precincts—Red, fallow, and roe deer—the wolf—Technical names for the young deer—And for the antlers of the stag—Other technical terms used in woodcraft—The Forest Courts—Woodmote, Swanimote, and the Court of Justice Seat—Forest officers—The grand battue—for killing stag, boar, and hare—by forming a *tinchel* or ring of beaters—The earliest book on Hunting—James I., "The British Nimrod"—his hunting-grounds near London—The introduction of Fox-hunting and of Coursing—Fox-hunting, a brief history of it—The ideal sport of modern country life.

HUNTING is the oldest sport in the world, having its foundations in the daily necessities of primeval man, who hunted his meal before he ate it, and his clothing before he donned it. The excitement enjoyed in the chase of necessity was altogether too pleasurable to be relinquished by man when he became a civilised being; and to this day the sport of hunting wild creatures is as keenly followed, by those whose opportunities serve them, as ever it was.

The Ancient Britons, the earliest inhabitants of this country, were mighty hunters, those in the northern parts tilling no land, but depending almost entirely upon their prowess in the chase. Strabo says that the dogs bred in Britain at that time were highly esteemed on the Continent, on account of their excellent qualities in hunting; and these qualities, he seems to hint, were natural to them and not the effect of tutorage by their masters. Venison constituted the chief part of the early Briton's diet, and hence their possession of dogs naturally prone to the chase. It is noteworthy that they excluded the hare from their table, notwithstanding that the island abounded with these creatures. Cæsar is our informant on this point, and the inference is that their abstinence arose from some religious principle. The Romans, during their occupation of Britain, do not seem to have imposed any restrictions upon hunting; the maxim honoured by them was that wild beasts, birds, and fishes became the property of those who first could take them.

The Germanic peoples, being much more strongly attached to the sports of the field than the Romans, restricted the natural rights which the people claimed of hunting. Hence among the Anglo-Saxons the privilege of hunting was in time withdrawn from the people, till it became the sole prerogative of the Crown, to be extended at the royal pleasure to the ranks of those already favoured and ennobled.

Asser assures us that Alfred the Great as a boy "was a most expert and active hunter, and excelled in all branches of that most noble art." Athelstan, having signally overcome Constantine, King of Wales, imposed on him a heavy tribute, which included, among other valuables, "hawks and sharp-scented dogs fit for hunting of wild beasts." His successor, King Edgar, remitted a pecuniary portion of this tribute on condition of receiving annually the skins of three hundred wolves. The Danes, being of the same common origin, were equally addicted to the sports of the chase, and we find King Canute, whose edicts were generally of a mild character, imposing most severe restrictions upon the pursuit of game. Edward the Confessor, whose amusements were generally more fitted to the cloister than the field, took great delight in following a pack of swift hounds, and cheering them on lustily with his voice. In the famous Bayeux tapestry Harold is represented with his hounds by his side, and a hawk upon his hand. The boar, be it noted, seems to have been regularly hunted by our Saxon progenitors.

It is a matter of history that with the Norman conquerors came the most severe penalties for infringing the hunting privileges of the King and the nobles. It became a greater crime to kill one of the King's deer than to commit a murder. The forest laws of this period were most iniquitous in their severities.

John of Salisbury, a twelfth-century writer, tells us that "husbandmen with their harmless flocks and herds, were driven from their well-cultivated fields, their meadows and their pastures, that wild beasts might range through them uninterrupted." In no direction was Norman tyranny exhibited with so much inhumanity as in the conservation of the woodland privileges of these haughty Nimrods.

Before proceeding farther it may be well here to explain the distinctions which existed between a "Forest" and a "Chase," and the other forest franchises which were then in existence in this country under Anglo-Norman administration. Such distinctions were, of course, purely legal; nature itself was exhibited much the same way in a forest as in a chase, or in territories by whatever name men might choose to call those respective sylvan areas which they punctiliously graded for their own social convenience.

A Forest was the highest franchise anciently known in England. Only the King could make a Forest. But sometimes a subject might be seized of a Forest, by grant of the Crown, or by prescription. For instance, the Earls of Lancaster had a Forest at Needwood in Staffordshire, and executed the Forest Laws within it as fully as the King himself. The Duke of Gloucester, in the time of Richard II., likewise held the Forest of Dean by special grant. But these were quite exceptional.

A Chase came second in degree, and was the franchise which was usually possessed by the greater barons of England; as Cannock Chase, with its full baronial franchise granted to the Lord Bishop of Lichfield, which actually lay inside the "Royal Forest of Cannock," whose far-extended boundaries encompassed not less than seven hays, or district bailiwicks. As the Forest Laws and the laws applicable to a Chase were different, there was in this inconvenient contiguity sufficient cause for constant friction between the royal officers of the forest and the woodland rangers of the lord bishop.

The term "forest" anciently meant, according to law, a territory of uncultivated ground "maintained for wild beasts and fowls of forest, chase, and warren, the meeres or boundaries of which are fixed and known, and to which are attached particular officers and laws." The latter clause was essential to the designation of a Forest. Without it, such a territory would be merely a Chase.

A Chase, in its legal aspect, was a privileged place for the preservation of deer and beasts of the forest, of a middle nature between a Forest and a Park. It was commonly less than a forest, and not endowed with so many liberties in respect of officers, laws, and courts; and yet it was of a larger compass than a park, having more officers and game than a park. It also differed from a park in that it was not enclosed; yet it was bound to have certain metes and bounds, although it might be in other men's grounds, as well as in one's own.

Thirdly came the Park, the essential feature of which was that it was always enclosed. The right to a park was granted to nobles whose territorial holdings were large, but not so vast as those who ranked themselves next to royalty. The first to empark land was also a Norman—no less than Henry I., who put a wall seven miles in length round his Woodstock domain in Oxfordshire.

The last of the four forest franchises was that known as Free Warren. This was a privilege granted by the monarch to a subject for the preservation and custody of "beasts, and fowls of warren"; a warren was the preserve of the smaller creatures, in fur and feather, which have been carefully enumerated by that legal luminary, Coke, to include "hare, coney (rabbit), roe; partridge, quail, rail; pheasant, woodcock, mallard, heron," &c., &c.

The franchise of Free Warren, or the right to take small game, was one usually possessed by the lord of the manor. It was not always the case; as, for instance, when a manor happened to be situated within the metes and bounds of a royal forest.

As a rule, however, the last two franchises were held after the thirteenth century by most lords of manors. Yet they were held only by special grant and favour of the Crown, it being an old legal axiom that by right "all wild beasts and fowls of chase and warren do belong to the King."

From the legal we proceed now to consider the physical aspect of the subject.

A Forest was a territory of both woods and pastures, with all the rights of chase and warren reserved for the King's pleasure of hunting. The boundaries which were set to a royal forest might consist of a hill, or stream, or highway, or aught else; but they were supposed to be known by every resident in the locality, and were regarded in the eye of the law as if they were a wall. These boundaries were made known to the public by ceremonious perambulations of them by the forest officials at set times.

The term "forest" does not imply that the whole area so-called was covered with trees. It simply meant that it was land kept purposely out of cultivation in order to maintain beasts and birds of the forest. There might actually be towns and villages within the legal confines of a "forest," as is well known was the case of the New Forest in Hampshire.

The bounds of a forest were carefully fixed and then made known, because there were so many offences against the Forest Laws which it was possible to commit within its prescribed limits, and for which grievous and oppressive penalties were inflicted. The whole code made transgressors of any one who did the least thing to interfere with the special privilege of the King and those invited by him to participate in the sports of the chase.

Forest growth consisted of "Vert" and "Covert"; that is, of "green food" for the deer, and "cover" for them in the shape of tree, bush, and underwood.

"Vert," from the Latin *Viridis*, meant every tree, underwood, or bush growing in a forest, and which might cover or feed deer. Fern and heather did not count, but all fruit-bearing trees, including oak and beech, were accounted special vert.

No man might cut timber, even in his own freehold, except under the inspection of the Forester or Woodward. All fences had to be kept low, so that the deer might leap them. Pasture was allowed to cattle, but not to sheep, as they bit too close. Goats were forbidden, as they damaged the herbage.

In the forest jargon of those times the forest trees were called Over Vert—or, in the Norman tongue, "Haut-Bois." The underwood was designated in good Saxon-English the Nether Vert; but the Norman noble spoke of it as "Sous-Bois." Trees bearing fruits, as pears, crabs, hips and haws whereon deer might feed were those distinguished as Special-Vert.

The word "forest" is derived from a French source, and means "out-of-doors," "abroad," being allied to the word foreign; or from the Latin *foris*, because "outside" the jurisdiction of the common law—a fact to which allusion has already been made, differentiating "chase," &c.

To "disafforest" a tract of land, was to remove it from the jurisdiction of the Forest Courts—a process which overtook all these royal preserves in due time.

The "Purlieus" of a forest consisted of the surrounding territory which had been disafforested. A "Purlieu-man" or freeholder within the purlieus, might hunt on his own lands, but was bound to call off his dogs as soon as the feet of the flying quarry touched the sacred precincts of the forest itself.

From inanimate nature we next proceed to the consideration of the animated inhabitants of the forest.

The stag or hart was regarded as the "royal beast" of the forest; until the reign of Henry II. the penalty for killing one was the loss of life or members. After this reign fines and imprisonments were substituted for the barbarous punishments before in force.

The red deer (hart and hind), the noblest of our wild animals, are now to be found only on Exmoor. Fallow deer ("buck and doe"), are kept in our English parks, but are more tame than wild. The roe deer, smallest of the group, do not herd, but mate singly, and live in solitude; they are becoming exceedingly scarce in England.

In venery the male and female both of the red deer and of the fallow deer were accounted as different beasts, owing to their having entirely different seasons; the season of the hind and doe beginning when that of the hart and buck ends.

The "Fence Moneth" or close time for fawning, comprised fifteen days before Midsummer and fifteen after, during which month it was strictly forbidden to all and sundry "to haunt the forest."

The beasts of the forest were the hind, the hare, the boar, and the wolf. The birds then mostly prized were the pheasant and the partridge.

Although the wolf was originally recognised as a beast of the forest, its destructiveness led to its extermination. At first the killing of a wolf within the compass of a royal forest was accounted a "trespass" only, and a nominal fine was inflicted in punishment. In 1289 Edward I. issued a mandate for the destruction of wolves in a number of English counties, but the last wolf found roaming in England was not killed till more than two centuries afterwards.

The wild creatures of the wood were strictly classified in the etiquette of the hunt. For instance, the law recognised as beasts of Venery (*i.e.*, the forest)—Hart, Hind, Hare, Boar, and Wolf.

The recognised beasts of the Chase (*i.e.*, the field) were Buck, Doe, Fox, Marten, and Roe. The terminology of the chase was, in all particulars, punctiliously precise.

The forester, according to Venery, or the recognised code of the chase, had special names for the venison of the Common Red Deer, according to his age; as thus:—

A hart of the first year was a Calf.

A hart of the second year was a Broket.

A hart of the third year was a Spayad or Spire.

A hart of the fourth year was a Staggard.

A hart of the fifth year was a Stag.

A hart of the sixth year was a Hart.

A "Hart Royal" was one that having escaped pursuit of King or Queen no subject might molest. A "Hart Royal Proclaimed" was one made so by special proclamation.

The growth of the Antlers was noted by special names for them, as they developed their points, increasing the number of tynes year after year, till maturity was reached. Thus, Spring by Spring :—

The Brocket had a beam—one straight unbranched horn.

The Spayard had also a Brow-antler—a small branch pointing forward.

The Staggard had a Tress—an extra front branch.

The Stag had a Brow-antler doubled to form Brow and Bez-tyne : also the top of the main beam divided into Sur-royals.

The Hart had Sur-royals becoming more numerous, and the whole antler heavier.

The Great Hart had ten or more points, each larger and longer than before.

A Buck from a fawn became a Pricket, a Sorel, a Sore, and in its fifth year a full-grown Buck. The Roe in the first year was a Kid ; then successively became a Girle, a Hemuse, and in the fourth year a Buck.

Many other terms used in woodcraft were equally precise. To be correct in expression, it was imperative to speak in such phrases as :—

"A Bevy of Roes."

"A Richesse of Martens."

"A Lease of Bucks."

"A Hart harbouring."

"A Buck lodging" ; also, he might be "dislodged."

"A Hare being seated" ; also he might be "started."

A Woodman, who was a stickler for forest etiquette, would also say :—

"A Hart belloweth."

"A Buck groaneth."

"A Boar freameth."

With similar punctiliousness of expression he would say that—

"A Hart had a Tail."

"A Roe had a 'Single,' or a 'Sengill.'"

"A Boar had a Wreath."

"A Fox had a Bush" (not a "brush" as it is now); or, alluding to the use to which it is often put, it might be called a "Holy Water Sprinkler."

"To blowe a Seeke" was to sound a huntsman's horn such as when they seek a deer.

"To blowe a Recheate," was the sound which a huntsman blew to call back his hounds from a false scent.

"To blowe a Morte" was to blow on the horn the particular air used when a deer was killed or being killed.

When hunting was a knightly accomplishment and an essential part of a gentleman's education, it was necessary his ear should be trained to all these blasts in venery; nay, more than that; he was not only expected to be versed in all this lore of the chase, but he was not deemed perfect in his woodcraft unless with his hunting-knife he could make all the approved cuts on the carcase of the fallen stag.

Here are yet other ancient terms, which are now all but unintelligible, except to the initiated :—

"Stable stand" was where the lord stood in order to shoot the driven deer.

"To drive the Wanlass" (or "windass") was to drive deer to a stand while the lord shot at the same.

A "Buck-Stall" was a toil in which to take deer, and could be kept only by one possessing his own park.

The term venison meant really the flesh of any animal taken in hunting; but as the common people accounted nothing as venison but the flesh of red and fallow deer, this sense became generally adopted.

It is almost impossible to realise the state of England under the old Forest Laws; as Sir Walter Scott puts it, in "The Talisman"—

> "By my faith! there is something in these words *Vert* and *Venison* that turns the very brains of our Norman princes."

And again in the same work—

> "I wot well it is said abroad that we of the line of Anjou resent offences against our forest laws as highly as we would treason against our crown."

Hence to afford that close, stringent, and effective protection to the preserved denizens of the forest, there was provided a most elaborate machinery, consisting of special courts with an army of executive officers.

The lowest of these was the Court of Attachment, otherwise the Wood Mote, held every forty days, for dealing with the offences of minor trespassers. If a Forester found a man trespassing on the Vert of the forest he attached him by his body, and caused him to find pledges to appear before this primary court for trial, and (if guilty) commitment. If the offence was against the Venison; if there were any overt sign of having been engaged in killing an animal, as blood on the hands or clothes; or of having any part of a newly slain animal in his possession, he was said to be "taken red-handed" or "taken with the manner," and was scarcely open to bail; but in any case this court was only one of inquest.

The next higher tribunal was the Court of Swanimote (evidently of Saxon origin, from *Swein*, a free tenant, and *mote*, a court) comprising the freeholders living within the forest area, and presided over by the Chief Warden.

The judges were the Verderers elected in full county; and associated with them were representatives of the townships contiguous to the scene of the trespass complained of. This court met three times a year, when all the forest officers were generally present, the dates of meeting being fixed for definite objects. The first meeting, fifteen days before Midsummer, marked the season for preserving the deer during the time of fawning; the second, a fortnight before Michaelmas, was for pasturing domestic sheep and cattle, so far as it could be permitted in the forest without detriment to the wild animals; and the last court of the year was on St. Martin's Day (November 11th) when the Agisters saw to the pannage, or profitable consumption of acorns and beech-nuts by the swine.

The highest forest tribunal was the Court of Justice Seat, which sat only once in three years. The King sent round his Forest Justices, with powers of justice-seat to hear pleas of the Crown. These sent out warrants both to the Sheriffs of counties and to the Chief Wardens of Forests, summoning every one who held land within the forest to appear before them; and their function was not so much to try offenders as to fix the fines and punishments of those previously convicted at Swanimote.

The officers of the forest comprised—

1. The Steward, or Chief Forester.
2. The Forester, or Ranger.
3. The Verderers.
4. The Reguarders.
5. The Agisters.
6. The Woodwards.

The last four classes were chiefly concerned in preserving the woods, the timber, and the herbage; in regulating the pannage and tillage (so much of these as was allowed); preventing the erection of fences or the destruction of underwood; noting the keeping of hawks; "expediting" or maiming the forefeet of dogs (for none within the precincts of a royal forest were allowed to keep dogs capable of chasing a wild beast); and generally in guarding against encroachments, and the numerous trespasses contrary to forest law. The freeholders had generally certain rights of pasture though under very stringent regulations and restrictions.

The Steward, Chief Forester, or Chief Warden—for by these various titles he was indifferently known—was of noble family, and held this high office by grant of the Crown; he was sometimes called "the Rider" by the people. His was a position of great honour and authority.

Under him were Rangers, often of knightly rank, who also were sometimes popularly styled "Ryders" too. And so on, down to subordinates whose duties corresponded with those of our modern gamekeepers. The woodwards had charge only of the woods and vert, and wore a hatchet as a badge of office. Every forest officer, down to the lowest, had power to arrest a malefactor. Forest law did not apply to a "Chase"—only to the royal recreation grounds; but for the infinity of other interesting details concerning this complicated system, the reader must be referred to Manwood's "History of the Forest Laws."

In the reign of Henry III., when many forests were disafforested, the clergy actually protested against amelioration of the severities of the Forest Laws. The first of our innumerable Game Acts was passed in 1496.

At a grand battue the hunt was as mimic warfare; and the arms employed by the hunters were not unlike those used by the soldier, the equipment including bows and shafts, boar spears, sharp swords, hunting-knives, and other tools of the chase. To take part there were helpers on foot to lead the dogs; there were drivers and beaters to rouse the game, and dislodge the beasts from dingles and thickets. As at Chevy Chase—

"The drivers through the wood went
 For to raise the deer,
Bowmen bickered upon the bent
 With their broad arrows clear.
Greyhounds through the groves glent
 For to kill the deer."

All these efforts of the noble huntsmen were mainly directed against the noble stag. For the stag was accounted the monarch of the woods. Was it not one of these hunted creatures the melancholy Jaques, wandering in the Forest of Arden, encountered?—

"A poor sequestered stag,
That from the hunter's aim had ta'en a hurt,
Did come to languish; and, indeed, my lord,
The wretched animal heav'd forth such groans
That their discharges did stretch his leathern coat
Almost to bursting; and the big round tears
Cours'd one another down his innocent nose
In piteous chase; and thus the hairy fool
Stood on the extremest verge of the swift brook,
Augmenting it with tears."

By the Forest Law of William the Conqueror (1087) the Wild Boar was included (with the Stag and the Roebuck) in one of those ferocious decrees which characterised the Norman rule in England; it was ordered that any found guilty of killing a boar should have their eyes put out. The Wild Boar seems to have become extinct in this country during the reign of Charles I.; that monarch attempted to remedy the defect by turning out some wild swine into the New Forest, but during the Civil War they were all killed, and since that time England has known them no more.

The Hare has long been, and still remains, a much-hunted animal. Our modern minstrel, Wordsworth, sings :—

> "Up, Timothy, up with your staff and away,
> Not a soul will remain in the village to-day;
> The hare has just started from Hamilton grounds
> And Skiddaw is glad with the cry of the hounds."

The Beagle, most diminutive of the hounds, seems to have been used for hunting hares and conies.

The younger inhabitants of the surrounding villages were usually requisitioned to assist in the old-time battues ; their duty being to form a ring of wide extent, technically called a *tinchel,* and by advancing and narrowing their circle by degrees, to drive the alarmed animals of every kind before them ; all of which as they broke from the cover on to the open, became the objects of the bow or the javelin, or such other missile weapons as were carried by the hunters ; some were run down and worried by large greyhounds, or not unfrequently brought to bay, and then killed by the more important personages of the hunt. These marksmen stood with bow bent or javelin poised, their well-bitted horses held firmly in hand all the while they kept their eager watch for the expected game ; sometimes the noble steeds were thrown on their haunches at the exciting moment when a rustle in the underwood gave warning that the prey was about to break forth and rush from cover. Then, perhaps, a headlong flight commenced, and the noisy clatter of the chase was kept up mile after mile, over moorland and heath, the solitudes of which were broken for a brief space by the clanging of hoofs, the yelping of dogs, and the ringing blasts of the bugles; till at last the whole chorus of the hunt died gradually away again in the farthest distance. Such was the scene at an old baronial hunt.

After the decay of Feudalism hunting was still kept up by the nobility and landed gentry as much as ever; though now it was unaccompanied by the ferocities of the ancient Forest Laws.

The earliest known treatise on the subject was "The Art of Hunting, which Mr. William Twici, huntsman to the King of England, made for the instruction of Others." The work was in French, and the writer was William Twety, Grand Huntsman to Edward II. The next in point of time was, perhaps, the "Book of St. Albans," to which allusion is made elsewhere.

Though the chase of the stag held the foremost place in olden times as "the goodliest, statelyst, and most manly," yet the hunting of the hare was considered the prime test of a huntsman's qualities; because, said Twici, the Edwardian authority previously noted, "she is the most marvellous beast which is on this earth"; in proof of which he quaintly recounts the superstition of the time that the hare had the power of changing its sex when hunted; he goes on to name other "marvels" of its subtlety and craft, which included "doublings and crossings," tricky running, and other cunning wiles whereby to evade the pursuing hounds.

James I., in his formal advice to his son and heir, says: "I cannot omit here the hunting, namely, with running houndes, which is the most honourable and noblest sort thereof; for it is a theivish forme of hunting to shoote with gunnes and bowes; and greyhound hunting is not so martial a game."

James I. has been styled the British Nimrod. "My health," he would say, "is necessary for the state; the chase is necessary for my health; *ergo* it is doing the public a service if I hunt." And hunt he did, very much; chiefly pursuing his sport in his own parks. Our modern English sovereigns have contented themselves with one pack of buck-hounds; but the Stuart Solomon maintained never less than seven—his hunting-lodges being situated at Royston, Hitchenbrooke, Theobalds, Windsor, Newmarket, Nonsuch, and Hampton Court, to say nothing of other hounds kept for hunting the great woodlands around Newington, and at St. John's Wood. Even in these suburbs of London he kept up an expensive staff of foresters and keepers to preserve pheasants, hares and conies, which in the goodly company of great stags and fallow deer swarmed their leafy coverts. We read of him hunting the stag from Highgate to St. John's Wood; and of his son, Charles I., a few years later, unharbouring a buck from a secluded dingle at Newington, where just previously a few trembling Puritans had assembled for secret worship in the deadly fear of Archbishop Laud. It is difficult to realise these now thickly populated suburbs as royal hunting grounds of great sylvan beauty.

King James had distinct packs of hounds for the several kinds of chase in which he indulged—stag, red deer, roebuck, fox, wolf, hares, and others—besides ban, bear, and bull dogs with a nobleman for their official keeper; and teams of spaniels which were indispensable to the superb hawking establishment he also maintained.

All this necessarily demanded a large suite of attendants; there were Masters of the Game, Sergeants of the Staghounds, Lumbermen of the Buckhounds, Yeomen and Pages of the Leash, and keepers of all sorts and grades.

From the State Papers of the period we are enabled to get an occasional glimpse of James on the occasion of these [illegible]ng parties in which he so much delighted. [illegible]y responding to the sharp sting of Ripon rowels, says [illegible] descriptive writer, we witness the pure-blooded iron-grey that usually carried this royal Nimrod, dash along at the head of the field. "Down the steep, along the valley, through the centre of the shallow river-bed, sweep onwards the gallant cavalcade, scattering the shingle with their horses' hoofs, and throwing up the water in broad, glistening sheets. A bugle-note from some distant forester falls on the ear. The game's 'at soil.' Another five minutes' sweep round that elbow of the stream, and there stands our 'hart of grease,' knee-deep in the amber pool, his broad dun haunches firm against the lichen-covered rock; his beamy antlers lowering from side to side, as the clustering hounds struggle and swim around him, straining their blood-shot eyes. The King, pleased and flushed with excitement, his hunting garb soiled with mire and bogwater from spur to bonnet plume, runs up just in time to witness the finish; for Bran and Buscar, Ringwood and Jewell, the prime leaders of the royal pack, have fastened upon the quarry's throat. And when the deer has been broken up, and whilst the foresters all unbonneted wind the customary *mort* upon their horns, the royal woodsman plunges his unbooted limbs into the beast's warm and reeking entrails"—for, strange though it may appear, this is the extraordinary panacea recommended by the Court physician for the cure of those gouty and rheumatic twinges which at times remind the haughty monarch that he is not exempt from the ills to which human flesh is heir.

Such is a verbal picture of a royal hunt, within a fifty-mile radius of London, less than three centuries ago.

At the present day there are a number of staghounds kept up in different parts of England, at the head of the

THE STAG TAKING SOIL.

*Printed for Carington Bowles in St Pauls Church Yard London.*

list being the royal pack which hunts the country around Windsor. The modern practice of conveying the quarry to the meet in a closed cart, and turning down a half-tame deer to be hunted has, in recent years, aroused an outcry of cruelty; and there has been a well-voiced demand for the abolition of the Royal Buckhounds in consequence.

The term "Buckhound" is applied to the royal pack of staghounds, which are large-sized foxhounds; the Mastership of the Buckhounds is usually held by a prominent nobleman who now goes in and out of office with the Government, although between 1366 and 1633 the Mastership was hereditary in the Brocas family.

In no other district of the British Isles can the sport of hunting the wild red deer be now enjoyed to perfection except on Exmoor, where the unique wildness and picturesqueness of the scenery lends a fascination to it, and where it has been conducted precisely in the same manner since the days of Queen Elizabeth.

Burton, in his "Anatomy of Melancholy" (1660), in giving his views on the sports of his day, says:—

"Hunting and hawking are honest recreations and fit for some great men, but not for every base inferior person, who, while they maintain their faulkoner, and dogs, and hunting nags, their wealth runs away with their hounds, and their fortunes fly away with their hawks."

So that hunting had then become a means of extravagance, leading the landed gentry to live beyond their incomes two and a half centuries ago.

This was the period when the stag was yielding the pride of place to the fox. When Milton speaks of

> "Oft list'ning how the hounds and horn
> Cheerly rouse the slumbering morn"

he doubtless has in his mind's eye the chase of the stag or buck; for when he wrote "L'Allegro" in 1636, fox-hunting, as practised in England now, was quite unknown.

The coursing, or hunting of hares by the aid of the speedy greyhound, is comparatively new as an English sport, though Coursing was known to the ancient Greeks. Late in the sixteenth century the Duke of Norfolk framed "the laws of the leash" on principles so admirable that they have been largely adhered to ever since.

It was Lord Oxford, however, who has been called the "father of modern coursing"; he founded the first club for the sport at Swaffham, in the county of Norfolk, in 1776. One of the most prominent clubs, the Ashdown Park Club, was established soon afterwards, by the Earl of Craven, in 1780. Many other societies were subsequently formed, but it was not till after the passing of Game Laws of 1831 that coursing became more general.

At a coursing meeting two greyhounds are slipped, and the judge, in deciding which is the winner, has one uniform principle to guide him—the dog which does most towards the killing, though he may not actually kill the hare, is declared the victor. The points he goes by are "speed," for which one, two, or three points may be allowed; the "go-bye," two or three points; the "turn," or the bringing of the hare round at not less than a right-angle, one point; the "wrench," or bringing the hare round at less than a right-angle, half-a-point; the "kill," one or two points, or sometimes less; and the "trip," where the hare is thrown off his legs, one point.

The Waterloo Cup, which is run for annually in the early spring of the year, on the "plains" of Altcar in Lancashire, land belonging to Lord Sefton, is the most famous coursing meeting of the present day. This prize, designated sometimes "The Blue Ribbon of the Leash," was instituted in 1836. The first ground over which

THE COURSER.

*[From a painting by G. H. Laperte. Published, 1828, by Sherwood & Co.]*

"inclosed" coursing took place was at Plumpton, in Sussex, in 1876.

The Greyhound hunts by sight, and conquers by superior speed. It was formerly customary to hunt the hare with Beagles, the most diminutive of the hounds. The Beagle is prized for its keenness of scent and its perseverance in following the trail; if distanced by the hare at first it is sure to kill it in the end; and the cry of the dog while hunting is considered quite musical.

The Beagle has been superseded by the Harrier, a dog something like a small-sized foxhound, and though deficient in speed, a hound capable of hunting on a much colder scent. Beagles and Harriers are hunted in packs, and it is customary to follow them on foot, using leaping poles, as when out with Otter hounds.

In the Middle Ages the fox was merely hunted for extermination; being regarded as vermin, it was deemed legitimate to accomplish his death by any means, and the usual practice was to drive him either into nets or into ground and then dig him out.

Even when regarded as a "beast of the chase," he was classed in an inferior rank, and dubbed the "beast of stinking flight." Records show that the fox was hunted in the time of Edward I., that monarch maintaining an officer, one William de Foxhunte, to superintend an establishment of six couple of foxhounds, two boys, and a horse to carry the nets.

It was not till the middle of the seventeenth century that the fox attained to that greater dignity which made the hunting of him to be regarded as a worthy branch of sport. By the time of William III. several packs of staghounds had been changed for foxhounds. The first to make the change—just prior to 1689—was the Charlton Hunt (now the Goodwood) in Sussex.

Among other old-established packs of foxhounds are

the Sinnington (Yorkshire) Hounds, the descendants of the Duke of Buckingham's pack which hunted the Hambleton country in 1686; the Quorn Hunt established by Mr. Boothby in 1698; the famous Belvoir pack established by the third Duke of Rutland in 1740; and the Pytchley Hounds, of which Lord Spencer was the first master in 1750.

It was about 1762 that the Duke of Beaufort changed his pack from staghounds to foxhounds; and as the eighteenth century wore on an increased importance gradually but steadily accrued to the sport, till there was scarcely a part of the country that was not regularly hunted. The Berkeley country extended from Bristol to London; the Cottesmore area covered a larger slice of Leicestershire than it does now; while the Duke of Beaufort hunted from Badminton to Chipping Norton. These are merely a few of the leading establishments which have had an unbroken existence from the earliest period of fox-hunting. At the present time there are upwards of 150 packs in the country.

It has been claimed by some authorities that the first steady pack of foxhounds was got together by Squire Fownes, of Stepleton, Dorsetshire, in 1730. Before this pack was raised the hounds that hunted Cranbourn Chase are said to have hunted all the animals promiscuously, except the deer, from which of course they were steadily kept.

The county of Leicester, which is pastoral, with the town of Melton Mowbray as a centre, is now accounted the headquarters of the sport. The locality is one that presents two kinds of fences which try the mettle of both man and horse to leap them in good style.

One is the ox-fence, which is used as the only effective barrier against the roaming of cattle from their pastures, during the season of the gadfly; the hunter confronted

*Figures by Morland* *Landscape by Girtin*

**THE EARTH STOPPER.**

[*Published, 1805, by J. Wheble, Warwick Square.*]

*To face page 47*

by one of these has to clear in one flying leap a wide ditch, bordered by a strong blackthorn hedge, and beyond that a four-foot rail.

The other kind is called the bullfinch-fence. This is of more frequent occurrence, and consists of a high and thick quick-set hedge of long growth, with a ditch on one side of it. The horseman has to charge it at full speed in order to push his way through, and the bushes close upon him again immediately, leaving no more trace than if a bird had hopped through.

The Melton Mowbray country is thronged with sporting visitors during the season, who spend at least some £100,000 a year here. In the vicinity is the celebrated Quorn pack of hounds, so called from Quorndon Hall (formerly the residence of a very well-known hunting man, Mr. Meynell), and the foremost pack of foxhounds in England.

The majority of packs are maintained by subscriptions; and a considerable sum per year is required for the purpose. There are expenses connected with stables and kennels; money is required for the keep of horses and hounds, and the payment of stable-men, kennel-men, feeders and helpers, the whipper-in who manages the kennel staff, and sometimes a stud-groom, and hunt servants of all kinds. Sometimes the coverts have to be rented; and nearly always compensation has to be paid to farmers for damage done by the "preserved" foxes.

It has been estimated that it requires at least £1,800 for the upkeep of a pack, hunting three times a week during the season; and that not less than a quarter of a million of money a year is spent in this country on the pursuit of fox-hunting. Some packs have been maintained solely at the expense of one individual; as those of Sir Watkins Wynne, and of Earl Fitzwilliam, both of which have afforded gratuitous sport to the neighbours of these wealthy and enthusiastic fox-hunters.

Fox-hunting is pre-eminently the sport of the English country gentleman. It is a sport which requires considerable pecuniary means to bear the expenses it entails, and the possession of an amount of physical courage and activity for the hard riding it necessitates. To be "M.F.H." requires a very ample income indeed; and when no one will undertake the heavy liability of a Master, the pack is generally managed by a committee.

Of all hunting enthusiasts, none have been more distinguished in the annals of the sport than the celebrated Assheton Smith, of Tedworth, in Hampshire, who, possessed of a fine estate, and endowed with great strength and courage, was a Master of Hounds for no less than fifty years, regularly riding hard after them till he reached the age of eighty.

The fox-hunting season extends from the latter part of October to the beginning of April, the period when the fields are clear of their produce—although cub-hunting for trying the puppies is commenced much earlier.

At one time it was customary for the hounds to meet early in the morning; as the old hunting-song has it—

> "Do you ken John Peel at the break of the day
> With his horse and his hounds in the morning?"

but now the fashionable hour is about ten or eleven o'clock. And if attention to detail would ensure the success of a run, the enthusiastic hunter would never fail to enjoy it; for in the earliest hours of the morning the gamekeepers on all the surrounding estates have been requisitioned for "earth stopping," and other preliminaries of a precautionary nature.

As the hour fixed for the meet approaches, the assembly of the mass of sturdy dogs, with a forest of tails waving in eager anticipation of the run, though every animal is under the strictest control, and the grouping of a gallant

The Rondezvous

To face page 49

body of red-coated, well-mounted horsemen, all lend colour and animation to the picturesqueness of the scene.

While the huntsmen wait about, the dogs proceed to "draw" some adjacent wood, or spinney, or gorse ; the fox being tracked by his "drag"—that is, the scent left by Reynard on the ground as he returned from his nightly prowl in search of prey—and, when found, he is allowed a little law ere the Whipper-in gives the "Halloa!" announcing the fact, for fear he may be frightened by the cry and turn back.

Then is the stirring moment, to see the grand burst when the fox has started, and the cry of "Tallyho! Gone away!" breaks forth from every throat. With the hounds in full cry the hunt sweeps over hill and dale till it is lost to sight and sound in the far and fading distance.

The success of a run depends much upon the prevailing atmospheric conditions. If it is dry, or a sharp northerly breeze prevails, the scent or exhalation from the hunted animal is rarefied and dissipated, and leaves nothing for the dogs to trace. The best conditions are a moist air, without actual rain, and a gentle gale from south or west, which induce the scent to cling to the soil and the vegetation ; or, better still, when it is suspended in the air at a little distance from the earth, and thus enables the dogs to follow it breast high at full speed, without having to keep their noses close to the ground.

"A southerly wind and a cloudy sky
  Proclaim a hunting morning ;
Before the sun rises we'll nimbly fly,
  Dull sleep and a downy bed scorning.
    To horse, my boys, to horse, away ;
    The chase admits of no delay!

On horseback we've got, together we'll trot;
On horseback, on horseback, together we'll trot.
Leave off your chat, see the cover appear;
The hound that strikes first, cheer him without fear;
Drag on him! ah, wind him, my steady good hounds,
Drag on him! ah, wind him, the cover resounds."

Such is the commencement of another famous hunting lay. But it has been contended that the author of this well-known song could not have been a practical fox-hunter, as the conditions here set forth are not invariably the best, so many unknown causes being found to affect the scent.

Other things, too, may mar the success of a run; the fox may baffle the hounds by returning to cover, or sometimes may run back right into the mouths of the dogs. Or some horseman, more eager than sportsman-like, may over-ride the hounds, or hinder them by some unpardonable *gaucherie* of the hunting-field.

All these things are anathema to the fox-hunter. On the other hand, the very yelping of the dogs is as music, "glorious music," in his ears, and he will dilate with rapture on the cry of a pack. Did not Sir Roger de Coverley decline a hound sent to him as a present, informing the sender, with all courtesy, that the dog in question was an excellent "bass," but that at present he wanted only a "counter-tenor"! And if it were required to demonstrate the intense hold which this pursuit gets upon the typical country gentleman, there is the case in Fielding's novel, "Tom Jones," of Squire Weston being drawn from the serious and urgent quest of his eloping daughter, to join incontinently in the merry, mad chase of a pack of hounds, which happened to cross his path! Could infatuation any further go than this?

T. Cook, Sculp.

DEATH OF THE FOX.

*[From a much admired painting in the Exhibition at the Royal Academy. Published 1793, by J. Wheble, Warwick Square.]*

# III

## HAWKING

Falconry preceded the invention of the fire-arm—Introduced into England in eighth century—The legend of St. Edmund the Martyr—A favourite sport under the Plantagenets—Followed by nobles, the clergy, and the privileged citizens of London—The ancient love of hawk and hound—Till the time of James I. —The decline of Falconry—A hawking party—The equipment of the bird—Hawking custom—The Anglo-Norman laws—The high value of trained birds—The various species of hawks reserved to the different social grades—More pedantic hunting jargon—The Hereditary Grand Falconer of England.

HAWKING can only be considered a modern invention when put in comparison with hunting.

By Hawking is meant the art of training and flying hawks for the purpose of catching other birds. It is frequently called Falconry; the person charged with the care of the hawks was not called a hawker, but always designated a falconer.

Falconry was a favourite sport in the far-away times before the invention of the firearm had enabled man to attack elusive game on the wing; for feathered game, that was inaccessible to the arrow, was never out of the range of a swift-winged falcon. In olden times, therefore, this sport occupied the place now filled by modern shooting.

Hawking was introduced into this country during the Saxon era, probably about the eighth century; and a romantic legend pretends to connect the martyrdom of St. Edmund, King of East Anglia, with this pastime.

A Danish chieftain of high rank, named Lothbroc, hawking near the western coasts of Denmark, was dismayed to find his bird, in the keen pursuit of her game, fall into the sea. Anxious for the safety of the hawk, he quickly launched a small boat with the intention of recovering her. But a storm suddenly arose which blew him out to sea, and after suffering much hardship he was eventually stranded on the coast of Norfolk, at a place called Rodham. Here he was seized by the inhabitants and sent prisoner to the Court of King Edmund.

The King received him favourably, and soon became particularly attached to him on account of his skill in training and flying hawks. Edmund's partiality, however, roused the jealousy of Beoric, the King's falconer, who took the opportunity to murder the Dane as he was exercising his birds in the midst of a wood. The secreted body being discovered by the vigilance of a favourite spaniel, the crime was brought home to Beoric, who was condemned to be put in an open boat—the same in which the murdered man had been carried to England—without rudder, oar, mast, or sail, and abandoned to the mercy of the waves. Watchful fate wafted the culprit to the very point of land from which Lothbroc had started ; when he landed he was apprehended by the Danes and taken before two of their chieftains, Hinguar and Hubba—no other than the sons of the ill-fated Lothbroc.

The crafty Anglian, discovering this relationship, sought to gain their favour by recounting the murder of their father, who (he falsely affirmed) was executed at the command of King Edmund ; for opposing which, and for endeavouring to save the life of the Danish nobleman, he said he had been committed to the dangers of the deep ; but providentially he had escaped them, spared to wreak a just vengeance on the perfidious Anglians. Incited by this villain, the Danes undertook that invasion of East Anglia which resulted, not only in the pillage and devastation of the country, but in the particularly dastardly martyrdom of King Edmund, who was tied to a tree and shot to death with arrows. Such is one variant of the legend of Bury St. Edmunds.

That studious King, Edward the Confessor, was addicted to Hawking as an agreeable outdoor exercise; and Alfred the Great is reported to have written a treatise on the subject.

Among the hardier barons of the early Anglo-Norman period the sport is said to have been despised as effeminate, and relegated chiefly to the amusement of ladies. And it long remained one of the most popular outdoor amusements enjoyed by the fair sex. The training of a hawk for the field was reckoned an essential part of the education of a young Saxon nobleman; but it was not till a considerable interval after the Conquest that Hawking became again a favourite pastime, and then always reserved exclusively to the upper classes. King John was partial to fine horses, staunch hounds, and good hawks. These creatures were sometimes received in large payments, instead of money, or accepted as presents fit for a noble.

In the time of Edward I. the amusement was reduced to a perfect science, regular rules being formulated for its practice; and the Master of the Game under Henry IV. revised and expanded these rules for the use of Henry, Prince of Wales, the popular "Madcap Harry."

According to Froissart, when King Edward III. invaded France, he was accompanied by no less than thirty falconers on horseback; his fondness for the sport could not induce him to forego it, even during an arduous campaign in a foreign country.

Hawking was much followed by the clergy, notwithstanding that it was forbidden to them by the canons of the Church; and as they persisted in the pursuit of this fashionable amusement they were frequently lashed most severely by the moralists and censorious rhymsters of the period.

The citizens of London were exceptionally favoured by certain concessions made to them under royal charter, in respect of this aristocratic sport.

Persons of high rank rarely appeared in public without their dogs and their hawks; the latter they even carried with them on their longest journeys. Hawks have been carried into battle; and men taken prisoners with them have been known to decline to purchase freedom by parting with a favourite bird. Such a sacrifice was deemed ignominious. These birds were considered as ensigns of nobility, and it was accounted dishonourable for a man of rank to give up his hawk. Hounds and hawks were even taken to church occasionally, to the unseemly interruption of divine service. Thus Sebastian Brant's work, "Stultifera Navis" ("The Ship of Fools"), translated from the German by Alexander Barclay (1508) hath it—

> "Into the Church then comes another sotte
> Withouten devotion, jetting up and down,
> Or to be seene, and showe his garded cote.
> Another on his fiste a sparhawke or fawcome—"
>
> &c., &c.

There is an amazing story (*Gentleman's Magazine*, 1793) to the effect that a favourite hawk of James I., lost in 1610, was found at the Cape of Good Hope, alive and sound, in 1792. A gold collar on its neck was engraved—"This goodlie hawk doth belong to his most excellent majestie, James, King of England, A.D. 1610."

A. Cooper, R.A., Pinx. E. Hacker, Sculp.

MY LADY'S HOBBY.

[*Published by Rogerson & Tuxford, 246 Strand.*]

*To face page 55*

A reference to Sir Anthony Weldon's history of the Court of that monarch discloses an account of King James going forth from Newmarket that year, to witness the flight of some special birds; one he witnessed was "the most stateliest flight of the world for the high mountee"; for "the kite went to such a mountee, as all the field lost sight of kite and hawke and all, and neither kite nor hawke were either seen or heard of to this present, which made all the Court conjecture it a very ill omen." The cult of Hawking, it may be mentioned, was not without its own special group of superstitions.

The pursuit of the pastime was one which involved considerable expense; the practice of it was overlaid with a jargon of terms which were necessary to be learnt by one who would fit himself for the company of others in the field; in fact, in the course of centuries Hawking became a semi-science which required no small effort of study to master.

Falconry held despotic sway for many centuries, but was never more fashionable than in the Stuart period. To such a height was the amusement then carried, no gentleman was deemed completely dressed for company unless a glove were on his left hand, and a hawk sitting upon it. He who bore the hawk in the most graceful manner was considered the most accomplished cavalier; and to please the ladies it was the practice to play flirting tricks with the plumes of the birds, just as the ladies did with their fans.

Old John Aubrey, the antiquary, says (1678): "In the last age every gentleman-like man kept a sparrow-hawk, and the priest a hobby; as Dame Berners teaches us (who wrote a treatise on Field Sports, *temp.* Henry VI.), it was a divertisement for young gentlewomen to manne sparrow-hawks and merlins."

The decline of Falconry was brought about by the

perfecting of the hand-gun, musket, or fowling-piece. And the fall was very rapid; the sport was at its zenith at the commencement of the seventeenth century, and by the end of it was rarely practised. A few years afterwards it was hardly known.

And, though ousted by firearms, it is curious to note that towards the last it actually became a custom to fire off pistols, in order to make the quarry rise on the wing, that the trained bird might deliver its attack.

In later times a few hawks were trained in the neighbourhood of Bridport, Dorsetshire, for the taking of landrails in the hemp and flax fields near that town. This was scarcely sport, however.

A hawking party was a merry sight at any season, and was particularly exhilarating when seen cantering over a carpet of dry leaves in autumn, perhaps wending a way to some pool or water where there was the likelihood of abundant game. There, if a large party, it would break up into sets for the better working of the hunt.

The sport was one which could be pursued either on horseback or on foot; if it were open country the former method was employed, but through the woods and coverts it was necessary to proceed on foot, and to employ a stout pole for leaping across the ditches and rivulets.

It is related of Henry VIII., that one day hawking on foot in the neighbourhood of Hitchen, he was leaping across a storm-flooded ditch when his pole broke, and he was precipitated head-first into the mud; and we learn that it was only the promptitude of an attendant footman which saved the burly Harry from an untimely death by suffocation.

Each rider in a mounted party carried a hooded falcon on his or her wrist, protected from the sharp talons of the bird by a leather gauntlet; and on arrival at the haunt of the game, when a heavy-winged heron or a flight of noisy ducks rose from the water, removed the hood of the bird, gave it sight of the quarry, and let it slip in pursuit.

For when a hawk was not flying at her game she was hoodwinked with a hood or cap fitted on the head for that purpose. When carried "on the fist," as the phrase was, the bird was held captive by little straps of leather called jesses, having one end attached to the creature's legs, and the other allowing knots to appear between the middle and the little fingers of the hand that held them, so that lunes or small thongs of leather might be fastened to them by two tyrrits (or slip-rings), the lunes being kept loosely wound round the little finger.

Jesses might sometimes be made of silk. To each leg of the bird was fastened also a tiny tinkling bell, attached by leathers called bewits. The bells were equal in weight, but one was a semitone below the other; for they were sonorous, shrill, and musical, though not of a size to impede the flight. These bells were often of silver, and always of fine make and design, the best coming from Milan. A character in one of Thomas Heywood's old plays, speaking of a hawk's flight, is made to utter this opinion—

> "Her bels, Sir Francis, had not both one waight
> Nor was one semitune above the other.
> Mei thinkes these Milanes bels do sound too full
> And spoile the mounting of your hawke."

In a flight of hawks it was sometimes arranged that the different bells varied in tone, so a babel of sweet sounds might be produced.

To the bewits was attached the creance, a long thread by which the bird, in tutoring, was drawn back after being allowed to make a short, tentative flight. Says Othello, speaking of his wife—

> " If I do prove her haggard
> Though that her jesses were my dear heart-strings
> I'd whistle her off, and let her down the wind
> To prey at fortune."

Hawks and falcons were caught young, and trained for the purpose by a man called a falconer. The swift, keen-sighted bird when properly trained swept through the air in pursuit of its quarry, soared high above it, and then, descending with a sudden swoop, struck his fatal talons and yet more fearful beak into its back and head, and bore the victim dead to the ground.

A hawking costume included a large purse, suspended from the girdle, in which to carry the implements of the chase, or to stow the hood and the jesses when they were removed from the hawk.

The hood was made of leather or velvet, often enriched with needlework, and surmounted with a tuft of feathers. This crest was not only an ornament, but was useful to take hold of while unhooding the bird.

Only persons of rank were permitted to keep hawks under the early Anglo-Norman laws; but a clause in the Forest Charter which King John was forced to sign granted to every freeman the privilege of having "airies of hawks, sparrow-hawks, falcons, and eagles in his own woods." In the reign of Edward III. it was ordered by statute that any person finding a hawk, tercelet, laner, or other species of hawk, was to take it to the Sheriff, who was to endeavour to find the owner by proclamation throughout his county; failing which, after four months, it might be given to the finder, providing he was a person of rank, and paid the Sheriff's expenses in the matter. Concealment was made a felony

A SPORTSMAN OF THE 16th CENTURY.

*To face page 58*

and severely punished. A bishop of Ely once solemnly excommunicated the persons who stole his hawks while he was conducting divine service, accounting the miscreant's crime as equivalent to sacrilege. The laws of England relating to falconry always prohibitive and arbitrary, were often as capricious as they were severe, being altered from time to time, till the reign of Elizabeth, to which period they made it a felony punishable by both fine and imprisonment even to destroy the eggs of these much-prized birds.

After the amelioration of these severities in Elizabeth's reign, the beginning of the seventeenth century found the price of these birds, when they changed hands, reaching a high figure. Indeed it was always considered a favour to sell; and this no doubt because of the incredible pains, the incessant watchfulness by night as well as by day, always necessary for the correct training and exercising of them.

A perfectly trained hawk was deemed a present fit for a king or an emperor; and skilful falconers were often rewarded in a princely manner. In the reign of James I. Sir Thomas Monson gave a thousand pounds for a cast of hawks. (A cast of hawks of toure, says an old book on this subject, signifies two, and a lese three.)

It was the close and continuous attention bestowed on a favourite bird which in time subdued its natural wildness, and made it familiar with its master. It was deemed no loss of dignity for the greatest noble to cut up the meat for the food of his favourite bird.

In training a bird to fly at game, an instrument called a "lure" was used. It was made in the shape of a bird's pair of wings, being formed in part of wing-feathers, inserted in a pad of leather or velvet, quilted with needlework, and having on the centre of the shoulder, or top, a swivel-hook to which a cord was attached.

This lure being thrown into the air, and guided like a boy's kite by a string, the fierce bird was taught to fly at and strike it, as if it were a real bird. At the same time he was just as carefully taught to desist, and return to his master's wrist at the call of his whistle.

> "The eager hawk, with sudden sight of lure,
> Doth stoop, in hope to have his wished prey;
> So many men do stoop to sights unsure;
> And courteous speech doth keep them at the bay.
>
> Let such beware, lest friendly looks be like
> The lure, to which the soaring hawk did strike."

Of the numerous species of hawks the Peregrine Falcon was the most celebrated among falconers, being esteemed for its superior dash and courage. The female is much the larger and more powerful bird, and is called the Falcon, while the male is known as the Tiercel. One caught wild in full plumage and intractable was termed a Haggard; and, in the reverse of this, one perfectly trained, docile, and tractable was called a Gentle.

The Jer-falcon, or Noble, was also much prized for its fire and dash in the pursuit of its quarry. The Saker Falcon, of South-eastern Europe, belongs to this species. Another European hawk was the Lanneret, which again was inferior in size to its female, the Lanner. The Goshawk and the Sparrow-hawk have very short wings, and are therefore inferior to the true falcons in the power of flight. They were called "hawks of the fist," as they were flown at game from the hand, instead of soaring down on the quarry from above. The Goshawk was chiefly employed to take hares and rabbits.

The Hobby and the Merlin are among the smaller falcons of the British Isles. The Kestrel belongs to the short-toed hawks, and is less fierce than the nobler ones mentioned. In Falconry the birds were esteemed and graded according to their size and ferocity in attack.

The etiquette of the sport assigned to different ranks of persons different sorts of hawks. For instance, an old authority on Hawking placed the different ranks of men and the different species of bird proper to be used by them in the order following :—

For an Emperor—the eagle, the vulture, and the merloun.
For a King—the Ger-faulcon and the tercel of the Ger-faulcon.
For a Prince—the faulcon gentle and the tercel gentle.
For a Duke—the faulcon of the rock.
For an Earl—the faulcon peregrine.
For a Baron—the bastard.
For a Knight—the sacre and the sacret.
For an Esquire—the lanere and the laneret.
For a Lady—the marylon.
For a Young Man—the hobby.
For a Yeoman—the gos-hawk.
For a Poor Man—the tercel.
For a Priest—the sparrow-hawk.
For a Holy Water Clerk—the musket.
For a Knave or Servant—the kestrel.

This was the strict book-lore of the subject, the pedantry of the *dilettanti* who delighted in inventing technicalities and multiplying nice distinctions. The higher clergy were allowed to use the birds pertaining to their rank :—

"These abbots and priors do against their rights,
They ride with hawk and hound and counterfeit knights."

Fines were imposed on those who carried hawks awarded by the laws of the chase to persons of a higher rank.

Equally quaint and curious were the terms to be used (if one was to be regarded as strictly proper and no tyro in the sport) to apply to the different kinds of birds hunted, when they were found in flocks. We are gravely instructed to speak only of "a sege of herons, and of bitterns; an herd of swans, of cranes, and of curlews; a dopping of sheldrakes; a spring of teals; a covert of cootes; a gaggle of geese; a badelynge of ducks; a sord or sute of mallards; a muster of peacocks; a nye of pheasants; a bevy of quails; a covey of partridges; a congregation of plovers; a flight of doves; a dule of turtles; a walk of snipes; a fall of woodcocks; a brood of hens; a building of rooks; a murmuration of starlings; an exaltation of larks; a flight of swallows; a host of sparrows; a watch of nightingales; and a charm of goldfinches." And never, unless we would betray a most lamentable ignorance, should we speak of a "flock," or in such general terms, when alluding to any of these specific birds.

The house in which tame hawks were kept was designated a mew; it was the name given by falconers to the place where they mewed or confined their birds during the period of moulting. The King's hawks were kept at Charing Cross from 1377 till 1537, when Henry VIII. had them removed elsewhere, and built his stables on the site. Hence the modern use of the word "mews" for stabling.

The Duke of St. Albans is to this day Hereditary Grand Falconer to the King, a sinecure to which is attached a salary of £1,200 a year; such was the dignity of the sport in olden times when this office was instituted.

A. Cooper, R.A., Del. J. H. Engleheart, Sculp.

THE QUARRY.

[*Published, 1856, by Rogerson & Tuxford, 246 Strand.*]

*To face page 62*

## IV

## JOUSTING (THE TOURNAMENT)

A knightly sport—The institution of chivalry—The education of a gentleman—Fighting the Pel—Tilting at the Quintain—The page becomes an esquire—The office of an esquire—The admission to knighthood—The Tournament—The Joust—The Round Table of Kenilworth—The Round Table of Windsor—And the Order of the Garter—The lance and the mode of combat—The fight *à l'outrance*—The *mclée*—The disgrace of being unhorsed —The lists—The laws of the Tournament—The proclamation—The arms used—And method of procedure—"The dagger of mercy"—The charge—The "chaplet of honour" for the victor —The occasions for holding tournaments—The attempt of Richard I. to fix the localities for them—The presiding "Queen of Beauty"—The judicial combat—And the "joyous passage of arms"—Knight errantry—A bride offered and won as a tournament prize—The celebration of Queen Eleanor's coronation (1236)—A meeting in honour of Alice Perrers (1374)—Froissart's account of England's acceptance of a French challenge outside Calais (1389)—The return compliment at Smithfield in the following year (1390)—A notable tournament on London Bridge —Richard Beauchamp, Earl of Warwick, a model of English chivalry—The excrescences of chivalry—Fantastic ceremonial —Decline from lofty ideals—The satire of "Don Quixote"—And of the ballad "The Tournament of Tottenham"—English chivalry inferior in its romance owing to democratic tendencies —The Tudor revival—The last royal tournament—A nineteenth century attempt at revival—The great Eglinton tournament— —An anachronism and a travesty.

THE Tournament, or Tourney, was the great sport of the Middle Ages reserved for the knightly class. This was no sport for the common people to engage in, except as spectators. It was one of the means used for the promotion of chivalry, and received the encouragement of sovereigns to supply themselves with faithful supporters and to counteract the independent spirit of feudalism.

As the Knight was a warrior always, even in the piping times of peace he was ever preparing for war. His education was purely military, and even his sports were adapted to the same end. "Chivalry," as synonymous with knighthood, is a word derived from Chevalier, an obvious corruption of Caballarii, the name of a body of Knights instituted by Charlemagne. What Scott does not hesitate to call "the brilliant but useless character of a knight of romance" was "realised and revived" in the person of Richard the Lion Heart; and in the same chapter ("Ivanhoe," xli.) he mentions the interesting fact that shields with armorial bearings (so prominent as accessories to the chivalry of later generations) were then novelties to the Normans and totally unknown among the Saxon nobles.

The accomplished Knight cultivated an active sense of justice, and an ardent indignation against wrong; as Chaucer wrote—

> ". . . he loved chevalrie
> Trouthe and honour, fredom and curtesie."

The education of a gentleman's son had sole reference to the military training which would best fit him to maintain the independence of his country and uphold the honour of his family. Until the age of seven he lived entirely among the females of his family, and then he became a page or varlet.

If the father were too poor to give the necessary training in his own hall at home, the boy went to be educated, in company with others like himself, in the castle of some great noble. During his noviciate the boy's mind was instilled with admiration of the knightly character and of all the chivalrous virtues, while his body was daily improved in strength, dexterity, and hardihood by the practice of physical exercises.

One of these was *Fighting at the Pel,* or the stump of a tree marked with the different parts of the human body, which he was taught to attack both with the edge and the point of his sword, till he could strike any point instantaneously, at the same time covering himself from pretended attack with equal alertness and dexterity. This course was to prepare him for the hand-to-hand combat on foot.

To teach him his duty on horseback—that is, to acquire a firm seat and aim a strong and steady blow, he practised *Tilting at the Quintain.* This was a pole set up firmly in the earth, to which a shield was strongly bound with thongs of leather. Against this shield he was expected to ride at full career, and with his lance endeavour to strike it to the earth.

Later the target was transformed into the wooden figure of a Saracen, armed with sword and shield, and revolving on a spindle. The learner's object now was to strike the figure full in the face or breast; but if he missed his aim or struck aslant, the apparatus was so designed that the figure wheeled rapidly round and caught him a sharp blow with its wooden sword.

At the age of fourteen the page was admitted by a religious ceremony to the dignity of an Esquire, the priest girding him with a sword. Besides the sports designed to make an expert mounted warrior of him, he now shared in the sports of Hunting and Hawking.

The Squires were divided into classes, according to their offices; the highest was the Squire of the Body, the personal attendant on the Knight, and who was therefore called the Squire of Honour. They were all accustomed to obedience and courteous demeanour. As a Squire was not allowed to wear such costly dresses or so much armour as a Knight, it was always a point of honour with a Knight never to attack an Esquire.

In time of war each Squire rendered some specific service to his Knight; one led his horse, others carried appointed portions of his arms or armour, and in the action they warded off blows aimed at their master.

At the age of twenty-one the Squire was duly admitted to Knighthood under a combination of civil and religious ceremonies. For days before, his shield had been hanging in a neighbouring church as a sign of his intention to compete in this great game of chivalry. If any stain lay on his knighthood, a lady, by touching the shield with a wand, could prevent him from a share in the jousting. And if, when he had entered the lists, he was rude to a lady, or broke in any way the rules of the tilt-yard, he was beaten from the lists with the ashwood lances of the knights.

Tournaments were held in France and Normandy before the Conquest, at which period they seem to have been practically unknown in England.

Tournaments were a powerful incentive to emulation; and, says an authority, "every scenic performance of modern times must be tame in comparison of these animating spectacles." They were introduced into England about the middle of the eleventh century, immediately after the Norman Conquest. The word Tournament, or tournoyement, which signifies to turn or wheel about in a circular manner, comes from the French word *tournoi*.

In the Tournament parties of mounted knights, clad in complete armour, and known only by the devices emblazoned on their shields (or sometimes by the favours of their mistresses), encountered each other with lances and swords to display their skill in arms, and establish their prowess and bravery.

If it were a single combat between two knights, it was termed a Joust, or Just. The Joust, or separate trial of skill, according to the laws of chivalry, might be made exclusive of the Tournament.

The curious appellation of The Round Table was given to the Joust during the reign of Henry III. The name was derived from a fraternity of Knights who frequently jousted with each other, and afterwards feasted together, sitting down to a round table in order to set aside, amongst men equally brave and honourable, all distinctions of rank and quality—after the Arthurian legend.

In the time of Edward I., Roger de Mortimer, a nobleman of great opulence, established a Round Table at Kenilworth. This institution, which included a hundred knights and as many ladies, entertained at the founder's expense, acquired considerable fame at home and abroad, and brought a great influx of foreign knights, who came to initiate themselves, or to make some public proof of their prowess.

Edward III. erected a splendid Table at Windsor, upon the same model, but on a more extensive scale. In jealousy, Philip de Valois instituted a Round Table for France, to intercept the German and Italian knights on their way to England. This rivalry had the effect of destroying both establishments, for presently nothing further is heard of them. It is claimed, however, that in England the Order of the Garter took the place of, and was in direct succession to, the Knighthood of the Round Table.

The arm commonly used in Jousting was a spear without an iron head; the excellency of the tilting was estimated according to the accuracy, or otherwise, with which the performer struck the front of his opponent's helmet, the object being to force him backwards from his horse, or shatter the spear by the force of the contact.

The modes of combat were various. Sometimes there was a joust with pointless lances; sometimes a hand-to-hand encounter with blunt two-handed swords. But when the spears or swords were sharpened, then the combat was *à l'outrance*, to be fought to the death. When each knight did not select his antagonist, but one party challenged the other generally, and so fought, it was called a *melée*. In the *melée*, thus hurled together by the signal of the dropping of the princely president's baton, the two parties rushed at each other and hacked away with sword, axe, and mace, gashing limbs and breaking bones in the fury of the fray.

At all times it was regarded as a disgrace to be unhorsed, by whatever means that form of discomfiture might be effected. It is on record that at a tournament in Savoy Edward I. was once attacked by an opponent who discarded his arms and clung round the King's neck, hoping to drag him to the ground by sheer weight. But the sturdy monarch turned the tables by putting spurs to his horse and dragging his assailant from the saddle.

The place of combat was called the Lists, a large open space surrounded by ropes or a railing, outside which were erected temporary galleries for the spectators, among whom were conspicuously seated the ladies, the supreme judges of the tournament. Sometimes the pavilions were erected with gorgeous magnificence, and subsequently provided the accommodation for the rich banquets with which the day's entertainments were not unfrequently brought to a close.

It was a considerable time after the establishment of Jousts and Tournaments before Lists and Barriers were used; at first the combatants contented themselves with being stationed at four angles of an open space, whence they rode in parties one against another. A cord was

A MÊLÉE IN THE 14th CENTURY.
[*From a manuscript in the British Museum.*]

THE JOUST WITH BARRIERS, 15th CENTURY.
[*From a manuscript in the British Museum.*]

[*From Jusserand's "Les Sports et Jeux d'Exercice."*]

*To face page 68*

stretched in front of the different companies, "and when the tyme was," says an ancient MS., "the cordes were cutt, and the trumpettes blew up for every man to do his devoir" (his duty).

As the pastime was accompanied by much danger, they invented in France the double lists, where the knights might run from one end to the other, without coming in contact, except with their lances. Other nations followed the French example, and the usage of Lists and Barriers soon became universal.

The Barrier was a boarded railing, erected longitudinally in the middle of the Lists, some four or five feet in height, and open at both ends.

Of laws and ordinances for regulating this feudal form of dissipation there was a fairly comprehensive code.

Proclamation was always made of the place appointed for the parade of arms; and two days before it was held the two barons (or governors) of the tournament, were at their respective lodges (or pavilions) to which their arms were attached, and before which their banners were set up; so that all who wished to be admitted as combatants on either side, could in like manner set up their shields and banners in front of the parades allotted to them. On the evening of the day they showed themselves in their stations, and exposed their helmets to public view. On the morrow every champion was due on his parade by the hour of ten in the morning.

All arms, banners, and helmets were examined, and approved or rejected, as found to be in accordance with the ordinances of chivalry, or otherwise. Any knight who was not in his station when the two barons (the challenger and acceptor) nailed their banners to their respective pavilions, forfeited all privileges, and was not permitted to tourney.

The combatants were notified to arm themselves by

the king-at-arms and the heralds crying aloud—"To achievement, knights and esquires, to achievement!" Presently the heralds cried, "Come forth, knights and esquires, come forth!" and the two barons having taken their places in the lists, each of them facing his own parade, the champions of both parties proceeded to arrange themselves, every one by the side of his banner, a cord being stretched between them till the commencement of the sports was formally announced.

As a rule the combatants were armed each with a pointless sword, having the edge rebated, and with a baston or truncheon hanging from the saddle-bow. Either weapon was used, as long as the governors of the tournament gave permission by the cry of the heralds—"Laissiez les aler!" (Let them go on).

After the combatants had sufficiently vindicated their prowess the heralds called them to "Ployer vos baniers" (fold up the banners); which was the signal for the conclusion of the tourney.

Every knight or esquire performing in the tournament was allowed the use of one page, armed, within the lists, to wait upon him, or give him his sword or truncheon, as occasion might require; or in case of an accident to his armour, to amend and adjust the same.

The laws of the Tournament permitted a combatant to unhelm himself at pleasure, if incommoded by the heat—for a tilting helmet was extremely heavy and unwieldy; and no one was suffered to assault him until he had replaced his helmet, which he was always bound to do at command of the governor of the entertainment.

The kings-at-arms, and the heralds who proclaimed the tournament, had the privilege of wearing the blazon of arms of those by whom the sport was instituted; they were entitled to six ells of scarlet cloth as their fee, and to have all their expenses defrayed so long as the tournament lasted; the helmet of every knight making his first essay in the tournament became their perquisite; and for affixing the blazon of arms to the pavilions they claimed six crowns as "nail money."

The kings-at-arms held the banners of the two chief barons on the day of the tournament; the other heralds held the banners of their confederates, according to their rank.

Richard I. imposed a tax upon all, according to their quality, who engaged in these encounters; an earl paying a fine of twenty marks for the privilege of entering the field as a combatant, a baron ten, and a knight four or two, according to his possessions. It is not known how long these imposts were collected, and by the time of Henry V. many of the old ordinances were altered or abrogated. It had then become necessary to legislate against any combatant being allowed to enter the lists with more than three esquires; to regulate the amount of armour worn in the lists; and to restrict the arms carried by attendant non-combatants.

Almost with the sun, on the morning of a great tournament, arose the noise of clanking hammers around the tents of the rival knights, at each end of the lists, as the armourers closed the rivets of the plate-armour in which each knight was clad from head to heel for the encounter. As the visor was closed upon his features the top of his tilting helmet was surmounted by a "crest," consisting of some favour or special badge or some distinguishing device by which he could be identified even in the confusion of battle or *melée*. The heavy, rigid armour was worn over a dress of soft leather.

The weapon mostly used in the tourney was a long lance; in addition to which were also worn a big two-handed sword, and the "dagger of mercy" with which a fallen foe could be dispatched if he did not yield. The weapons of attack varied slightly with the changes in the kinds of armour worn at different periods; the favourite arm, the long tapering tilting-spear, not being introduced till the latter half of the thirteenth century.

The shock with which two heavily armed horsemen, thundering towards each other at full speed, met in the centre of the lists, has been well described as that "of a thunderbolt."

Lances were shivered, sometimes to the very grasp; and according to the address of the respective riders, one or both knights might be unhorsed, or the steeds made to recoil backwards upon their haunches.

If by the dexterous use of bit and spur both resumed their stations at opposite ends again, fresh lances were served to them by the attendants, and the breathless silence into which the spectators had been hushed by the crisis just passed gave way to loud plaudits as they prepared to ride to the next attack.

Again the trumpets sounded, the spears were once more lowered and placed in the rests; the spurs were dug into the flanks of the horses, and the champions rode at each other again at full gallop.

The lance was sometimes aimed at the centre of the opponent's shield; and sometimes at the more difficult mark, his helmet, to hit which made the shock more irresistible.

Sometimes saddle-girths burst, or other misadventure overtook the most brave; sometimes the rider was stunned, or hurled to the dust, or even slain; but for the victor in the lists was reserved a triumph commensurate to the deadly earnestness of this gladiatorial form of contest.

At the termination of the encounter was heard the din of martial music, and "Honour to the sons of the brave" resounded as the conqueror was led by the Marshals of the Lists to receive the prize—the chaplet of honour—from the hands of his mistress or the appointed Queen of Love and Beauty. Then the welkin rang with the plaudits of the multitude as the wreath of victory was placed on his brow; and victory in a tournament was thus made little less glorious than the moment of victory on the sanguinary field of battle.

Such celebrations were held on notable public or private occasions; as at the friendly meetings of two great sovereigns—the Field of the Cloth of Gold in 1520, to wit—at the coronation of a King, or the rejoicing over a great national victory; or even at the marriage of a wealthy heiress. But whatever the occasion, everything was done to give it wide renown, and to signalise it as an event to be long afterwards remembered.

King Richard I. had attempted to fix the localities for holding tournaments in England, specifying that, at the meetings for such purpose, the peace should not be broken, nor justice hindered, nor damage done to the royal forests. The places selected by him were five in number, namely—between Sarum and Wilton; between Warwick and Kenilworth; between Stamford and Wallingford; between Brackley and Mixbury; and between Tickhill and Blyth in Yorkshire.

In the days of chivalry ladies presided as judges paramount over these sports. Esteemed as paragons of beauty and virtue, the spirit of romance substituted them in place of the true knight's tutelar saint, to whom he paid his vows, and addressed himself in the hour of peril.

In the Tournament they not only distributed the prizes, but were invested with the power of remitting the punishment of offenders; it was peculiarly in their honour, to win some mark of their favour, that the joust was most frequently undertaken—as, for example, when a lady's hero undertook some achievement on her behalf, and as a proof of his devotion to her.

The encounters invariably took place before large bodies of spectators, sometimes sovereign princes and their noblest barons; and always were present that which was most distinguished amongst the rank and beauty of the fair sex. When, therefore, a lot of fearless and fiery-spirited knights thus fought in the presence of so many witnesses of their valour, there was always a danger of the combat becoming too serious; in which case the Sovereign, if he were present, or the Marshal of the Tournament, would stay the fight by crying "Hoo!" and throwing down his truncheon in the midst. Thus, in Scene 3, Act I of *Richard II.*, the whole of which is an admirable illustration of the customary proceedings at the Lists (except that in this case it was no sport that was intended, but a trial by combat, a part of the English judicial system of the time), the Lord Marshal exclaims—

"Stay, the King hath thrown his warder down!"

Of the etiquette and forms of procedure observed at the judicial combat in the lists—the throwing down of the gage, the herald's challenge, the acceptance of the champion for the appellant, and the recognition of the judgment of God in the result—all these may be learnt very pleasantly by reading the penultimate chapter of "Ivanhoe."

In an ordinary "Joyous Passage of Arms," however, although lances might be shattered, knights dismounted, armour pierced or dinted, or even blood let and limbs broken, life was not intentionally taken, nor was aught done but what knightly prowess, blended with gentle courtesy, permitted in the exhibition of such desperate exercises of martial skill.

Besides the regular tourney, single combats were often fought between knights who would tilt against each other on the highway or wherever they met. The famous battle of Otterbourne, as sung in the ballad of Chevy Chase, is illustrative of this chivalrous but deadly sport—

> "When Percy wi' the Douglas met
> I wat he was fu' fain;
> They swakked their swords till sair they swat,
> And the blood ran down like rain."

Besides these accidental meetings, which were never neglected as opportunities for fighting out old-standing feuds, and were not, therefore, unlike the vendetta, there was what was known as Knight Errantry—the common practice of lusty knights wandering abroad in search of adventures, such as rescuing fair damsels in distress, or releasing unfortunate captives from the clutches of their oppressors. It was the essence of chivalry to espouse the cause of the weak and the oppressed; but this romantic roving of errant knights, who often displayed more valour than discretion, not infrequently led to worse situations than their ill-directed actions had tried to relieve. In fact, so many follies and extravagances came to be committed in the name of Knight Errantry, that the institution at last more richly earned the ridicule rather than merited the approbation of the world.

The Tournament has supplied a large proportion of the romance which distinguishes the history of mediæval times; for, as just stated, no festive occasion at which it was desired to bring together a large assemblage of nobles, and offer them entertainment congenial to their tastes, was deemed complete without one of these martial displays.

Not the least romantic tale of Tilting left on record by the chroniclers of old is one told of a Shropshire manor to the following effect :—

The wide-stretching territory of this county was bestowed by the Norman Conqueror on Roger de Montgomery, a faithful follower who had defeated Eric the Forester, the Saxon Earl of Shrewsbury, and driven him to seek shelter in the fastnesses of Wales beyond the wall of castles which then formed the frontier between the two countries. At a later period, one of the Montgomery's successors having forfeited the manor of Whittington, this Shropshire holding was conferred on William Peveril of the Peak, to whose romantic soul we owe this typical tale of chivalry.

Peveril had a daughter, the Lady Melette, the fame of whose beauty had attracted many a mailed suitor across the wildest tracts of Derbyshire to the lone castle of the Peak. Animated by the chivalric spirit of the age, the lord of the Peak proclaimed a great tilting match, the prize of which should be nothing less than the Lady Melette, with Whittington Manor as a dowry.

Such a rare opportunity of winning fame and fortune at one stroke drew a crowd of knights across the brown, barren moors and stony hills of Derbyshire to show their prowess in the lists set up under the grim stronghold perched high on the frowning rock above Castleton.

And long afterwards did Norman minstrel and English rhymer sing the story of that brilliant passage of arms, telling how among all the gallant knights who attended that famous tourney was Guarine de Metz, Sheriff of Shropshire, bearing a silver shield; and how he by his skill and bravery honourably won the noble guerdon.

The family of Warren, says the romance, held Whittington for nearly four hundred years; and as they had won it by the lance, they failed not to encourage similar exploits of chivalry under its old grey towers; and of each successor to him who had espoused the fair Melette it was proudly sung by the troubador how he—

> "Oft to his rich domain
> Welcomed many a crested knight,
> Welcomed many a lady bright—
> Fitz-Guarine of Lorraine."

In this romance perhaps fiction is artistically blended with fact; but our other illustrations may be accepted as unadulterated history.

The first historic occasion to supply us with a fitting illustration was the coronation of Queen Eleanor, consort of Henry III., in 1236, when "goodly jousts and other royal solemnities" were held in Tothill Fields, Westminster. For two centuries afterwards the same site was used for the tilting in "appeals by combat," to which allusion has been made. Stow, the historian, says, referring to one of these law cases of 1571, "it was thought good the Court should sit in Tuthill Fields, where was prepared one plot of ground, one and twenty yardes square, double railed, for the combate."

A grand tournament was proclaimed in London in 1330 to celebrate the birth of an heir to the crown of England, the child who was afterwards that ornament to chivalry, the Black Prince. The jousting was held in Cheapside, the highway being strewn with sand, and an ornate wooden tower was erected in that thoroughfare for the accommodation of Queen Philippa and her ladies. But the fair company had scarce taken their seats when the whole scaffolding suddenly gave way, precipitating the royal lady and every one else upon it to the ground. Though no one was injured the rage of King Edward may be imagined ; and it was only at the earnest solicitation of his beloved consort that the wretched carpenter was spared his life, and it was on her knees that the angelic Queen had to pacify her incensed husband.

A less worthy occasion for holding a tournament was that in 1374, when Edward III., then sixty-two years of age, being enamoured of Alice Perrers, thought to amuse her by organising a seven days' festival in Smithfield. At the joustings there got up in her honour, the fair Alice sat beside her elderly lover in a magnificent car, as the "Lady of the Sun" ; and each day her escort to and from the festive scene consisted of a long train of plumed knights (who evidently had no prudishness in their composition, but were bravely determined to keep their gallant King in good countenance), each cavalier leading by the bridle a beautiful palfrey on which was mounted a fair damsel.

In the "Chronicles" of Froissart may be read how the high enterprise of three valiant knights, chamberlains to Charles VI., took upon themselves in 1389 to do deeds of arms on the frontiers of Calais, challenging to "abide all knights and squires, strangers, for the term of thirty days, whosoever would joust with them jousts of peace or of war."

These gallant Frenchmen undertook to meet at St. Inglevere, outside Calais, for thirty days, Fridays excepted, and to "deliver from their vows all manner of knights and squires, gentlemen, strangers of any manner or nation, that will come thither for the breaking of five spears, either sharp or rockets, at their pleasure."

"And," continued their widely proclaimed challenge, "outside our lodgings shall be shields of our arms, both the shields of peace and of war ; and whosoever will joust, let him come or send the day before, and with a rod touch which shield he please ; if he touch the shield of war, the next day he shall joust in jousts mortal with which of the three he will, and if he touch the shield of peace he shall have jousts of peace; and all such knights, strangers, as will joust, to bring some nobleman on their side, who shall be instructed by us what ought to be done in the case.

"And we entreat all knights, squires, strangers that will come and joust, that they think not nor imagine of us that we do this for any pride, hatred, or ill-will; but all only we do it to have their honourable company and acquaintance, the which with our entire hearts we desire."

In the wording of this clause will be observed the true niceties of a fine knightly courtesy, the expression of a delicacy of feeling well calculated even at that critical time, when a three years' truce had been concluded between England and France, to attract to the Lists of St. Inglevere some of the flower of English knighthood.

"None of our shields," they announced, "shall be covered with iron or steel, nor none of theirs that will come to joust with us, nor shall there be any manner of frauds, advantage or evil service"—shields, it should be explained, were at this period made of courbouilli, a preparation of leather; and rockets, it may be added, were pointless lances.

The challenge thus written, in round, clerkly style, and couched in all knightly courtesy, fixed the time of meeting for May 20th following; and though issued to all comers, was specially promulgated in England; and 'tis little wonder then that on the appointed day there issued from the gates of Calais—the lists were just over the English frontier—no less than sixty English knights and nobles, clad in full panoply of war, and all prepared for the jousting.

For further particulars of this notable episode in the

history of English chivalry the reader is referred to the pages of Froissart, who is always a vivid and a picturesque writer. Suffice it to say here, that after four days' tilting these memorable jousts came to a satisfactory conclusion ; for though the French champions seem to have had the best of the courses run, the English knights came away perfectly satisfied, taking a most friendly leave of their courteous and gallant opponents, "thanking them greatly for their pastime," and promising to send other English gentlemen to do deeds of arms at any like entertainment in the near future. The whole incident is a good specimen of its kind, illustrating, as it does, the true spirit of chivalry as it was cultivated in its palmiest days.

The compliment was returned the following year (1390) when the young and prodigal King of England, Richard II., sought to rival the splendid jousts which had been given by Charles of France in honour of his bride's entry into Paris. Heralds were sent throughout England, Scotland, France, Flanders, Hainault, and Germany, inviting sixty knights to tilt at Smithfield, commencing on the Sunday after Michaelmas.

The Sunday was the feast of the challengers, and about three o'clock on that day there issued forth from the Tower sixty barbed coursers, in full trappings, each attended by a squire of honour, and after them sixty ladies of rank, elegantly and richly dressed, mounted on palfreys, and each leading by a silver chain a knight completely armed for tilting. The procession, accompanied by trumpeters and minstrels, passed on to Smithfield through the plaudits of the people who thronged the streets. The tilters were entertained to a grand supper every night at the bishop's palace, where the King and Queen were lodged ; and dancing was afterwards kept up till daybreak. On the Tuesday the King entertained all the foreign knights and squires, and the Queen their ladies; on the Friday a similar compliment was paid them by the Duke of Lancaster; and on the Saturday they visited Windsor Castle on the invitation of their royal hosts.

The year 1390 also saw a remarkable tournament on London Bridge. It appears that Sir David Lindsay, of Glenesk, who had married a daughter of Robert II. of Scotland, challenged to the jousts Lord Wells, the English Ambassador to the Court of Scotland; no mean antagonist, for the Scottish poet, Wyntoun, describes him as—

> "Manful, stout, and of good pith,
> And high of heart he was therewith."

His challenger arrived from Scotland with twenty-nine attendants and thirty horses; the King presided in person at the tournament, seated in a splendid pavilion designated by the contemporary writers "a summer castle."

At the first shock the lances splintered to fragments; but as the Scotsman's firm seat was totally unaffected the crowd shouted out that he was tied to his saddle. Whereupon the redoubtable Sir David leaped off his charger, vaulted on again, and dashed on to the next collision. At the third crash Lord Wells was unseated with a heavy fall; and at the final grapple Sir David Lindsay, fastening his dagger into the armour of his antagonist, lifted the English knight from the ground, and dashed him, completely vanquished, to the earth again.

The stout and valiant Scotsman pursued his advantage no further, but generously threw himself on his fallen antagonist and embraced him as he revived to consciousness. And during the three months of Lord Wells' subsequent illness, the courteous Sir David Lindsay failed not to visit him every day. For he fought (says his biographer) "without anger, and only for glory."

And to perpetuate the memory of his glorious victory on London Bridge, the Scottish knight afterwards founded a chantry at Dundee.

Among Englishmen of that period, not a less worthy exemplar of true knighthood was to be found in the person of the irreproachable Richard Beauchamp, Earl of Warwick, who, after the fashion of the age, spent a large portion of his life in the business of foreign wars, relieved only by the recreation of jousts and tournaments.

The actual life of Earl Richard, who was created a Knight of the Bath by Henry IV., and was a favourite of Henry V., the latter committing to him the tutelage of the infant Henry VI., reads like one long romance. This romantic career embraces, among other stirring episodes, his capture of Glendower's banner; an adventurous pilgrimage to the Holy Land; the quelling of two rebellions in Rome; his victories over the champions of foreign tournaments, including Sir Randolph Malot at Verona, and a grand duke at Constance—at which latter place, in admiration of his courage, the Empress took his badge from one of his knightly retinue to pin it, and wear it proudly, on her own dress; his feats of arms at Jerusalem and Venice, in Germany and Russia; his gallantry in painting three shields with the devices of three different ladies, and sending them as challenges to the French King's Court, where they were accepted by the "Chevalier Rouge," the "Chevalier Blanc," and Sir Collard Fines, each of whom he defeated, wearing each time a different coat of arms; his keeping joust in London against all comers at the coronation of Queen Joan of Navarre, and his negotiation of the famous marriage treaty between Henry V. and Catherine of France, after the crowning victory of Agincourt; his departure to take up the governorship of Calais with all the gorgeous pageantry of the Middle Ages, "in his cote bete with fine gold," and on board a ship with "the great stremour forty yerdis in length and eight yerdis in bredth, with a grete Beare and Gryfon holding a Ragged Staff," and with "the grete Cross of St. George" on the other mast; his entertainment at Calais of Henry V. and the Emperor Sigismund, the latter telling the King that "no other sovereign had such a knight for wisdom, nurture, and manhood, and if curtesy were lost it would be found in him." This noble model of English chivalry died Regent of France, in 1439; and his body was brought with much worshipful pomp and stately ceremony to Warwick, where in St. Mary's Church may be seen his sepulchral hearse of brass—a work of art as superb as befits the glorious career it commemorates.

Chivalry, like most other human institutions, deteriorated with age; and as time went on its inherent virtues were sapped by the growth of what were mere excrescences. Tournaments were held with lavish magnificence as an avowed method of keeping up the tone of chivalrous feeling—thus confusing the material with the essential. Fantastical ceremonies were invented, and meaningless pageantry indulged in; and among other ridiculous innovations the peacock, the swan, and the pheasant—birds of high fame in romance—received the homage of every "true" knight. And thus it came about that a Knight would make his vows, formally swearing "before God, my Creator, in the first place, and the glorious Virgin, His Mother, in the next, and before the Ladies, and the Pheasant" (or whichever of these birds was present), and so on.

Chivalry, as it was first instituted, cultivated an exquisite sense of honour with emulous valour, and sought to soften some of the rough usages of war by the practice of courtesy, magnanimity, and munificence ; taught a devotion and a gallantry towards woman, and a reverence towards religion ; it consistently bred a fine disdain of all that was false, perjured, disloyal, and recreant.

But in course of time an undue thirst for military renown had obscured the best principles of knighthood ; and gallantry—a word which came to signify valour, merely because none but a true knight was supposed capable of showing extreme respect to the fair sex—had led to dissoluteness of life. Then much that was false to chivalry—as mistaking ceremonious politeness for spontaneous modesty ; and allowing an avaricious ransoming of prisoners to take the place of that old princely courtesy of entertaining one's captives—much of this spurious stuff was wrought up into the most popular romances of the later Middle Ages.

When therefore Chivalry fell away from its high ideals and lofty principles, such models of fictitious heroism set up by the writers of romance availed little towards setting it upon its pedestal again. Knight Errantry had performed its best exploits for the love of justice, and in vindication of right. But when roving knighthood became a profession it cannot be conceived to have any existence outside the precincts of romance. Then there were the absurdities of Knight Errantry to which passing allusion has been made. How these reaped a full harvest of well-merited ridicule may be read in Cervantes' unmerciful satire, "The Adventures of Don Quixote," which appeared in 1605, when Chivalry was decadent if not moribund, and than which there is nothing finer in the whole range of imported literature.

The hero, a Spanish gentleman whose pedigree was equalled only by his poverty, living at a period when the last dying glories of the Tournament and Knight Errantry had flickered out, muddled his brains by reading books of chivalry, till nothing could content him but he must turn knight errant himself, and set forth in search of adventures. How Don Quixote scoured bright his great-great-grandfather's rusty armour, furbished up his arms, and mounted his wretched steed, all skin and bone, upon whom he bestowed the stately name Rozinante; how he chose a good-looking country girl who lived hard by, and bestowed upon her the high-sounding title of Dulcinea del Toboso, to represent the lady of noble birth for the love of whom he might perform such wondrous deeds as knights-errant of old were wont; how he got himself dubbed knight as nearly to the usages of ancient chivalry as it could be managed; how he attached to himself, to act as his squire, a shallow-brained labourer named Sancho Panza; and all the other whimsical extravagances in his absurd scheme for roving about to redress wrongs and relieve oppression by the prowess of his knightly arms; all these vain imaginings and grotesque efforts result in nothing (so far as the purpose of this work is concerned), except poor Quixote's tilting at a windmill which his poor addled brain mistook for a monstrous giant! And, fittingly, his epitaph ran—

> "Wrongs to redress, his sword he drew,
> And many a caitiff giant slew;
> His days of life though madness stain'd,
> In death his sober senses he regain'd."

Much earlier than Cervantes, perhaps more than a century earlier, an English rhymster had belittled the ceremonial practices of Chivalry in a mock-heroic description of the "Tournament of Tottenham," a ballad so named and now preserved in the "Percy Reliques."

The full title is "The Turnament of Tottenham, or the wooeing, and wedding of Tibbe, the Reeve's daughter there." The poem is descriptive of the contest between half a dozen lusty bachelors bearing such palpably unaristocratic names as Perkyn, Hawkyn, Dawkyn, and Tomkyn, all of them hailing from such-like country places as Hackenaye, for the hand of the fair Tibbe, a rustic maiden, the daughter of the reeve or manciple of the place, whose marriage portion was a grey mare, a spotted sow, a dun cow, a brode hen, and similarly desirable live stock. The scene of the conflict was the Croft at Tottenham; and the quaint old rhymster flowingly describes the rushing of the doughty warriors upon each other in the lists, the broken pates and fractured limbs, the falls from clumsy horses more accustomed to the plough than the joust, and the ultimate winning of the fair Tibbe by the bold Perkyn. Then we have the carrying home of the drunken and defeated combatants, and all winds up to the sound of wedding bells, and the living-happy-ever-afterwards of Perkyn and Tibbe. All these incidents are described in a style that slily but very richly burlesques the inflated ballad of romance—the grandiloquent composition which portrayed or pretended to portray the genuine tournaments of knights and heroes. But the real humour of it all is recognised in the attempted imitation, by a parcel of country bumpkins, of all the solemnities and fopperies of the legitimate tournament, from the challenge and the oaths on entering the lists, through the various accidents of the encounter, to the victor leading off his prize, and the magnificent feasting which invariably ended it all.

In the English romances of ancient chivalry there exists a marked inferiority as compared with the old romances of the Continent. The cause for this is apparently found in the fact that Chivalry, being an institution which distinctly made for the separation of the classes, failed to thrive in a country where the laws had assumed a democratic tendency.

The decline of the royal tournaments had set in during the Wars of the Roses. Having then waned from their ancient lustre, they were kindled afresh for a brief space, only to expire under the Tudor monarchs. They had lost much of the old spirit of chivalry, and the Tudor revival, in the face of the newer ideals of the Renaissance, was somewhat artificial.

The Tilt-yard at Whitehall adjoined the old Banqueting House, where, running in a northerly direction, was a long range of building devoted to purposes of exercise and recreation, and including the Tennis Court, the Bowling Alley, the Manège or Riding School, and the Cock-pit. The approach to the courtyard was by two fine gates; one of extraordinary beauty, designed by Holbein, was commonly known as the Cock-pit Gate.

These buildings were mostly erected by Henry VIII., a monarch so fond of robust sports and manly exercises of all kinds that a Tilt-yard was indispensable to him. At the south end of this enclosure was a magnificent lofty pavilion for the royal ladies—a veritable "Fortress of Perfect Beauty" as it has been called when occupied by a full bevy of Court beauties—while on the others the gallery was arranged in two tiers of seats, and partitioned off, like boxes in a theatre.

In the reign of Henry VIII. joustings were frequently held at Greenwich Palace; as notably on the May-day of 1511, when, for that holiday and the two days ensuing, the King, Sir Edward Howard, Charles Brandon, and Sir Edward Nevill, as challengers held the field against all comers. "On the other parte the Marquis Dorset, the Earls of Essex and Devonshire, with others, as defendauntes, ranne againste them, so that many a sore stripe was given and many a staffe broken." Jousts were also held here in 1516, 1517, and 1526. At a grand May-day Tournament held at Greenwich in 1536 a tragic incident occurred. The King observing Queen Anne Boleyn to drop her handkerchief, and interpreting this as a private signal to one of her admirers, hastily took his departure while the sports were at their height, without uttering a word to the Queen or anybody else, greatly to the surprise and chagrin of the tilters. In great ill-humour he hastened to London, accompanied only by six domestics; the same night Anne Boleyn was arrested, and by the 19th of the month, as history tells us, she had lost her head on Tower Hill.

That was the end of Henry's second wife; it was in honour of his fourth spouse, Anne of Cleves, that another noteworthy tournament was held on the May-day of 1540. These splendid joustings took place at Westminster, the challengers being headed by Sir John Dudley, and the defenders by the gallant and accomplished Earl of Surrey.

"This entertainment," writes Lucy Aiken, "was continued for several successive days, during which the challengers, according to the costly fashion of ancient hospitality, kept open house at their common charge and feasted the King and Queen, the members of both Houses of Parliament, and the Lord Mayor and Aldermen of London with their wives."

The lion-hearted Elizabeth encouraged a taste for this chivalrous sport, and joustings took place at various times throughout her long reign. Both the Queen's favourites, the Earl of Leicester and the Earl of Essex, were distinguished for knightly prowess, and splintered many a lance in her honour, while in the gallant Sir Philip Sidney she possessed a perfect mirror of chivalry.

Yet in spite of Elizabeth's efforts to maintain its

splendour undiminished, the star of chivalry was rapidly declining, to disappear for ever in the reign of her successor.

The last Royal Tournament held in England was that at the old Whitehall Tilt-yard, in which Prince Charles took a part somewhat to the annoyance of his father. For James I. was a monarch of constitutional timidity; a prince who rejoiced not in the glitter of burnished steel, the clash of arms, the rude encounter, and all the nerve-trying circumstances inseparable from the arena of martial sport.

He ridiculed the Court of Honour and declared the laws of chivalry obsolete. Nevertheless, the trials of skill and strength in the tilt-yard were still considered fashionable; and much against his inclination, the King was compelled to witness them on special occasions, as the welcoming of some important visitor, or on the anniversaries of his succession to the English throne.

His eldest son, Prince Henry, whose career was so brief and whose early death left Charles heir to the throne, inured himself betimes to the weight of armour, and made himself expert in the use of all weapons—he could couch the lance, wield the sword, swing the battle-axe or the mace, and toss the pike, better than any youth of his years.

Prince Charles, though less martial in his tastes and of a more reflective cast of mind, also cultivated the accomplishments proper to knighthood. And so in the days ere he was called to fill the throne he took his share in the tournament, perhaps gravely, but as became a knight and a prince. From that throne he was dragged, amidst civil strife and discord, to the bloody scaffold at Whitehall, close to that very arena where he had once engaged in mimic strife to the bruit of kettledrum, the fanfare of trumpets, and the cheers of a fickle multitude;

marched slowly in solemn silence to bare his neck for the axe where once he had pranced on a richly-caparisoned steed, accoutred from head to foot in magnificent armour.

The final extinction of the Tournament had at last been hastened by the looming shadow of the approaching Civil War. Nor when peace was afterwards restored and tranquillity once more reigned, could there ever have been any hope of its resuscitation ; for had not the musket and the pistol proved the lance and plate-armour to be obsolete, the class prerogatives claimed for chivalry would never have been allowed by the new democracy that was born of Cromwell's "New Model" army.

And now we come to an extraordinary attempt to revive the Tournament in modern times. The glamour which the historical romances of Sir Walter Scott have thrown over their readers from time to time may be judged by the influence which "Ivanhoe" seems to have exercised upon the youthful Lord Eglinton in 1839, only seven years after the great novelist's death, and while the fascination of his personality was still fresh.

The Earl of Eglinton, through his admiration for the writings of Scott, became fired with a desire to revive the glories of the Tournament and to recall to life the long-dead days of chivalry; to see in actuality upon his own castle grounds all the stirring scenes and picturesque incidents as had been depicted by the magic pen of the great romancer for the plain of Ashby-de-la-Zouch. The earl was a young nobleman of ancient lineage and ample possessions, and well calculated in every way to give effect to his romantic proposals.

Near the main entrance of his castle at Eglinton, a magnificent Ayrshire home, erected in 1798, was an ideal site for a tilting-ground. On its northern side it sloped gently upwards, thus providing naturally an admirable stance for the spectators to view the sport. The other sides of the enclosure were bounded by the river Lugton, and the noble castle formed a fitting background for the enactment of the coming pageant. The surrounding scenery of this natural amphitheatre was of the most picturesque description.

The arena set out for the tilting was 650 feet in length and 250 feet in breadth ; a stout barrier standing four feet from the ground was run along the centre of the enclosure for the purpose of preventing the horses of the knights colliding with each other when their riders were charging.

The long south side of the arena was occupied by a large gallery consisting of a central main structure and two wings, the former accommodating a thousand spectators, and the wings about the same number between them. The centre, which was the Pavilion of the Queen of Beauty, was elegantly finished in the Gothic style, with gilded pinnacles and other richly painted ornamentations. No expense was spared, and the costly trappings were those which had been used recently at Queen Victoria's Coronation.

There was a Pavilion for the Lord of the Tournament (Lord Eglinton himself), and there were separate tents for each of the knights, all after the best models obtainable, and arranged for effect and administration as in the days of ancient chivalry. Every care was taken to ensure correctness of technical detail, and at the same time to construct the whole pageant as an artistic and harmonious picture.

Open house was kept at the Castle, with banquets and balls every night. One writer with special knowledge has left it on record that "everything that art and wealth could produce was lavished on the Castle . . . which had been specially furnished and decorated for the occasion . . . and Eglinton was garnished and beautified as probably no other dwelling in Scotland was ever adorned."

Nearly two years were occupied in making the necessary preparations, and the public, who felt that a new pleasure had been invented for them, eagerly anticipated the pageant. The procession from the Castle included not only the principal lady guests to occupy the central gallery, all clad in fourteenth-century costumes, but men-at-arms in demi-suits of armour, musicians, trumpeters, banner bearers, marshals, heralds, pursuivants, a knight-marshal, a judge of the peace, a jester, a chamberlain, servitors, halberdiers, archers, swordsmen, liveried retainers, and all the motley crew which went to make such gatherings in the olden times a gorgeous picture that was a feast of colour. There were fifteen Knights and twice as many Esquires and Pages in attendance upon them, all in full or demi-armour.

The *rôle* of Queen of Beauty was filled by Lady Seymour, a granddaughter of the brilliant Richard Brinsley Sheridan, and one well equipped by nature to do honour to it.

The Knights were the Marquis of Waterford; the Earls of Eglinton, Craven, and Cassilis; Viscounts Alford and Glenlyon; Captains Gage, Fairlie and Beresford; Sirs Frederick Johnstone and Francis Hopkins; and Messrs. Boothby, Jerningham, Lamb, and Lechmere. The Squires and Pages were all gentlemen of fortune and position.

Each Knight bore a chivalric appellation. There was a Knight of the Dragon, of the Griffin; of the Black Lion, of the Dolphin; of the Crane, and the Swan, and the Ram; of the White Rose, the Golden Lion, and the Burning Tower; of the Stag's Head, of the Lion's

Paw, and so on, these devices being emblazoned on the trappings of the respective combatants and their retainers.

When all was ready the Knights issued forth from their Pavilions, two and two, paid their devoirs to the fair ladies in the galleries, and then fought to the sound of the heralds' trumpets. The fighting consisted of each Knight galloping against his opponent full tilt and striking his armour with his lance.

But it has to be confessed that the lances were made of wood which would easily splinter, and no great danger was incurred by any one of the performers. After several couples had jousted, the final passage was run by the Earl of Eglinton against the Marquis of Waterford, otherwise the Knight of the Dragon, both contestants most gorgeously arrayed, and attended by no fewer than eight Esquires and Pages.

After breaking two lances against each other it is not surprising to learn that the Earl—and host—was declared the best Knight of the day, and was rewarded by the Queen of Beauty with a crown of victory, according to ancient custom.

All this sounds exquisitely romantic. But something remains to be told. First of all, the weather was so unseasonable, and apparently so fiendishly and persistently malevolent, as to mar the whole of the proceedings from beginning to end. There was to have been four days' jousting—the last four days in August—but the rain was almost incessant, each succeeding day proving no better than its predecessor, till the ground was sodden and flooded, and the atmosphere thoroughly chilled. Gaily-caparisoned horses had to plash through seas of mud, the colouring of the beautiful dresses was lost in the lowering and uncongenial gloom, and the proceedings had practically to be abandoned—a lamentable conclusion to a most costly undertaking.

Then the anachronisms which transpired were enough to send a shudder through the frame of the least sensitive of antiquarians. Fourteenth-century ladies hoisted umbrellas, and palfreys with antique trappings had to give way to modern covered vehicles. Outside the show, among the tents of ancient chivalry was one labelled "The Reporters' Gallery," for the special use of nineteenth-century journalists. And, lastly, it scarcely squares with one's idea of the eternal fitness of things to learn that so many thousands of spectators were carried to the scene by the Ardrossan Railway, and that the canny company seized the opportunity to treble their ordinary fares for the occasion.

Notwithstanding the drawbacks here enumerated, it is calculated that no less than two hundred thousand persons availed themselves of this opportunity of viewing the representation of an ancient Tournament; they came from all parts of the United Kingdom, from the United States of America, and from nearly every country in Europe. Among the large and distinguished company entertained in the Castle was no less a personage than Prince Louis Napoleon, afterwards Emperor Napoleon III. of France.

Even if it be allowed that the Eglinton Tournament was a success as a pageant, it must be confessed that as an exhibition of legitimate tilting (that is, jousting in armour) it was a hollow mockery. And a little reflection will show that it could never have been anything else.

It seems to have been forgotten that to engage successfully in the mimic battle of the mediæval tournament men were specially trained almost from infancy to manhood; and, moreover, that this branch of instruction filled almost exclusively the educational curriculum of the Knight of old.

Again, the wearing of armour alone, apart from the

effort of fighting in it, called for an amount of strength, and such powers of endurance as must have proved a heavy strain, even upon a man inured to it by a life-long training. It is well known that an armoured knight struck from his horse, though quite unhurt, was often unable to get up from the ground without assistance.

As Cervantes brought a crushing ridicule on Knight Errantry by his writing, none the less did Lord Eglinton bring a withering derision on the Tournament, by the ill-starred travesty of a revival. There is not likely to be any more tilting in real armour seen in this country.

# V

## TILTING AT THE QUINTAIN

A yeoman's sport—And a preparation for the knightly tournament—The Welsh "Gwyntyn"—Practised by the Londoners—Fighting the pel—A human quintain—Tilting at the ring—The water quintain.

THE Quintain was a sport of the same military nature, in which the youthful yeomen of old England substituted a sandbag for the Saracen and shield of the knightly form of the game.

Two large poles being driven in the ground, far enough apart to allow a man on horseback to ride full speed between them, an immense, heavy sandbag was fixed on a pivot at the top of these in such a manner as to swing round very freely, and backward and forward, with amazing rapidity. The sport was for the horseman, facing the sandbag, to dash forward at full speed, hurling a javelin at the bag with all his might, and after striking it, to pass between the poles before it could resume its original position. If unsuccessful, however, the bag would strike a blow sufficient to dismount the unlucky wight.

Another variant of the game was to have a cross-post turning upon a pin on the top of a single upright; at one end of the revolving cross-post was a broad board or a shield, and at the other a heavy sandbag; and the

THE QUINTAIN, OFFHAM, KENT.
[*Photo: Pictorial Agency.*]

THE GAME OF PALL MALL. (*See page* 145.)

*To face page* 97

play was to tilt against the shield with a stout lance, and pass by before the sandbag, spinning round, should strike the tilter to the earth.

It has been said that combating the Quintain was anciently the practice of tyros in chivalry, preparatory to engaging in the Tournament. The earliest form of the game was merely to stick a staff or spear in the earth, and hang a shield upon it to aim at; and the dexterity of the player was exercised in the attempt to strike the shield so as to break the ligatures and throw it to the ground.

In process of time this diversion was improved in the manner already mentioned; a human figure carved in wood was substituted, generally in the resemblance of a formidable Turk, with a shield in his left hand, and brandishing a sword or a club in his right.

This was the most popular form of the game, and in running at this figure the horseman aimed his lance to strike on the forehead between the eyes, or on the nose; for if he struck wide of these, especially on the shield, the figure wheeled on its pivot with such velocity as to deal the competitor a severe blow on the back with its wooden sabre—to the amusement of the onlookers.

The sport is supposed to have had a classic origin as one of the Olympic games, and to have been introduced into this country by the Romans, from whom the Britons learnt it. Its name has been derived from "quintus," because the game was celebrated every fifth year of the Olympics; and again the Welsh name for it, "Gwyntyn," is said to mean literally "a vane"—the authorities are at variance about the word.

Of the actual thing itself very few examples remain in existence. The Quintain preserved on Offham Green, Kent, is but a replica of the ancient original, though as a relic it is scarcely less interesting on that account.

The sport seems to have survived as one peculiar to wedding festivities, and among the last places where it was thus celebrated was Blackthorn, in Oxfordshire, where it was indulged in with "much solemnity and mirth" on the village green. Ben Jonson says—

> "At Quintin he
> In honour of his bridal-tee
> Hath challenged either wide countee."

In Roberts's "Popular Antiquities of Wales," we read: "On the day of the ceremony, the nuptial presents having previously been made, and the marriage privately celebrated at an early hour, the signal to the friends of the bridegroom was given by the piper mounted on a horse trained for that purpose; and the cavalcade being all mounted set off at full speed, with the piper playing in the midst of them, for the house of the bride.

"The friends of the bride in the meantime having raised various obstructions to prevent their access to the house of the bride, such as ropes of straw across the road, and blocking up the regular way with the quintain; each rider in passing which struck the flat side, and if not dexterous was overtaken, and perhaps dismounted, by the sandbag, and so became a fair object for laughter.

"The Gwyntyn was also guarded by champions of the opposite party, who, if it were passed successfully, challenged the adventurers to a trial of skill at one of the twenty-four games—a challenge which could not be declined, and hence to guard the gwyntyn was a service of high adventure."

The principle of the Quintain, it will be observed,

was to endanger the awkward or inefficient tilter in some way, and bring his lack of skill into contempt. In 1827 there was revived by Viscount Gage, at his seat, Firle Place, Sussex, yet another form of the game.

"Two Quintains, consisting of two logs of wood, each fashioned in the resemblance of the head and body of a man, were set upright on a high bench, on which they were kept by a chain passing from each through the platform, and having attached to it a weight, so that if not struck fully and forcibly the figure resumed its seat. One was also divided in the middle, and the upper part being fixed on a pivot, turned, if not struck in the centre, and requited its assailant by a blow with a staff on which was suspended a small bag of flour."

Dr. Watts describes it as "a ludicrous and sportive way of tilting or running on horseback at some mark hung on high, movable and turning round; which, while the riders strike at it with lances, unless they ride quickly off, the versatile beam strikes upon their shoulders."

Shakespeare mentions the subject thus in *As You Like It*:—

"My better parts
Are all thrown down, and that which here stands up
Is but a Quintain, a mere lifeless block."

Speaking generally, it may be said that a Quintain was some sort of a lifeless butt or mark set up for a mounted man to exercise his strength, dexterity, and horsemanship against. Many of the squires and yeomen of Richard the Lion-heart held it in great esteem, and in the competitions of the time he who executed his feat of horsemanship in the most graceful manner was awarded the prize of a peacock.

Says Matthew Paris, writing of the time of Henry III.:

"The young Londoners, who were expert horsemen, assembled together to run at the quintain, setting up a peacock as the reward of the best player." On one occasion, the King being in residence at Westminster, went to see this pastime, when a *fracas* arose, and the citizens gave the King's domestics a severe drubbing for their insolent behaviour on the field of sport.

For several centuries after this, tilting at the Quintain was a favourite sport of the youths of London and Westminster.

*Fighting the Pel* has been mentioned as a part of the education of the Knight. It should be added that the pel, pile, or pale was also set up as a mark to cast at with spears.

Old treatises on the sport of fighting the Quintain advised the use of arms of double weight, in order that the warrior might acquire strength to give greater facility in wielding weapons of ordinary size. One poet adds—

"And sixty pounds of weight 'tis good to bear."

An occasional form of this sport substituted a Human Quintain to be tilted at. A fully armed man sat firmly on a heavy block; and assuming an alert, defensive attitude, with a shield held in front of him, he parried the blows of the youthful tilter.

Also in place of a Quintain a ring was sometimes used to tilt at. The ring was suspended from a cross-bar overhead, by means of two springs clipping a socket-holder. Riding full speed with couched lance, if the point fairly entered the ring, it came away readily enough, and remained on the top of the lance, a counter and a trophy in the game.

Another variant of the sport was the Water Quintain. In this aquatic form of the game there was substituted for the shield a large square board, set on the top of a mast appearing some five or six feet above water, in mid-stream. The spearman stood up in a boat, which was rowed swiftly past the board; and any lack of dexterity on his part usually precipitated him into the water, to his own discomfiture and the amusement of the spectators.

## VI

### ARCHERY

The national pastime for centuries—The long-bow and the cross-bow—An insight into the points and technicalities of Archery through the exploits of that prince of archers, Robin Hood, *alias* Locksley (an extract from Scott's "Ivanhoe")—The make of the bow—Of the arrow—The targets—Archery butts—Archery encouraged by municipalities and school foundations—The five points, Standing, Nocking, Drawing, Holding, and Loosing—Shooting at rovers—Military Archery—The prowess of English bowmen—Practice enforced by law—Holiday Shooting in the olden times—Bishop Latimer on Archery—The Yeomen of the Guard—Michael Drayton on English Archery—The long-bow gradually superseded by the arquebus—Archery as a modern recreation—Some ancient and fashionable toxophilite clubs.

FOR centuries the chief national pastime of this country was Shooting with the Long-bow.

The Bow is among the inventions of antiquity, and of all the projectile weapons of man it has been the most universal, remaining almost to the present day a recognised portion of the military equipment of China.

The invention of the Cross-bow, or Arbalist, has been attributed to the Normans, who are said to have used it with marked effect at the Battle of Hastings. Be that as it may, it is certain that from that historic epoch the Long-bow became the most popular, if not the national weapon of the Englishman.

While the arrow sped from the Long-bow was designated a "shaft," that shot from the Cross-bow was called a "bolt." Hence the old English proverb, "I will either make a shaft or a bolt of it," signifying the determination that a thing shall not go unused. The shaft was an ell, or a cloth-yard, in length.

The Arbalist, which came to be made of steel, fitted to a stock of wood, had some such machine as a spanner or a ratchet for bending it, or the larger kinds a windlass; and the bolt adapted to it was termed a "quarrel," from its square or diamond-shaped head.

The English Long-bow was probably a gradual development of the Saxon bow, a short weapon little better than a toy, used almost exclusively for sporting purposes, and seldom if ever employed in warfare. An illuminated manuscript of the eighth century, preserved in the Cottonian Library, shows two Saxon sportsmen, one with his dog in search of the wild deer, the other shooting wild-fowl, and both armed with short, clumsy-looking bows, the strings of which are not attached to the extremities, but allowed to play at some little distance from them. In to all which, they were evidently effective weapons in the hands of a marksman, if we may judge by the number of birds which are depicted as adorning the girdle of the fowler.

Almost ere Saxon and Norman had united to produce the Englishman, the Long-bow had found favour in the land; that is, if we are to credit the word-picture painted for us by Sir Walter Scott, in that incomparable romance of chivalric days, "Ivanhoe."

Everybody has read the novel, and it may be easy to recall the test to which the archery of Robin Hood was put by the tyrannical Prince John. The great outlaw was then passing under the *alias* of Locksley—a name probably chosen because one of the many traditions which clustered around the romantic life-story of that popular hero fixed his birthplace at Loxley, a village on the borders of Needwood Forest in Staffordshire.

The episode is given not only with that air of reality

which distinguishes all Scott's fiction, but also with a wealth of descriptive detail which makes it an apt illustration for our present purposes; and which at the same time overbears nearly every attempt at abridgment, a process which scarcely fails to rob it of some point or other.

"'Fellow,' said Prince John, 'I guessed by thy insolent babble thou wert no true lover of the long-bow, and I see thou darest not adventure thy skill among such merry-men as stand yonder.'

"'Under favour, sir,' replied the yeoman, 'I have another reason for refraining to shoot, besides the fearing discomfiture and disgrace.'

"'And what is thy other reason?' said Prince John, who, for some cause which perhaps he could not himself have explained, felt a painful curiosity respecting this individual.

"'Because,' replied the woodman, 'I know not if these yeomen and I are used to shoot at the same marks; and because, moreover, I know not how your Grace might relish the winning of a third prize by one who has unwittingly fallen under your displeasure.'

"Prince John coloured as he put the question, 'What is thy name, yeoman?'

"'Locksley,' answered the yeoman.

"'Then, Locksley,' said Prince John, 'thou shalt shoot in thy turn, when these yeomen have displayed their skill. If thou carriest the prize, I will add to it twenty nobles; but if thou losest it, thou shalt be stripped of thy Lincoln green, and scourged out of the lists with bowstrings, for a wordy and insolent braggart.'

"'And how if I refuse to shoot on such a wager? Your Grace's power, supported as it is by so many men-at-arms, may indeed easily strip and scourge me, but cannot compel me to bend or to draw my bow.'

"'If thou refusest my fair proffer,' said the Prince, 'the provost of the lists shall cut thy bow-string, break thy bow and arrows, and expel thee from our presence as a faint-hearted craven.'

"'This is no fair chance you put on me, proud Prince,' said the yeoman, 'to compel me to peril myself against the best archers of Leicester and Staffordshire, under the penalty of infamy if they should overshoot me. Nevertheless, I will obey your pleasure.'

"A target was placed at the upper end of the southern avenue which let to the lists. The archers, having previously determined by lot their order of precedence, were to shoot each three shafts in succession. The sports were regulated by an officer of inferior rank, termed the Provost of the Games; for the high rank of the marshals of the lists would have been held degraded, had they condescended to superintend the sports of the yeomanry.

"One by one the archers, stepping forward, delivered their shafts yeomanlike and bravely. Of twenty-four arrows, shot in succession, ten were fixed in the target, and the others ranged so near it, that, considering the distance of the mark, it was accounted good archery. Of the ten shafts which hit the target, two within the inner ring were shot by Hubert, a forester in the service of Malvoisin, who was accordingly pronounced victorious.

"'Now, Locksley,' said Prince John to the bold yeoman, with a bitter smile, 'wilt thou try conclusions with Hubert, or wilt thou yield up bow, baldric, and quiver to the provost of the sports?'

"'Sith it be no better,' said Locksley, 'I am content to try my fortune ; on condition that when I have shot two shafts at yonder mark of Hubert's, he shall be bound to shoot one at that which I shall propose.'

"'That is but fair,' answered Prince John, 'and it shall not be refused thee.—If thou dost beat this braggart, Hubert, I will fill the bugle with silver pennies for thee.'

"'A man can do but his best,' answered Hubert ; 'but my grandsire drew a good long-bow at Hastings, and I trust not to dishonour his memory.'

"The former target was now removed, and a fresh one of the same size placed in its room. Hubert, who, as victor in the first trial of skill, had the right to shoot first, took his aim with great deliberation, long measuring the distance with his eye, while he held in his hand his bended bow, with the arrow placed on the string.

At length he made a step forward, and raising the bow at the full stretch of his left arm, till the centre or grasping-place was nigh level with his face, he drew his bow-string to his ear. The arrow whistled through the air, and alighted within the inner ring of the target, but not quite in the centre.

"'You have not allowed for the wind, Hubert,' said his antagonist, bending his bow, 'or that had been a better shot.'

"So saying, and without showing the least anxiety to pause upon his aim, Locksley stepped to the appointed station, and shot his arrow as carelessly, in appearance, as if he had not even looked at the mark. He was speaking almost at the instant that the shaft left the bow-string ; yet it alighted in the target two inches nearer to the white spot which marked the centre than that of Hubert.

"Hubert resumed his place, and, not neglecting the caution which he had received from his adversary, he made the necessary allowance for a very light air of wind, which had just arisen, and shot so successfully that his arrow alighted in the very centre of the target.

"'A Hubert! a Hubert!' shouted the populace, more interested in a known person than in a stranger. 'In the clout!—in the clout!—a Hubert for ever!'

"'Thou canst not mend that shot, Locksley,' said the prince, with an insulting smile.

"'I will notch his shaft for him, however,' replied Locksley.

"And letting fly his arrow with a little more precaution than before, it lighted right upon that of his competitor, which it split to shivers. The people who stood around were so astonished at his wonderful dexterity, that they could not even give vent to their surprise in their usual clamour. 'This must be the fiend, and no man of flesh and blood,' whispered the yeomen to each other; 'such archery was never seen since a bow was first bent in Britain.'

"'And now,' said Locksley, 'I will crave your Grace's permission to plant such a mark as is used in the North Country; and welcome every brave yeoman who shall try a shot at it to win a smile from the bonnie lass he loves best.'

* * * *

"Locksley returned almost instantly with a willow wand about six feet in length, perfectly straight, and rather thicker than a man's thumb. He began to peel this with great composure, observing, at the same time, that to ask a good woodsman to shoot at a target so broad as had hitherto been used was to put shame upon his skill.

"'For his own part,' he said, 'and in the land where he was bred, men would as soon take for their mark King Arthur's round-table, which held sixty knights around it. A child of seven years old,' he said, 'might hit yonder target with a headless shaft; but,' added he, walking deliberately to the other end of the lists, and sticking the willow wand upright in the ground, 'he that hits that rod at five-score yards, I call him an archer fit to bear both bow and quiver before a king, though it were the stout King Richard himself.'

"'My grandsire,' said Hubert, 'drew a good bow at the Battle of Hastings, and never shot at such a mark in his life; and neither will I. If this yeoman can cleave that rod, I give him the bucklers,—or rather, I yield to the Evil One that is in him, and not to any human skill: a man can but do his best, and I will not shoot where I am sure to miss. I might as well shoot at the edge of our parson's whittle, or at a wheat straw, or at a sunbeam, as at a twinkling white streak which I can hardly see.'

* * * *

"Locksley proceeded to change the string of his weapon which he thought was no longer truly round, having been a little frayed by the two former shots. He then took his aim with some deliberation, and the multitude awaited the event in breathless silence.

"The archer vindicated their opinion of his skill;—his arrow split the willow rod against which it was aimed! A jubilee of acclamations followed; and even Prince John, in admiration of Locksley's skill, lost for an instant his dislike to his person."

Such is Scott's vivid picture, his remarkably realistic description of an Archery contest in the olden time. In a later chapter we are not surprised to learn that, after the custom of the period, the doughty champion had been fitted pat with an eke-name—his admirers had dubbed him Cleave-the-Wand.

We have thus pleasantly obtained an insight into the ancient practice of Archery, and have incidentally made ourselves acquainted with not a few technicalities and points of detail in connection therewith. As to the material used in the construction of bows, and the wearing of Lincoln Green cloth by bowmen of the woodlands, Scott has a further allusion.

In a subsequent passage the novelist makes Isaac of York, in a fit of gratitude, offer to Robin, whom he had previously known under the name of Diccon Bend-the-bow, a present of "merchandises" which he thought would be peculiarly acceptable to that Prince of Archers—to wit, "one hundred yards of Lincoln Green to make doublets to thy men, and a hundred staves of Spanish yew to make bows, and a hundred silken bowstrings, tough round and sound."

Bows were made some six feet in length, or about the height of the bowman when held in the correct vertical position for aiming. The material used was lancewood, hickory, or yew. It is to the compulsory laws of feudal times that we owe the presence of so many old yew-trees in our churchyards at the present day; for it was ordered that this wood should be thus cultivated in order that there should be no lack of material in any of the ten thousand parishes of England for making bows wherewith to arm the nation's staunchest defenders. It is scarcely a quip to say the English yeoman was a "yewman."

An arrow-maker was called a Fletcher, though more properly the name signifies the one who put on the feather, rather than the one who made the shaft and barbed it. On the exterior stone walls of some ancient village churches in this country may still be seen the grooves made centuries ago by the regular sharpening there of arrow-heads.

Gleanings from old ballads, too, may often be found very informative on some of these points, where poetic extravagance has not been unduly allowed to supplant the plain truth. Ordinarily the missile was correctly described as a "gray-goose shaft"; but sometimes the romancist and the minstrel speak of "a silver-headed arrow flighted with peacock's feathers."

Fittingly on gay and particularly festive occasions the targets were garlands of roses hung from the branches of trees; while the prizes ranged from a pair of gloves, or a ring of bright red gold, to a pipe of wine, a great white bull, or a prancing steed ready saddled and bridled for the winner to ride proudly away.

At less heroic competitions, the unskilled shot matches among themselves for the paltry wager of a penny, the less proficient being handicapped to the extent of three shots to one; while the loon who failed to shoot within reasonable distance of the target got a sound buffet on the head. So, at least, the old balladists tell us.

On the other hand, if we are to accept an Old Play as sufficient warranty—a marksman's skill, if not his good deeds, lived after him:

"... And is old Double dead? See, see, he drew a good bow: and dead? He shot a fine shoot. John of Gaunt loved him well, and betted much money on his head. Dead! he would have clapt in the clout at twelve score, and carried you a forehand shaft a fourteen, and a fourteen-and-a-half, that it would have done a man's heart good to see."

Archery Butts were of turf, and ordinarily were placed eleven-score yards apart—a twelve-score shot was accounted a long flight—the shooting taking place from each end in turn. Every parish was required by law to provide its own "buttes," and to this day these ancient shooting-places can be identified by such place-names as "Robin Hood's Butts," "Bassett's Budds," "the Butcroft," or the "Black Butts"; while Churchwarden's Accounts show that these ranges were kept in repair at the public cost to the very close of the seventeenth century.

The ancient practice was to affix a target to the butts by a minute peg displaying a small white mark in the centre; and it was reckoned a gallant shot which placed an arrow quivering in the "blanc" from a distance of four-score yards.

During the shooting all the spectators were cleared from the target end except the marker, who carried a white wand as his symbol of office. As arrows were dear enough not to be lightly lost, competitors were allowed to fetch back any of their discharged arrows that had missed. This they did entirely at their own risk, having to listen for, and give heed to, the warning word "Fast!" which was always uttered as the competitor steadied himself to take aim.

The use of the long-bow appears to have been encouraged in an exceedingly quaint manner at Chester. One of several Shrove Tuesday customs in that city had been for the Saddlers' Company to present to the Drapers "a painted ball of wood, with flowers and arms," which the Master, mounted upon horseback, proffered on the point of a spear in the presence of the Mayor. About 1540 it was agreed in lieu of this to present a ball of silver, valued at 3s. 4d., to be competed for in a race on horseback. And, what is more to the point, it was directed that every man who had been married within the year should give an arrow of silver, in place of the balls of silk and velvet, which according to custom they had hitherto presented to be competed for by shooting with the long-bow.

The original deed founding Harrow School in 1590 discloses Archery as a branch of education at that time. "You shall allow your child at all times bows, shafts, bowstrings, and bracer to exercise shooting." At this foundation was held an annual competition for a silver arrow, and the competitors were attired of white, green, or scarlet satin. Every hit was saluted with a flourish of hunting horns, and the champion shot was escorted home by a procession of the whole school with music and acclamations.

The celebrated scholar Roger Ascham, in his "Toxophilus, the Schole of Shootinge," published in 1545, names as the five important points in Archery—Standing, Nocking, Drawing, Holding, and Loosing.

In Standing the feet were to be planted firmly on the ground, the left foot a little in advance, and the whole of the left side presented to the target; the face looked over the left shoulder, the head and neck being inclined slightly forward.

By Nocking is meant the placing of the arrow in position on the bow. The shaft was set straight across the bow, neither too high nor too low, and drawn back to the bow's cer tre, the nocking point being marked by a coloured silk. Care was taken to nock with the cock feather upwards, and no feathers ruffled.

In Nocking the bow was held obliquely, but in Drawing it was raised to the perpendicular, ready for shooting; the arrow on the string was drawn back to the ear with the right hand, till the pile, or arrow-head, reached the left, or bow-hand; the eye of the marksman was all the time fixed steadily on the gold centre, or bull's-eye.

The Drawing having been accomplished with three fingers (Archery gloves were made with three stalls for that intent), the Holding was not to occupy too long, as hesitancy was considered conducive to the spoiling of both the shot and the bow.

The Loosing was to be quick and hard, so that it might be without twitches, yet soft and gentle that the shaft might fly truly. And, of course, the last three movements were continuous.

Roving, or Shooting at Rovers, was wandering about and taking a sudden shot at any object which struck the eye. Flight Shooting was a trial of strength, rather than of skill, to see how far an arrow could be sped.

To understand the popularity and national importance of Archery a little more than passing attention must be given to the Long-bow as a weapon of war.

The military effectiveness of Archery was found in the sustained discharges of arrows "wholly together," so that they fell thick and sharp as hail; or in what we should now call "volley" firing.

In battle the archers were drawn up in open lines, one behind the other, so as to resemble the form of the spikes of a portcullis or a harrow. They necessarily fought on foot, though when their importance was fully recognised every knight was anxious to mount a few of them on horseback, so that they might attend him in all his expeditions.

Thus Chaucer's knight was attended by his yeoman who carried under his belt—

> "A shefe of peacock's arwes bright and kene."

And—

> "In his hond he bare a mighty bowe."

Edward III. had a guard of one hundred and twenty archers, selected from the strongest men in his kingdom.

The glorious victories of Crecy, Poictiers, and Agincourt were largely attributable to the Englishmen's effective use of the Long-bow; the Cross-bows used by the French could not be so easily protected from the rain.

In the long-drawn-out Wars of the Roses, the ultimate triumph of the Yorkists over their rivals was gained by the superiority of the bands of bowmen they could usually manage to rally to their standard. An edict of that period unequivocally declared that on the due exercise and practice of Archery "the liberties and honour of England principally rested." And be it remembered that by this time the firearm had not only been introduced into warfare, but improved into the convenient form of a hand-gun.

Edward IV. ordained that every Englishman should have a bow of his own height; and whoso neglected to shoot a shaft on a holiday not only forfeited a halfpenny, but, such was public opinion, unmistakably fell in the estimation of his fellows.

On a great popular holiday in those times, although Archery was no part of a knightly accomplishment, even nobles and princes did not disdain to match themselves against the yeoman's cloth-yard. Many of the gentle youth of England, we may read, were trained from boyhood "to brace the bow without the use of gauntlets so that the string touch not the arms." It was necessary physically for the sinews of the bow-hand to acquire a particularly strong grasp.

Henry VIII. was a match for the best bowman in his kingdom—an accomplishment popularly believed to have been inherited from his father, the warlike Henry of Richmond. Bishop Latimer, preaching before Edward

VI., in 1549, said, "My father taught me to lay my body on my bow;" authoritatively adding for the edification of his hearers, "It is best to give the bow so much bending that the string need never touch the arm."

Another passage in his published sermons says that Archery "is a worthy game, a wholesome kind of exercise, and much commended in physic."

The same learned bishop, in his Sixth Sermon, boldly designated the bow "Goddes instrumente." And it speaks volumes for the universal favour in which this arm was then held that, in a period when class distinctions were rigidly observed, the gentry showed no compunctions about taking up a bow, which was not the customary weapon of the well-born, and entering freely into the open competitions for the prize of a "silver arrow" which were held at all great popular holiday meetings.

The fine of a halfpenny had been imposed on every able-bodied man who abstained from Archery practice after church on Sunday, from the warlike times of Edward III. This law was avowedly designed in the cause of national defence. A subsequent Act passed in 1525, "for the maintaining of artillery and the debarring of unlawful games," exempted judges and ecclesiastics, although the parochial clergy of England had not been unknown to take a regular part in these statutory martial exercises.

That famous regiment of Henry VIII., known as the Yeomen of the Guard, was composed entirely of bowmen. An old North Country ballad makes the connection of the yeoman with this weapon a commonplace:—

"Thus endeth the lives of these good yeomen,
God send them eternel Blysse;
And all that with a hand-bowe shoteth
That of heven may never mysse."

Michael Drayton, the Elizabethan poet, who wrote while the archer still remained a most important factor in the national fighting forces, gives us a good insight into the effectiveness of English Archery on the actual field of battle. In the ballad descriptive of the "Battle of Agincourt" he sings thus :—

"When from a meadow by,
Like a storm suddenly,
The English archery
  Struck the French horses.

With Spanish yew so strong,
Arrows a cloth-yard long,
That like to serpents stung,
  Piercing the weather;

None from his fellow starts,
But playing manly parts,
And like true English hearts
  Stuck close together.

When down their bows they threw
And forth their bilboes drew,
And on the French they flew,
  Not one was tardy."

With the invention of the arquebus and other improved forms of portable firearms, the decline of the Long-bow as a weapon set in. But it died hard. Charles I., in the fourth year of his reign, granted a commission under the Great Seal for enforcing the use of the Long-bow. In 1643 the Earl of Essex called upon all well-affected persons to assist in raising a company of archers for the King's service; and, difficult as it may be to realise, at the siege of Worcester in 1651 bows and arrows were in actual use. And this was the last great national event in which the arrow was used as a warlike projectile.

Since that period Archery can claim to rank only as a

THE TOXOPHILITE GROUND AT BAYSWATER, 1830.

[*From a picture by R. Cruikshank. Reproduced by kind permission of the owner, C. J. Longman, Esq.*]

*To face page* 115

recreation. As a modern lawn game it is well calculated to train the hand and judgment to act instinctively (as in getting the proper elevation, and making allowances for side-winds), and to give a strong arm and a correct eye.

The modern practice is to set up a pair of targets, one at opposite ends, some sixty or a hundred yards apart; a party of eight or less shoot from immediately in front of one target at the other; and when one "end" is over, shooting back at the other, in order of merit, the highest scorer going first, and the lowest last.

The target (a thick coil of straw faced by a covering painted with concentric circles of different colours) has a gold bull's-eye, and the scoring is allowed to count thus: the gold centre, 9; the red ring next it, 7; the inner white, 5; the black, 3; and the outer white, 1.

A few of the older county clubs of toxophilites boast quite venerable histories. Yorkshire boasts an ancient club in the Scorton Archers, who are recorded as having met at that place, near Richmond, as far back as May 14, 1673, and to have met annually ever since, except for a brief break (1799–1809) during the Napoleonic Wars. The place of meeting has sometimes been changed to other parts of the districts, as to Settle, to Eryholme, and to Richmond; in fact it has been allowed as a privilege to the champion shot to name the rendezvous for the following year.

But the same quaint ceremonies have always been observed; each archer is allowed to send trial arrows to find the range, the target being set a hundred yards away. The first prize is, as usual, a silver arrow, and the second a silver bugle, the winners becoming respectively captain and lieutenant for the ensuing year. There are other prizes, and an "antient horn spoon" goes to the worst shot of the meet.

In Warwickshire exists an Archery Club known as the Woodmen of Arden, constituted of the nobility and gentry of the neighbourhood. They practise on what is known as the old Forest Ground at Meriden, in that portion of the Shakespeare country called the Forest of Arden, with headquarters at the Forest Hall in that parish. At this place is deposited a horn said to have been used by Robin Hood, who is traditionally stated to have competed here. The Archery meetings in their present form were revived in 1785; and it is an interesting fact that since 1745 the office of Bowman to the Club has been held by the great-grandfather, grandfather, and father of the present holder, Mr. F. W. Thompson. The King's Bodyguard of Archers of Scotland compete here every three years for the Scotch Bowl; the Woodmen of Arden likewise going to Scotland every three years alternately for the same purpose.

Towards the close of the eighteenth century there was a revival of Archery as a fashionable amusement among the county families of Staffordshire. In 1791 they established a society called the Staffordshire Bowmen, which held its meetings every three weeks during the summer season at Sandon. It languished during the disturbed period of the Napoleonic Wars, but was resuscitated in 1821, and for a number of years its meetings were well attended, particularly on Grand Target days.

The Kentish Bowmen, and other county clubs, have been similarly successful in keeping up locally the popularity of what was once the chief national sport of the English people.

## VII

## SHOOTING

A brief history of Shooting—The gun in succession to the hawk—Snap shooting supersedes netting—The "hedge sportsman"—Shooting becomes a national sport in the eighteenth century—The Shooting seasons—Battue shooting—Minor shooting—Pigeon-shooting—Trapping the birds—Nefarious practices—Lead to the decline of Pigeon-shooting.

SHOOTING as a sport is naturally of late development, the use of gunpowder having been restricted to military purposes for several centuries after its invention. The first sporting gun dates from the middle of the seventeenth century, towards the end of which the gentry had begun to amuse themselves with "shooting at the popinjay," a mark made in the form of a bird.

To shoot at a living thing rather than at an inanimate object seems always to afford the marksman a much keener sense of satisfaction. The propensity to kill something is very strong in the human breast, unrefined and unreclaimed from the last vestiges of savagery.

To shoot birds on the wing with arrows sped from a bow was scarcely possible. Grouse were invariably taken by hawking or by netting till about 1725. In fact shooting flying was not sufficiently practicable to become popular till much later in the same century, by which period a light and well-balanced gun had been produced which favoured the art of snap shooting.

After that nothing that wore feathers could hope to escape the attention of the sportsman armed with a gun.

The fowler who goes forth to search for the wild bird within its native haunts is not always the objectionable gunner.

> "See the flush't Woodcock thrill the grovy glades,
> Till Death arresting his swift flight invades;
> The Stock-doves fleet, the strong-pounc'd Mallard rise,
> The charge of Death o'ertakes them with surprise.
> Nor scapes the Lark that serenades the sun,
> The call of Fate commands the charmer down!"

The objectionable gunner is he who shirks the fatigue of the chase, and saving his own carcase from the risks of a hunt, takes a wanton delight in shooting innocent creatures which can be of no possible service to him, and whose lives are sacrificed merely to display his prowess as a death-dealer.

> "Tomtits and Sparrows, Pippits, Larks,
> Are all to him as easy marks."

Shooting as a national sport commenced in the eighteenth century, the objects of the gun being both game and vermin—chiefly pheasants, partridges, and hares in the one case, and foxes, martens, polecats, stoats, magpies, hawks, and owls in the other.

Grouse-shooting commences on August 12th and terminates December 10th; this moorland bird is found only in the northern half of the country. Partridge-shooting, practised over most of the cultivated land in England, begins September 1st, and the Pheasant-shooting season on October 1st: these two seasons terminate February 1st. Trained dogs are generally used to discover and to recover the game.

"Grouse-driving" is largely practised, the sportsmen

being hidden in various parts of the moor by peat-stacks, or furze, &c., while beaters drive the packs within range. Pheasant-shooting is of two kinds; there is the working of a cover with well-broken spaniels, and by battue. At the opening of the season, till the leaves are well off the trees, Pheasant-shooting is best practised in the open.

The battues are conducted in different ways; sometimes the plantation is surrounded by a net to prevent the birds from "running"; the sportsmen place themselves in advantageous positions commanding all the open spaces, so that even in the largest coverts a dozen guns get shots at nearly every living thing in it. A pair of guns are generally employed by each, and the marksman is often furnished with an attendant to look after them. The beating commences before the arrival of the sportsmen, and everything is done to ensure big bags.

Battue shooting has excited much controversy as to its legitimate position in sport; it is no doubt a plan whereby a party of several guns can obtain an equal amount of shooting, and there is generally a display of both bad and good shooting. But for the execution done it is a form of sport which entails comparatively little or no exertion.

Ground game is very plentiful in England, and the shooting of hares and rabbits is largely indulged in. The latter kind of shooting is sometimes assisted by the employment of ferrets to fetch the conies out of their holes.

For quick shooting the woodcock provides one of the best exercises; this bird in rising from the thick covert he haunts makes such rapid swerves that it is most difficult to hit him.

> "Where woodcocks dodge, there distance knows no laws,
> Necessity admits of no room to pause."

Snipe-shooting over boglands is a favourite pastime with the hardier class of gunners. Says Tom Hood—

> "There's a twofold sweetness in double pipes;
> And double barrel and double Snipes
> Give the sportsman a duplicate pleasure."

Rook-shooting, contrariwise, is just as tame; while again at the other extreme requiring hardihood on the part of the sportsman is the winter wild-fowling, either as the fen and shore shooting of aquatic birds, or their pursuit and slaughter in uncomfortable flat-bottomed craft called punts.

But wherever it is the gunner indulges his sporting proclivities, within the well-stocked covert, on the open moor, across the heavy snipe marsh, or lying *perdu* and half-frozen in a punt, his sport should be of the kind to give him a healthy amount of bodily fatigue, train him to an alertness of observation, and cultivate a quick and accurate style of marksmanship.

PIGEON-SHOOTING, and the shooting of other birds (generally small ones) from traps is still largely indulged in. Properly pursued and safeguarded from all the consequences of a culpable negligence, there need be no actual cruelty in this sport, though marksmanship may be cultivated just as well by the employment of clay birds or other inanimate objects thrown from spring traps.

In "Fifty Years of My Life," that all-round sportsman of the old school, Sir John Astley, describes the Great Derby Dove Handicap of 1863. There is nothing heroic or elevating about the narrative; the feature on which the writer seems to lay the greatest stress is the making of a betting book on the result.

It is always through indulgence in the gambling habit that the element of cruelty manages to creep into otherwise innocent pastimes. It is so in shooting matches.

J. Scott, Sculp.

DUCK SHOOTING.

[*Published, 1795, by J. Wheble, Warwick Square.*]

*To face page* 120

To win a wager some men will not only sacrifice their honour, but will give way to the most infamous of practices, from which they are not to be turned even by the innocent helplessness of a dove.

In trapping, at a properly conducted match, as each bird is taken from the open crate its wings are opened and smoothed out before being placed in the trap, thus affording it every possible chance of escape. The traps, sometimes five in number, are each connected by separate cords to an oblong box (fitted with an automatic arrangement), from the opposite end of which a cord is held by the "puller." The shooter takes up his position, at an average distance of twenty-five yards from the traps, and at the word "pull" the man in charge of the single cord releases one of the birds, but neither he (the puller) nor any person on the field can tell which of the five traps will be opened. As the bird flies from the trap the gun is fired, and immediately the bird touches the ground an exceedingly smart fox-terrier dog is slipped, gathers the bird, and returns to the man in charge of the slips, who, in case the pigeon is not killed outright, at once gives it the happy despatch; the average time between firing of shot and death of bird being fifteen seconds. But unfortunately for the "sport," some of the shadiest and most disreputable practices have crept into the code of its more vulgar votaries.

By arrangement between the "shot" and the man who puts the birds into the trap the pigeons may be made to fly to one side or the other, or else to pitch aimlessly about in the air, as mutually agreed upon in secret. This is accomplished in various ways; as by breaking a wing or plucking out some of the tail feathers, and applying caustic to the naked parts; by squirting tobacco-juice into the eyes; or even by piercing the bird's eye with a needle. By this latter atrocity the birds are said, in the slang of the Midlands to be "readied" or "ready-eyed." Or sometimes the traps have been "faked" so that the shooter should miss his mark; the birds being carefully sorted in such a way that a "swooper," or strong, active pigeon, would be slipped in after one or two slow or injured ones had been put up.

Little wonder, therefore, that Pigeon-shooting has been decried as brutal and degrading, and that the force of public opinion ultimately led to its abolition from Hurlingham, notwithstanding that Pigeon-shooting had been the very basis of the foundation of the famous Hurlingham Club. It was felt that the birds did not get "a sporting chance"; and although Pigeon-shooting still retains a high position on the Continent, and is still fairly popular in Yorkshire and Lancashire, it may now be looked upon as a rapidly declining English sport.

In hunting a wild animal or bird in its native haunts, in following it over heather and fallow, there is provided an outlet for the true sporting instinct—the instinct which helps to develop in man the qualities of courage, skill, wit, resource, alertness, and agility; which hardens the muscles, quickens the vision, and assists all the bodily faculties. Only in a very minor degree can this be said of Pigeon-shooting. It needs no courage, no strength of arm, and little resource to shoot a bird suddenly released from a trap a few yards off. Precision of aim and alertness are necessary, it is true, but little more. These qualities are requisite also, to an even greater extent, for success in bringing down clay pigeons—a development of the pastime which is not open to some of the solid objections raised against the practice of live Pigeon-shooting.

*Corbould, Del.* *Cook, Sculp.*

PIGEON SHOOTING AT THE WARREN HOUSE, BILLINGBEAR, BERKS.

## VIII

### HORSE-RACING

The "running horses" of antiquity—Races held by English nobles at Easter and Whitsuntide—The stable of Henry VIII.—Pedigree valued—The gambling element—Chester races the first regularly established—James I. the founder of English Horse-racing—Rise of Newmarket—The Rye House Plot—Patronage of the turf by Charles II., Anne, and the Prince Regent—York races—The St. Leger—The Derby—Royal Ascot—Glorious Goodwood—The classic ground of Newmarket Heath—The Jockey Club—Other ancient meetings—At Durham, Lincoln, Northampton, Aintree, &c.—The racing of donkeys and other animals in olden times—The modern gate meeting—The superiority of the English racer—Speed preferred to strength.

It was more requisite in former times that a man should be acquainted with the nature, powers, and characteristics of a horse than in these days of quick transit, by steam power or electricity. It is not surprising that from the earliest times the swiftness of the animal should have been appreciated by man, and a premium put upon "running horses."

It is not known for certain whether the ancient Britons raced the native horses yoked to their war-chariots, but the Romans, during their occupation of this country, are believed to have practised horse-racing with their military mounts.

Horse-racing would appear to have been known to the Anglo-Saxons, as King Athelstan made a present of a number of running horses, equipped with saddles and bridles, the latter fitted with bits of gold, to Hugh Capet, who subsequently became King of France.

The same Saxon monarch thought the preservation of the native breed of sufficient importance to call for a legal enactment to prevent the export of horses, excepting as presents; while at the same time he took steps for the introduction of foreign blood by importing "running horses" from Germany.

Fitzstephen, a writer of the time of Henry II., tells us that horses were regularly exposed for sale at Smithfield, and to test the qualities of the more valuable riding horses and charging steeds, they were often matched against each other and raced in the vicinity of the market.

To make a course for these impromptu races, the commoner horses were moved out of the way; the competing horses were ridden by jockeys of judgment, who steered them with brandished whips and bloody spurs, after the usually approved methods, though inspired only by the applause of the spectators and the hopes of victory.

We can learn nothing of prizes being offered at these informal market races, but it is clearly stated that the horses were not only willing, but often evinced a spirit of emulation, quivering with excitement, and actually seeming to enjoy the racing.

King John was so great a lover of swift horses that he frequently preferred fines to be paid to him in these rather than in money. Running horses are frequently mentioned in the items of royal expenditure at that period. One purchased for Edward III. was priced at twenty marks, and the £13 6s. 8d., into which this sum may be translated, represented perhaps twenty times that amount when compared with present values.

A little later it had become a custom for the nobility to race horses against each other at certain seasons of the year, particularly at Easter and Whitsuntide. Thus in the old romance of Sir Bevis of Southampton—

> "In somer at Whitsontyde
> When Knightes most on horsebacke ride;
> A cours, let they make on a daye
> Steedes, and Palfrayes, for to assaye;
> Which horse, that best may ren
> Three myles the cours was then,
> Who that might ryde him shoulde
> Have forty pounds of redy golde."

By that period the Welsh breed of horses had developed speed through the efforts of Roger de Belesme, Earl of Shrewsbury, in importing the swift and docile Spanish horse for stud purposes on his estates in Powysland. Horses from this part of the country had become celebrated throughout England for elegance and swiftness.

Among the many amusements of Henry VIII., Horse-racing held a place. In the household expenses of that amiable monarch may be found charges made for "Coursers, young horses, hunting geldings, hobies, Barbary horses, stallions, stalking horses," and other specimens of the noble equine race. Then appear, for the years 1529 and 1530, such items as "rewards paid to the boye that ranne the horse"; a sum paid as a reward to the keeper of the Barbary horse, evidently for winning; and similar entries of a like nature point unmistakably to the royal horses being put into competition with others. Henry VIII. was a great admirer of horses; he imported them from Turkey, Spain, Naples, and Flanders, and took various steps to improve the breed in England, even to regulating the proportion of sires to dams. It is manifest that a charger required for tilting, and carrying a weight of armour equivalent to that of a second man on its back, needed bone, strength, and stamina, even before speed. The late Sir John Gilbert, in his pictures of mounted knights, was always careful to depict the charger as a large, thick-set horse. When, at the commencement of the seventeenth century, Arab sires began to be imported into this country, it was clearly not in the interests of military mounts, but to improve the breed of what were then known as "bell-horses," otherwise race-horses, so called because the racecourse of the period was called a bell-course, on account of the prizes being invariably in the shape of a silver or a golden bell.

Not till the universal employment of firearms had made the carrying of a heavy panoply of mail no longer necessary, did it become possible to sacrifice the qualities of strength and endurance in a war-horse in favour of that speed and gainliness we recognise and admire in the light cavalry mounts of the present day.

We are let into the secrets of horse-breeding in Queen Elizabeth's time by Bishop Hall's satires, where he alludes to the folly of depending upon the lustre of ancestry rather than upon personal merit. He says:—

"Tell me, thou gentle Troian, dost thou prise
Thy brite beasts worth, by their dam's qualities?
Sayst thou this colt shall prove a swift-paced steed
Onely because a Jennet did him breed?
Or sayst thou this same horse shall win the prize
Because his dam was swiftest Trunchefice,
Or Runcevall his sire, himself a Galloway?
While like a tireling jade, he lags half-way!"

That betting has been almost inseparable from this sport from the very first, may also be gathered from contemporary writers; for does not Shakespeare allude to wagering with Barbary horses in *Hamlet?* And in his "Anatomy of Melancholy" Burton sarcastically writes (1660): "Horse-races are desports of great men, and good in themselves, though many gentlemen by such means gallop quite out of their fortunes." Yet, though the gambling evil had crept in, the racing of horses as first instituted may be regarded as a liberal pastime, honestly practised for the pleasure of it rather than for profit.

When, in the middle of the sixteenth century, the citizens of Chester substituted the emulative sport of Horse-racing for the annual Shrovetide Football on the Roodee, no longer bearable on account of the intolerable rowdyism which accompanied it, it was agreed that the usual prize-money should be applied to buy a silver bell, to be awarded to the rider whose horse should "run the best and farthest" at that customary holiday meeting of the early spring.

There is no present-day remnant of this ancient practice, but it may be explained that the Roodee, or Rood-eye (that is, "the Island of the Cross"), is a public open space by the side of the Dee, where now are held the annual races, which are so managed as to constitute a source of revenue to the city of Chester. The silver "glayves" appear to have been a prize in the shape of toy daggers or miniature swords. At a meeting of the Goldsmiths' Company on January 23, 1674, there was passed the following "regulation": "It was agreed that those who are to make the gleaves for that yeare shall take those gleaves that are left in any of the Brothers' hands in the yeare preceading, and to pay for every gleave tenn pence a peece, and to give twelve pence to those Brethren who do not make gleaves for that yeare."

For the first three-quarters of a century the bell seems to have been held only for the year, and returned to the Corporation at the end of the twelve months, to be re-offered for competition. Then the Chester contest became known as St. George's Race, and the prize St.

George's Bell. The latter was "of good value of eight or ten pounds," bought with "moneyes collected from the citizens" for that purpose.

It was to be given to the one "who won the last course or trayne" in a race "five times round the Roody," starting "from the new tower." It was in 1624, John Brereton, innkeeper, being Mayor of Chester, when these alterations in the conditions of running were made, it being then decided (on St. George's Day, April 29th) that in future the successful horseman should be awarded the prize absolutely, to hold as his own for ever.

As may be seen, the Chester races, the oldest regular event of their kind in England, were clearly established for amusement simply; there is found no mention of weighing the riders, loading them with weights, or any of the other niceties now observed at race meetings.

Nearly half a century afterwards (1665) there came a check to the prosperity of Chester Races. It appears that the Sheriffs of the city determined to forego their Calves-head Feast in order to provide with the cost of it a piece of plate to be run for on the Shrove Tuesday.

The High Sheriff himself became a competitor, and "borrowed a Barbary horse of Sir Thomas Middleton, which won him the plate." This proceeding may have been accepted as quite legitimate; but the same competitor holding the official position of Master of the Race, he in that capacity "would not suffer the horses of Master Massey, of Puddington, and of Sir Philip Egerton, of Oulton, to run, because they came the day after the time prefixed for the horses to be brought and kept in the city." We are not surprised after this to learn that this stickler for punctilio gave such offence to the gentry who had previously patronised the meeting, that the city historian has to record with regret that they had "relinquished our races ever since."

It was James I. to whom the "Turf" is mainly indebted for placing it upon a solid basis in this country. In Scotland the breed of horses is said to have been vastly improved by some Spanish stallions which had been thrown on the coast of Galloway, from a wrecked vessel of the Spanish Armada. The increase of speed and fire thus acquired had led to a spirit of wagering and gambling among the Scotch; and in 1621 it was found necessary to enact that no person should win more than a hundred marks, any surplus above that sum being cannily confiscated to the relief of the poor.

On James's accession to the throne of England, if he did not exactly originate the races at Newmarket, he accorded them his patronage, built himself a house in the town, and did much by his presence and countenance to set the institution of Horse-racing there on a sound and permanent foundation.

It is recorded that in the seventeenth century Horse-racing that had formerly been practised at Eastertide "was then put down" (the fact itself is unimpeachable, though the reason assigned by the old writer is suspicious) "as contrary to the holiness of the season." Yet towards the end of that century it was receiving, as due to "the sport of kings," the royal patronage. Is it not a matter of history that Charles II. was returning from Newmarket Races when it was designed by conspirators to murder him, near the Rye House, in 1683? It was only the accident of a fire occurring at his Newmarket palace, which caused his hasty and unexpected return to London, that upset the calculations of his enemies and so saved his life.

In a collection of songs, entitled "Pills to Purge Melancholy," published in 1719, is one called "New Market," the most famous place in England for the exhibition of race-horses in the exercise of their prowess.

10

The following extract from it shows that the pursuit of the sport was already accompanied by every species of gambling and chicanery known to the school of roguery :—

"Let cullies that lose at a race
Go venture at hazard to win,
Or he that is bubb'd at dice
Recover at Cocking again.
Let jades that are founder'd be bought;
Let jockeys play crimp to make sport.
Another makes racing a trade
And dreams of his projects to come;
And many a crimp match has made
By bubbing another man's groom."

The Commonwealth period was, of course, inimicable to this, as to all other sports. After the Restoration Charles II. was a great patron of racing, and at one time proposed to make Winchester the seat of this and other outdoor royal diversions—a change that would have proved disastrous to the future prospects of Newmarket. Strangely enough an Act was passed in this reign to restrain gaming and betting in racehorses to an excessive amount on credit.

Queen Anne kept and raced horses in her own name; and to this sovereign the Turf is indebted for several Royal Plates, though it is doubtful whether all the "royal plates" now in existence were originally gifts from the royal purse. This by the way.

George IV., when Prince of Wales, was much given to the sport, though nearly always unfortunate in his turf speculations. William IV. kept a racing stud. Queen Victoria in the earlier years of her reign often favoured the racecourse with her presence, particularly Royal Ascot.

The reign of James I. was epoch-making in the history of English Horse-racing, a number of popular meetings dating from that period. As previously mentioned, they were at first called bell-courses, on account of the prizes consisting of gold or silver bells. It is doubtless to that period we owe the nursery rhyme—

> "Bell-horses, bell-horses, what time of day?
> One o'clock, two o'clock, and three goes away!"

In addition to Newmarket the royal patronage of James' sons was bestowed on race meetings in Hyde Park, and at Datchet meads, near Windsor. A doggerel of the year 1690, signed with the name of Matthew Thomas Baskerville, belauds Burford Downs, in Oxfordshire, thus:—

> "Next for the glory of the place
> Here has been rode many a race—
> King Charles the Second I saw here
> (But I've forgotten in what year).
> The Duke of Monmouth here also
> Made his horse to swete and blow;
> Lovelace, Pembrook, and other gallants
> Have been venturing here their talents—"
> &c., &c.

About this period the earlier practice of offering bells as prizes was altered; it became the custom to offer cups or bowls, or other pieces of plate, generally of the value of a hundred guineas; and upon these trophies of victory were usually engraved the pedigree and achievements of the winning quadruped.

The royal patronage continued to be extended to the sport, William III. and his Queen making contributions in money and plate; and George I., while staying in the neighbourhood of Guildford, gave a hundred guineas to the race fund of that town. At Merrow, near this place, an old inn long bore the sign of "The Running Horse," conferred, no doubt, when Guildford races were in their zenith.

While some of the older race meetings have flourished and grown, others have died out of existence. It is recorded in 1646 that at Stamford, in Lincolnshire, it was the custom for "a concourse of noblemen and gentlemen to meet together in mirth and amity, for the exercise of their swift-running horses every Thursday in March." The prize was a silver cup, of the value of about £8, provided by the interest on a fund originally raised by these noble patrons of sport, and administered by the aldermen of the town for the time being.

Although Horse-racing may be said to have been established on a permanent basis in the reign of James I., the regular holding of race-meetings cannot all be referred to that or any one period. The first regular races, in point of date, were the Chester Races, which can be traced back to 1511, though perhaps they were not in those days an annual affair, or held at any regular interval.

In the racing world Chester ranks after Epsom, Ascot, York, and Doncaster. Its King's Plate was first run for in 1802, and the Chester Cup (instituted as the Tradesman's Cup) in 1824.

Of all Englishmen, none can exceed a Yorkshireman in his love of a good horse. As early as 1590 horse-races were held at York, the prize being a small gold or silver bell, which it was customary to attach to the headgear of the winning quadruped.

The racecourse at Knavesmire ("the swampy pasture-land for the poor householders' cattle") by the side of the river Ouse about a mile out of York, was first established in 1709; some writers, however, postpone the date to 1731, when the King's Guineas were first run for, affirming that previously the races were run over Clifton and Rawcliffe Ings, on the north-west of the city.

The Knavesmire racecourse, in the shape of a horseshoe and over a mile and three-quarters round, is considered one of the best in England for witnessing the racing from the inside. Queen Anne gave a cup for this meeting in 1713.

Of the two Yorkshire meetings, Doncaster claims precedence over York on account of the great St. Leger race which is run over its course. The earliest notice of a race over Doncaster Town Moor is in 1703. In 1716 the Corporation or Town Plate of £50 was given to be run for annually; and the race known as the "St. Leger" was established in 1778.

This important racing event was named after Colonel St. Leger, who lived at Park Hill, near Doncaster. He originated the sweepstakes for three-year-olds, on the conditions of a race held two years previously; and at a dinner held on the day of entry at the "Red Lion," Doncaster, in 1778, the chairman—the Marquis of Rockingham—proposed the race should be named after the Colonel. The compliment was passed, and as the St. Leger the race has been known ever since.

In 1803 the King's Plate was transferred from Burford to Doncaster, and this caused another day to be added to the previous three days' meeting; in 1825 the meeting was prolonged to a fifth day.

The course, which is about a mile out of the town, is a little under a mile and three-quarters round it; there are two meetings held here in the year—one in March, as well as the better known one in September.

The well-known sporting proclivities of the average Yorkshireman will account for the continued prosperity enjoyed by these two meetings, which rank among the principal racing events of the year.

The most popular race of all is the "Derby," run on Epsom Downs, in Surrey, within driving distance of the great Metropolis. Its features are the excellence of the horses engaged in the contest, the large amount of the stakes, the immense sums of money in wagers depending upon the result, and the countless thousands who make holiday to attend it.

The other national races have each their own peculiar features. Chester draws the majority of its visitors from its own citizens and the locality around it; the same may be said of Doncaster and of York; at Newmarket the attendance is most strongly marked by the professional feature; Royal Ascot and Princely Goodwood by the aristocratic and fashionable elements; but Epsom possesses a universality—it combines in the greatest degree the elements of each and all.

The "Derby Day" to many is the great festival of the year; on that day the Englishman visiting Epsom loses his taciturnity; on the road to and from London, crowded with every kind of vehicle from the family coach to the costermonger's cart, social barriers are broken down, good-humoured banter is indulged in, and perhaps no other drive can be found in England on all the other 364 days of the year so fraught with exuberant spirits and harmless merriment.

The village of Epsom first came into public notice by reason of its mineral waters, the medicinal qualities of which were discovered in the reign of Elizabeth. During the time of Charles II. it was at the height of its popularity as a fashionable watering-place. Its decline set in about the year 1800, when the practice of sea-bathing began to supersede the drinking of mineral waters among the leaders of society.

The precise period when Horse-racing began to be practised at Epsom is not known; but by 1725 Banstead Downs (as the place is often called) was famous for its horse matches.

By 1730 annual races had been instituted, and in

1743 the prizes had already become valuable. Year by year the prestige of the meeting rose, capital horses being entered, and good sport always shown. In 1780 the Derby Stakes were instituted, the sponsor of the event being the twelfth earl of Derby, a prominent and liberal patron of sport in those days.

The Derby, like the celebrated St. Leger, was not taken so much notice of the first few years it was run; but the disposal of stakes to the value of several thousands of pounds in a brief period of time, less than three minutes, has led to the prize being dubbed the "Blue Ribbon of the Turf." Another well-known race run at Epsom is the one open to three-year-old fillies—and therefore sometimes termed the Ladies' Race—established in 1779, and called the Oaks—a name derived from an ale-house of that sign, which once stood on Banstead Downs, and was enlarged and converted into a hunting-seat, and then sold to the Earl of Derby, the founder of this event.

The Epsom racecourse, which is on manorial land, is exactly a mile and a half in length, and is not reckoned by any means one of the best in the kingdom; the first half-mile is on the ascent, the next third of a mile is level ground, from the bend into the straight run home, and to within the distance, it is on the descent, and from this point the remainder is again on the ascent—a variation of level which often upsets calculations as to the results anticipated.

The Derby is always run on a Wednesday near the end of May or the beginning of June, and till recently it was customary, year after year, to adjourn Parliament for this great racing carnival. The Oaks is run on the Friday following. The expense of conducting this meeting is very heavy, but the public support is always forthcoming. The Grand Stand at Epsom will accommodate 5,000 spectators.

The race meeting next in importance to the Epsom carnival is that at Ascot, near Windsor. While the former is noted for being the saturnalia of a vast crowd, the latter is distinguished for its genteel quietness and aristocratic assemblage. The earliest racing recorded here was in 1727. In 1772 the famous race for a Gold Cup was instituted; followed in 1785 by the establishment of a Gold Plate of one hundred guineas in value. The value of the stakes has risen since to £11,000 or £12,000.

These races, being near Windsor Castle, have been regularly honoured with royal patronage; the course is kept up by the Master of the Buckhounds; and the certificate of having won a royal plate here must be signed by the Master of the Hounds instead of by the Lord Lieutenant of the County, as in all other cases. There is usually a procession of royal carriages from the Castle to the course when the monarch, accompanied by the Master of the Buckhounds, goes to witness these races.

The dukes of Richmond have always been keen sportsmen. The first duke was an enthusiastic follower of the Charlton Foxhounds—Charlton was the Melton Mowbray of its day—and purchased Goodwood at the beginning of the eighteenth century, chiefly as a hunting-seat and summer resort. In 1801 the third duke formed the now famous racecourse in the park, and the first meeting was arranged by the members of the local Hunt Club, and the officers of the Sussex Militia. A sum of £313 in public money was collected, the sweepstakes amounting to £300. The Prince of Wales, afterwards George IV., was to have graced the opening with his presence, but failed to appear at the last moment. The race meeting made but little progress under the fourth duke, who, notwithstanding that he was fond of racing and hunting, could find little time from his numerous political engagements to indulge his sporting proclivities. Upon his sudden death, in

Drawn & Etched by H. Alken Esq.

ASCOT RACES. *Tom & Bob winning the long odds from a knowing one*

London Pub.d by Jones & Co. June 22nd 1822

1819, and the succession of his son to the estates, the race meeting began to assume the dimensions and importance which is summed up in the appellation now generally applied to it—"Glorious Goodwood."

The classic ground of English Horse-racing is Newmarket. The town is in Suffolk, but the course is in Cambridgeshire; and it is unquestionably the finest course and training-ground in England, with a grassy stretch of four miles, possessing a peculiarly springy turf, the springiness being attributed to the work of myriads of earthworms. The course is divided into eighteen different lengths; here no crowds impede the view, none of the rowdyism or even the bustle of most other racecourses distracts the attention on this course. The spectators seldom exceed 500 in number, and they are mostly of the highest classes, the majority on horseback. The fair sex are seldom in evidence. Newmarket Heath is by no means an animated scene during any one of its many races. There is no Grand Stand, and no permanently fixed winning-post; the distance to be run is determined by the Judge's Chair being wheeled about from point to point on the course. The spectators are, consequently, under the necessity of moving from place to place in order to witness the various contests.

These racing grounds have been the property, since 1753, of the renowned Jockey Club, a powerful and influential corporate body controlling all the racing affairs of this country.

The Jockey Club, established in the time of George II., makes and administers arbitrarily all Turf laws; some of its transactions, it may be observed, being neither recognised nor governed by the constitutional laws of the land. Still, it is a most admirable body, always perfectly just and strictly honourable in its rulings; it is the recognised custodian of Turf morals, and hitherto has proved itself worthy of the responsibility. It has long maintained a firm hold on the confidence of the racing public ; and it will continue to enjoy that confidence so long as it upholds the purity of the sport committed to its charge. All race meetings of any importance in this country naturally place their management under Jockey Club rules ; all racing clubs and committees acknowledge its authority by a common consent born of long-established usage.

Some of the earliest public races known—some of them, indeed, earlier than James I.—were held at Garterley in Yorkshire, Theobalds in Enfield Chase, and at Croydon in Surrey. There is scarcely a trace of them left.

Durham Races are an old institution, dating probably from James I.; Lincoln and Northampton Races are both equally ancient; Newcastle Races date from 1695, and the Carlisle meeting from 1750. In Lancashire the racing at Manchester was established about 1730, while the annual races held on Aintree course at Liverpool are as modern as 1827. The Royal Purse of a hundred guineas annually run for at Aintree was originally presented by William IV.

In 1711 a selling race was advertised, in a paper called the *Post Boy*, to take place at Coleshill, near Birmingham. The race was open to any horse, mare, or gelding, that had not won above the value of five pounds, to carry ten stone weight if fourteen hands high, weight allowance for inches; the prize being a six-guinea plate, and the winner to be sold for ten pounds.

The advertisement also announced donkey races at the same meeting; it should not be omitted to mention that it was no uncommon thing for other animals than horses to be raced at those old country meetings. At the Whitsun Races at Northampton, in 1724, two bulls, four cows, and a calf were raced for five guineas. The cows threw

DUNGANNON BEATING ROCKINGHAM AT NEWMARKET.
[*Published, 1800, by J. Wheble, Warwick Square.*]

*To face page 138*

their riders, the calf fell down with his, and one of the bulls won before a vast concourse of people.

A large proportion of modern race meetings are conducted in a purely commercial spirit, as dividend-earning concerns, deriving their profit from the gate-money paid for admission. There is little of that sentiment attached to these gate-meetings which clings to the popular old races that have, for a century or two, been run on open common land just outside the walls of a sporting community.

All English race-horses are descended either from Arabian or from Barbary sires ; and in energy, swiftness, elegance, and grace, surpass their Eastern progenitors. The English racer is so far superior to other European breeds that it is usual on the courses of this country to allow foreign horses an advantage in the weight they carry.

This improvement in the breed, brought about by crossing the English stock with Arabian blood, was due to Mr. Darley, a gentleman belonging to a Yorkshire sporting family, and having commercial relations with the Levant. The offspring thus produced was the Duke of Devonshire's Flying Childers, the fleetest horse of his time, with a record of 4 miles 1 furlong 138 yards, run in 7½ minutes.

Descended from the same Arabian was the famous race-horse Eclipse, who could never meet an opponent sufficiently fleet to test his full powers. He became the sire of 334 winners ; after realising his owner a princely fortune he died in 1789 at the age of 75, and his skeleton is now preserved in the Museum at Oxford.

Speed is now considered more important than strength, though in handicapping race-horses consideration is given to age as well as to previous successes in determining what weight an animal shall carry in any given race.

## IX

### BALL PLAY

Universality of the toy—Ball play, an Easter church diversion—The Stool-ball of dairymaids—The original form of Cricket—Cambuca, the English Goff—Bandy, or Stow-ball—Shindy, or Hackie—Pall Mall—Ring-ball—Fives, or Hand Tennis—Cavanagh, the famous Fives champion—The Fives Court at Copenhagen House—Tennis, as developed from palm play to bat play—At first an outdoor game—"The game of Kings" patronised by Henry VIII., Charles I., and Charles II.—The latest development, Lawn Tennis (1872)—Rackets—The evolution of the game—Tavern racket courts—Played in the Fleet Prison (extract from "Pickwick")—Club-ball the forerunner of Rounders—Trap-ball—Nurr and Spell—Tip-cat—Shuttlecock and Battledore—Cup-and-ball.

BALL playing was at one time universal in every rank of life as an Easter Monday diversion. Even the clergy could not forego its delights, and actually made ball-playing a part of the church service at Easter-time. Thus at Chester Cathedral a ball was taken into the sacred edifice by the bishop or the dean, who, at the commencement of the antiphons began to dance, and tossed the ball to the choristers, and these in turn tossed it to each other during the whole time of the dancing and antiphonal chanting.

The size of the ball for church service was strictly regulated, and as it was tossed by the dean, or his representative, to each chorister in succession, the organ played lively music suitable to the dance as well as the

*Cook, Sculp.*

GRAND CRICKET MATCH, PLAYED IN LORD'S GROUND, MARY-LE-BONE, ON JUNE 20th AND FOLLOWING DAY BETWEEN THE EARLS OF WINCHILSEA AND DARNLEY FOR 1,000 GUINEAS.

[*Published, 1793, by J. Wheble, Warwick Square.*]

*To face page* 141

chanted antiphon. It was deemed an honour to throw the ball, and even archbishops performed this ceremony; so long as the ball was held in his hand the clergy danced round him, hand in hand, in a sort of joyful adoration.

At the conclusion of the service the clergy and choristers retired to partake of a feast, in which always figured a gammon of bacon to denote abhorrence of the Jews, and a tansy pudding, symbolical of the bitter herbs commanded at the paschal feast. Some of these customs are commemorated in an ancient rhyme :—

"At Stool-ball, Lucia, let us play,
For sugar, cakes, or wine ;
Or for a tansy let us pay,
The loss be thine and mine.
If thou, my dear, a winner be
At trundling of the ball,
The wager thou shalt have, and me,
And my misfortunes all."

STOOL-BALL, an old-fashioned game for girls and women, but in which men sometimes joined, was at the height of its popularity in the sixteenth century; it still survives in a modified form in some of the remoter villages of Sussex. It is said to have derived its name from the original practice of the milkmaids, who indulged in it, setting up their milking-stools to serve as wickets to bowl at—for in the realm of sport Stool-ball was to women what Cricket was to men.

"While Betty dances on the green
And Susan is at Stool-ball seen"

is one of the many allusions made by old writers to this game.

When both sexes joined in the game upon the village

greens of "Merrie England," was heard the old folk-song which ran—

"Down in a vale on a summer's day,
All the lads and lasses met to be merry;
A match for kisses at stool-ball to play,
And for cake, and ale, and sider, and perry.

*Chorus.* Come all,
Great, small,
Short, tall,
Away to stool-ball."

The game was played by two sides, varying in number from three or four to eight or ten a side. The ball employed was of the common white type used in trap-ball, about four inches in diameter. Originally it seems to have been stuffed with quills, and could be tossed as lightly as a shuttle-cock. Thus in "Ivanhoe" we read of "a service chucked from hand to hand like a shuttle-cock or stool-ball."

The stool, or wicket, was defended by a batsman who, as a rule, employed the bare hand as a bat; so that the village maids, as the poet tells us, were wont to—

"Gall their hands with stool-ball."

In the modern form of the game two pieces of board, eighteen inches by twelve, are fixed to two sticks three or four feet high, according to the size of the players. These sticks are stuck in the ground, sloping a little backwards, from ten to fifteen yards apart.

There are "lobbers" to throw the ball, which is driven from stool to stool. The bowler pitches the ball at the board or wicket, and if it hit, the striker is out; and the same is the case if the ball is caught after being struck by the batsman; there is "running out" and "stumping" while the batsmen are changing ends, exactly as in cricket. Some writers have traced the origin of Cricket to Stool-ball.

Most of the games played with a ball required a bat, or a club, for striking it.

The ancient game of GOLF was peculiar to Scotland, and the nearest approach to it in England seems to have been a game, or possibly a variety of games, in which a ball was struck at with a club.

In the reign of Edward III. (says Strutt, the well-known authority on "Sports and Pastimes") the Latin "Cambuca" was applied to a pastime which derived its denomination from the crooked club or bat with which it was played. The bat was also called a bandy, from its being bent, and hence the game itself is frequently written in English as "Bandy-ball."

The feudal period has not inaptly been described as one of amateur soldiering; at its height, in the reign just mentioned, royal proclamation was made prohibiting a number of games and recreations—among them Hand-ball, Football, Club-ball, and the English species of Golf called Cambuca—not on account of any particular evil tendency in themselves, but because they engrossed too much of the leisure of the populace, and so diverted their minds from pursuits of a more martial nature—which was not to be tolerated in those warlike times.

Early in the Stuart period, however, Golf itself seems to have been introduced into England by our Scottish monarch, James I. His eldest son, Henry, Prince of Wales, seems to have amused himself with this exercise, as the following anecdote of his juvenile days discloses:—

"At another time playing at Goff, a play not unlike to Pale-Maille, whilst his schoolmaster stood talking with another, and marked not his highness warning him to stand further off, the prince thinking he had gone aside, lifted up his goff-club to strike the ball. Meantyme one standing by said to him, 'Beware that you hit not Master Newton!' Wherewith he, drawing back his hand, said, 'Had I done so, I had but paid my debts.'"

In the English modification of Goff, the club employed was not unlike the bandy-stick; the handle of the instrument was straight, usually of ash, about four and a half feet in length; the curvature affixed to the bottom was faced with horn and backed with lead. The ball was small, but exceedingly hard, made with leather stuffed with feathers.

There were generally two players pitted against each other, each having his own bat and ball. The game consisted in driving the ball into certain holes made in the ground, the one who achieved that object in the fewest strokes attaining the victory.

When four persons played, two of them were sometimes partners, and used but one ball, which they struck alternately; but every man had his own bandy.

The goff-lengths, or the spaces between the first and last holes, sometimes extended to a distance of two or three miles; the number of the intervening holes, however, was optional; but the balls were always to be struck into the holes, and not beyond them.

In the sixteenth and seventeenth centuries this game was also known as Stow-ball.

BANDY has sometimes been known as Shindy, or Shinty; in old London it was called Hackie, while in Gloucestershire it seems to have been known as Not—a name probably borrowed from the fact that the ball was usually made of a knotty piece of wood.

Here it may be observed that the golf-ball, like the one just described in Stool-ball, seems in its original form to have been stuffed with quilled feathers. It was quite a revolution in the game, accompanied by not a little

GOLF.

[*From Walker's "Games and Sports,"* 1837.]

*To face page* 144

excitement, when in 1848 the gutta-percha ball was introduced at St. Andrews by John Campbell, of Saddle. However, Golf is scarcely an old English game, possessing an unbroken record as such—twenty years ago it would have been difficult to find golf-links south of the Tweed ; and so we pass on.

PALL-MALL seems to have been a game, the popularity of which was restricted to the Metropolis and to the seventeenth century. It has lent its name to Pall Mall, that well-known fashionable thoroughfare in London, which was originally nothing more than the avenue or alley in St. James's Park where this sport was regularly indulged in.

Under date April 2, 1661, Pepys makes this entry in his famous Diary :—

"To St. James's Park where I saw the Duke of York playing at Pelemele, the first time that I ever saw the sport."

Pall-mall is thus described by Cotgrave : "A game wherein a round box bowle is with a mallet strucke through a high arch of yron (standing at either end of an ally one) which he that can do at the fewest blowes, or at the number agreed on, winnes."

Although the game was a novelty to Pepys it was known in England, as appears from Prince Henry's acquaintance with it, quite half a century before the great diarist's time. There are various old spellings of the name, but it is clear that when resolved into its simplest form the term Pall is equivalent to Ball, and Mall is but an abbreviated form of the word Mallet. For, as a matter of fact, the game was played with a ball, and a mallet with which to drive it.

The full term Pall-mall was not only applied to the place in which the game was played, but sometimes to the stick employed. Thus a writer, of the year 1621, says: "A stroke with a paille-maile bettle upon a bowl makes it fly."

The game is believed to have been introduced from France at the beginning of the seventeenth century; and although it offered opportunities for social intercourse with agreeable exercise in the open air, it was practically unknown before the century terminated.

The tree-lined avenue originally used for the game, and now called Pall Mall, had become converted into a street even in the time of the Commonwealth. After the Restoration the Duke of York had the Mall specially prepared for this pastime. It is believed the sides of the alley were boarded to prevent the ball going astray; and the ground was strewn with finely powdered shells and then hardened into a smooth surface, which in dry weather, however, turned to dust and had a deadening effect on the ball. From Waller's poem on St. James's Park it would appear that Charles II. was an expert exponent of Pall-mall—

> "Here a well-polished Mall gives us the joy,
> To see our Prince his matchless force employ;
> His manly posture and his graceful mien,
> Vigour and youth in all his motions seen;
> No sooner has he touched the flying ball,
> But 'tis already more than half the Mall;
> And such a fury from his arm has got
> As from a smoking culverin 'twere shot."

The mallet in shape was not unlike that used in modern Croquet, of which Pall-mall was doubtless the precursor. The long, straight shaft was light compared with the head, the two striking faces of which were not parallel with it, but were slightly scooped in such a form that a good swinging blow would lift the ball well into the air. The object of the player was to drive the ball along the straight alley, and through a ring elevated on the cross-bar of a tall pole. It is not known whether clubs of different shapes were used, as in Golf; but it is not improbable. The victory rested with him who accomplished his purpose in the smallest number of strokes. Although there does not appear to have been any contest to secure possession of the ball, as in Bandy, we are said to have derived the word "pell-mell," meaning "headlong," or "in reckless confusion," from the way the players at this game rushed heedlessly to strike the ball.

In an old North of England game known as RING-BALL, the ring which the ball had to pass through was not elevated.

There was a special alley, as in Pall Mall, and near the bottom of it, at an equal distance from each side, was an iron ring standing on the ground, and turning with great facility on a swivel.

The two flat sides of this ring were distinguished from each other; if the player drove his ball through one, it was said to be lawful, and he passed on; but if through the other, the stroke was declared unlawful, and he was obliged to beat the ball back, and drive again till such time as he caused it to pass through the lawful way. This done he proceeded to the bottom of the ground, where he had to pass the ball through an arch of iron to complete the game. As usual, the victory fell to the player who accomplished all this in the fewest strokes.

FIVES, the old Hand-Tennis, was a very ancient ball game. Hand-ball was mentioned by Homer; and in France its equivalent, *jeu de la paume*, or Palm-play, consisted in receiving the ball and driving it back again with the palm of the hand. At least it was originally played with the naked hand, about the fourteenth century; then a protecting glove was used; and later, players took to the plan of binding cords and tendons round the striking-hand in order to make the ball rebound more forcibly; till eventually the racket was evolved.

The inventiveness displayed in this transition from the thick glove to a network of strings, and the adoption of the leverage afforded by the use of a handle, has been progressive, and the present Tennis racket is a great advance upon the original form of it mentioned by Shakespeare—

> "When we have match'd our rackets to these balls,
> We will . . . play a set."
>
> *Henry V.* i. 2.

English Hand-Tennis appears to have become better known as Fives from the practice of having five competitors in it. This is gathered from the following passage in an old chronicle, relating to Queen Elizabeth's entertainment at Elvetham in Hampshire, by the Earl of Hertford, during one of her Progresses: "After dinner about three o'clock, ten of his lordship's servants, all Somersetshire men, in a square greene court before her majesties windowe, did hang up lines, squaring out the forme of a tennis court, and making a cross line in the middle. In this square they, being stripped of their dublets, played five to five with hand-ball, at bord and cord, as they tearme it; to the great liking of her highness."

A line, called the cord, was traced up the wall, below which a player's stroke was accounted faulty.

Fives is a game which, to play it, requires a brick-built court, roughly resembling a small racket court; for it is really a form of Rackets played with the hands instead of a racket, or bat, though with a somewhat larger ball. Some courts have only one wall—that against which the ball is hit; some have three—a front and two side walls; others have a back wall as well, and are nearly or quite enclosed.

Still, a court occupies but little superficial space, and could readily be put in the odd corners and buttressed angles of large school buildings. It has even been suggested that a Fives Court could very profitably be made to fill up a corner on every cricket ground.

Fives is not a widely popular game, though it deserves to be. It calls for no over-exertion, and rarely gives rise to more than a gentle panting ; in the court partners and adversaries—the four-handed game is the best form of it —are all close together ; the noise of "palm play" does not drown the voice, so that there is plenty of opportunity for talk and chaff and laughter, without interference with the business-like part of the play.

Notwithstanding all this, Fives remains almost exclusively a schoolboy's game; it has not even taken very deep root at the universities, and at Cambridge a dozen courts are found sufficient for fifteen hundred undergraduates.

The game is now chiefly followed at the great public schools, where it is played, as a game should be, for its own sake. It can claim the proud distinction of being at this day purely an amateur's game, free from every taint or suspicion of professionalism, whatever it may have been in the past.

One of the most famous Hand Fives-players ever known was John Cavanagh, a memoir of whom, by Hazlitt, appeared in 1819, and an extract from which is subjoined :—

"He has no other wish, no other thought, from the moment the game begins but that of striking the ball, of placing it, of making it. This Cavanagh was sure to do.

"Whenever he touched the ball, there was an end of the chase. His eye was certain, his hand fatal, his presence of mind complete. He could do what he pleased, and he always knew exactly what to do. He saw the whole game, and played it ; took instant advantage of his adversary's weakness, and recovered balls, as if by a miracle and from sudden thought, that every one gave for lost.

"He had equal power and skill, quickness and judgment. He could either outwit his antagonist by finesse, or beat him by main strength. Sometimes when he seemed preparing to send the ball with the full swing of his arm, he would, by a slight turn of the wrist, drop it within an inch of the line. In general, the ball came from his hand, as from a racket, in a straight, horizontal line; so that it was in vain to attempt to overtake or stop it. As it was said of a great orator, that he was never at a loss for a word, and for the properest word, so Cavanagh always could tell the degree of force necessary to be given to a ball, and the precise direction in which it should be sent.

"He was the best uphill player in the world; even when his adversary was 14, he would play on the same or better; and as he never flung away the game through carelessness or conceit, he never gave it up through laziness or want of heart.

"The only peculiarity of his play was that he never volleyed, but let the balls hop; but if they rose an inch from the ground, he never missed having them. There was not only nobody equal, but nobody second to him. It is supposed he could give any other player half the game, or beat them with his left hand. His service was tremendous. He once played Woodward and Meredith together (two of the best players in England) in the Fives Court, St. Martin's Street, and made seven and twenty aces following by services alone—a thing unheard of."

Cavanagh was the admiration of all the Fives Courts in London at the close of the eighteenth century. At Copenhagen House he frequently played matches for wagers and dinners. The wall against which they were played was the one supporting the kitchen chimney, and when the walls resounded louder than usual not only did the cooks recognise the champion's play, but it is said the joints trembled on the spit!

From the year 1780 Fives-play was the chief diversion at Copenhagen House, a well-known tea-garden and pleasure resort at Islington, where Skittles and Dutch-pins were also popular games with the patrons of the place. It is to be regretted that this famous Fives Court was afterwards degraded into the Sunday rendezvous of all the dog-fighters in London—as many as sixty bull-

LONG OR OPEN TENNIS.
[*From Walker's "Games and Sports,"* 1837.]

*To face page* 151

dogs have been tied to the benches at a time—till in 1816 it was threatened to withdraw the license unless an end was put to the disgraceful disturbances caused by the dog-fighting matches held there.

From Fives to the consideration of TENNIS the transition is easy. The ball has given origin to quite a number of popular pastimes, most of them in the earlier stages of society, playable in the open air. It was at a late stage came the evolution of ball play which could be practised without interruption from the weather, as in a covered building.

There are allusions by the ancient Greeks to the tennis-court divided by a line stretched in the middle, and the players standing on either side with their rackets ready to receive and return the ball, which the rules of the game required to be stricken over the line. Hence arose the old proverb, "Thou hast stricken the ball under the line," meaning one had failed in his purpose.

In the sixteenth century tennis-courts were common in England. In the official register of Henry VII.'s expenditure, preserved in the Remembrancer's Office, it is set down—

> "Item, for the king's loss at tennis, XII*d.*
> for the loss of balls, III*d.*"

The loss of balls could not have occurred in a tennis-court, from which it may be inferred that as yet the game was played abroad. His son, the bluff King Hal, was much attached to the diversion; which "being perceived by certain craftie persons," says the contemporary chronicler, Hall, "they brought in Frenchmen and Lombards to make wagers with hym, and so he lost muche money; but when he perceyved theyr crafte, he eschued the company and let them go." He did not give up his tennis, however, for in the thirteenth year of his reign we find him, with the Emperor Maximilian as a partner, playing a match against the Prince of Orange and the Marquis of Brandenborow. It was this English monarch who erected at Whitehall not only a riding-school, a cock-pit, and bowling alleys, but "divers fair tennis-courts" as well. In the wardrobe rolls of Henry VIII. we find catalogued "tenes-cotes for the King, also tenes-drawers, and tenes-slippers." Charles II. also wore a special dress for playing tennis. The game was a favourite one with the princes and nobility of the period —the cost of having to provide a special building naturally had the effect of excluding all but the noble and wealthy from participation in it. Tennis has been called the "game of Kings."

There are known to have been covered courts for the game in Henry VIII.'s time at Richmond, at Greenwich, and at Oxford, while in different parts of London there were no less than fourteen. The oldest court yet extant is the one built at Hampton Court about 1526. Charles I., before and after his accession, played at tennis regularly; in 1619 we read of his playing a match at St. James's Palace at six o'clock in the morning.

That old gossip Pepys makes the following allusion in his Diary to the sportsmanship of Charles II.: "January 4, 1664. To the Tennis-court, and there saw the King at Tennis. But to see how the King's play was extolled, without any cause at all, was a loathsome sight; though sometimes, indeed, he did play very well, and deserved to be commended; but such open flattery is beastly." The Merry Monarch played frequently at the court in James Street, Haymarket, an historic building devoted to the game which was not converted to commercial purposes till 1866.

LAWN TENNIS is not one of the ancient pastimes; although it belongs to the great family of ball games, it is its youngest member, having been born no longer back than the year 1874. It may, perhaps, claim to have been suggested by the Elizabethan game played on "a square greene court" at Elvetham; anyway it was not till some thirty odd years ago that it was organised and put into shape by Major Wingfield; it immediately sprang into favour at all country houses, and was not long ere it had ousted Croquet from the lawns of villadom.

The game of Tennis has added a few items to our already rich but always accommodating English vocabulary. The phrase "Serve him out," now vulgarly employed to imply the taking of a mean advantage, originated in the attempt to beat a rival in this game on the "service" only, and winning the game without his having had a chance. A similar phrase, "Put him out," had its origin in the game of Fives. Then in the matter of scoring, "Love" is a corruption of *l'œuf*, the "duck egg," or round O, standing for nothing; while "Deuce" is *de unx*, an ounce off the total, or one short of the game, announced in that form as a warning to the adversary to play up if he hopes to win.

RACKETS is not unlike Tennis, and the two games have much in common, though the former seems never to have enjoyed the patronage of the noble and the mighty, nor even to have been regulated by rules which applied universally to every part of the country.

Rackets is but a slight development of the play made by children who, armed with a bat and ball, have discovered that hitting a ball to a distance involves the trouble of running after it to get it back. To enjoy the hitting of the ball without having to run after it every stroke, the intelligent child makes the happy discovery that its object may be attained by hitting the ball against a large wall, and awaiting its return on the rebound.

The formulation of rules, when this exercise is elevated

into an emulative game between two players, readily follows. The rule of equitable partition is first settled; there arises the regulation that neither shall have a greater share of hits than the other, and the principle of alternation is obtained. Equity next demands that the advantage of having the first hit and of standing in a certain place must be shared fairly. Then, more arbitrarily, it is agreed, in a praiseworthy desire to cultivate skill, that it shall be made a rule that the return, to be good in the counting of points, must be made before the ball has twice touched the floor. And thus (opines an acknowledged authority on the game) was the game of Rackets evolved.

There are the close-court game, and the open-court game played against a single wall; which latter requires much more skill and judgment.

The word "racket" has been derived from a word signifying "wrist," or from a word meaning "to dash against"; it has been traced from *reticulum*, "a little net"; and it has been suggested to be nothing more than the diminutive of *rack*, as "stretching" is the essence of a racket.

The racket used in this game is less unwieldy than that used in Tennis; the reason assigned for this is that it requires to be more handy in order to meet the faster flight of a ball which has, of necessity, to hit a wall before it returns to the opponent.

Till fifty or sixty years ago "Racket Courts" were not unfrequently attached to the larger and more important class of taverns in the towns. During the earlier half of the nineteenth century Rackets shared with Skittles the honour of being the most popular of tavern games.

And as tavern frequenters sometimes found their way to the debtors' prison, we are by no means surprised to read in Dickens's immortal story of "Pickwick" that a racket court in active use was to be found in the notorious Fleet prison.

> "The area formed by the wall in that part of the Fleet in which Mr. Pickwick stood was just wide enough to make a good racket court; one side being formed, of course, by the wall itself, and the other by that portion of the prison which looked (or rather which would have looked but for the wall) towards St. Paul's Cathedral.
>
> "Sauntering or sitting about, in every possible attitude of listless idleness, were a great number of debtors, some shabby, some smart, many dirty. Lolling from the windows which commanded a view of this promenade were a number of persons looking at the racket players, or watching the boys as they cried the game."

Hazlitt, after extolling the Fives-play of the celebrated Cavanagh, says: "The only person who seems to have excelled as much in another way was John Davis, the Racket player. It was remarked of him that he did not seem to follow the ball, but the ball seemed to follow him. Give him a foot of wall and he was sure to make the ball."

CLUB-BALL seems to have been the old English forerunner of the game now called Rounders. A bat or flat club was used to strike with; and the ball was sometimes bowled, or "fed" to the batsman; or sometimes the batsman held the ball as well, either throwing it into the air or casting it forcibly to the ground and catching it on the rebound before striking it.

Other players stood about to stop or catch the ball, but it is not known how the game was determined.

TRAP-BALL was not unlike this, except that to strike the ball away it was placed on a trap at the end of a lever of the first order; the batsman struck the other end of the lever smartly with his bat, which sent the ball into the air, where it had to be struck away by him with his bat before it fell to the ground.

The modern form of this trap, generally made of wood,

is that of a shoe, the heel part being for the reception of the ball. But the rustics of old time, being unable to buy apparatus, contented themselves with making a hole in the ground, and by way of a lever used the brisket-bone of an ox.

An old game called NORTHEN SPELL (or perhaps it should be Nurr and Spell, a spell being a trap, and a nurr a wooden ball) was played with a trap, bat, and ball ; but there was no stopping or catching the ball, the game being decided by the greatest distance a player could knock the ball in a given number of strokes, a cord with one end fast to the trap being used to measure each stroke before the ball was returned.

The well-known old English game of TIPCAT is but a modification of this, the cat being a piece of wood pointed at both ends into the shape of a double cone, doubtless an ingenious rustic contrivance to obviate the use of the trap and the ball. The player with his cudgel strikes smartly one end, or "tip," of the cat as it lies on the ground, which has the effect of making it rise, with a rotary motion, high enough for the player to strike it away before it falls to the ground again.

Mr. Flinders Petrie, the Egyptologist, has proved this game to be as old as the Pharaohs ; for among his discoveries of the antiquities of the Twelfth Dynasty—say of four thousand years ago—were not only balls of leather and of wood, but well-battered specimens of the ancient tipcat.

One way of playing Tipcat was to start from the centre of a large ring, and if the player failed to strike the cat, as it was tipped into the air beyond its limits, he was out ; otherwise he counted the aggregate of the distances he struck the cat away from the centre during his innings, against the aggregate of his opponent's innings.

The evolution of Tipcat from ball play seems to have

been by two easy stages: the first the use of a wooden missile; the second, the shaping of it into a "cat" to obviate the use of a lever trap for making the missile rise into the air for striking it away.

SHUTTLECOCK and BATTLEDORE, now a child's game, was a fashionable pastime among grown persons in the reign of James I.; as in a comedy printed in 1609 appears the line—

"To play at Shuttlecock methinkes is the game now."

The battledore, or beater, is analogous to the bat or racquet in the other games just treated; and the shuttlecock is nothing more than a ball flighted with feathers to keep it in position for being struck upwards again, as it flutters down after each stroke.

There is another game of this class which, like most of them, came to us from France, but with us has never been regarded as more than a mere infantile amusement, fit only for the nursery. This is CUP-AND-BALL, and the childishness of the game is at once betrayed by the fact that the ball is tied to the stick, so that it cannot possibly be lost. In France, during the reign of Henri III., this game (under the name of Bilboquet) became so fashionable a form of amusement that elegantly attired courtiers actually played it as they walked along the streets of Paris. The toy consists of a stick with one end pointed and the other having a hollow cup; and the object of the game is to swing the ball into the air, as far as the attaching string will permit, and make it alight in the cup; or, alternatively, to catch it on the point of the stick, by a little hole bored in the ball for that purpose. Although this absurd practice died out with the dissipated Henri of Valois, it suddenly came into vogue again a century later; and the great French dramatists of the period, Molière Racine, and Corneille, introduced characters into their pieces carrying the then fashionable bilboquets. Cup-and-Ball is far too inane ever to catch the fancy of the English adult; to the English temperament it has one fatal objection—it lacks the great essential of requiring some amount of bodily exertion.

# X

## FOOTBALL

Its antiquity—Shakespearean references to its roughness—Tabooed by James I.—"Balouns"—Football played as a Parish *v.* Parish scramble—At Derby, Corfe Castle, Ashbourne, Chester, in Cornwall, &c.—London apprentices played in Finsbury Fields—The London Irish in Copenhagen Fields—Poetical allusions—Camp ball—As a school game—The Eton Wall game—The Rugby School game—"Tom Brown's" first big-side match (extract from Thomas Hughes)—The "civilised" Association game—Its immense popularity.

FOOTBALL, of course, derives its name from the ball being driven about with the feet instead of with the hands.

If legendary lore were as reliable as it is interesting, the game could claim a most venerable antiquity. At Derby football was played as the memorial of a great rejoicing for a signal victory gained over the Roman legions in the third century. At Chester the first football used in an annual game, played for many centuries on the Roodee, was said to have been a Dane's head. In the Isle of Purbeck the free quarrymen have from time immemorial perpetuated their claim to a piece of land by kicking a football across it, in accordance with the quaint old tenure of the original grant.

Football makes its appearance among the popular pastimes of England in the reign of Edward III., when, in 1349, it was prohibited by public edict because it diverted time and attention from the more martial, useful, and patriotic exercises of those feudal times, such as Archery and Wrestling.

Although this was the earliest legal mention of the game by the popular name, it would appear that Edward II. had previously forbidden struggles over "grosses pelotes" (big-ball). Henry IV. and Henry VIII. also legislated against football playing.

Shakespeare, however, gives the game a far greater antiquity than this; and it will be observed that all his references stigmatise the game as a rough one, the players always lying under the imputation of being "base."

In *King Lear*, Kent says to Oswald, "Nor tripped neither, you base football player." This seems to imply that Football was played with too much roughness in the poet's time. Perhaps he had seen it played in the streets of Nuneaton and Atherstone at Shrovetide.

Even stronger, perhaps, is the evidence of a passage in "The Comedy of Errors." Says the Ephesian Dromio—

> "Am I so round with you as you with me,
> That like a football you do spurn me thus?
> You spurn me hence, and he will spurn me hither.
> If I last in this service, you must case me in leather."

In the sixteenth and seventeenth centuries Football was played in utter defiance of the law, which (by a statute of Elizabeth) forbade it under pain of imprisonment. The reason for this unquestionably was the extreme brutality of the game, hinted at by Kent in the foregoing quotation.

That timorous monarch, James I., was so impressed with the danger of the sport, that he felt impelled to declare in his "Basilikon Doron," or "Manual of Precepts," formulated for his son and successor—"From my court I debarre all rough and violent exercises, as the Football, meeter for lameing than making able the users thereof."

However rough the game, the "base" footballer had the hardihood to continue in the enjoyment of his strenuous sport, unaffected by the denunciations of King and Parliament, until the middle of the seventeenth century, when it began to decline, with other popular pastimes, owing to the spread and domination of Puritan influences. Burton, in his "Anatomy of Melancholy," had deprecated the too great popularity of this game, which he coupled with another called "Balouns," in which large hand-balls were knocked up into the air like shuttlecocks.

The game, as a set field sport, was played by two sides, with an equal number of competitors on each, playing between two goals placed some eighty or a hundred yards apart; each side simultaneously defending its own, and attacking the opponents' goal. The goal was usually a couple of stout sticks, driven into the ground some three feet apart.

The ball was a blown bladder (generally of the pig) cased in strong leather. Delivered into the middle of the ground, the object of each party was to drive it between the goal-sticks of their antagonists.

Although there was little hesitation about kicking each other's shins at this form of the game, there was another form which exhibited it in a yet more violent light—a form of Football played in an exceedingly rough-and-ready style, with little or no reference to set rules and regulations. There was a Lancashire form of challenge to—

"Try it out at Football, by the shinnes."

Sometimes towns and villages were matched against

each other, the whole of the able-bodied inhabitants taking part in the struggle, the goals usually being miles apart, and not infrequently consisting of natural objects, as boundary brooks or well-known trees. The favourite season for these inter-parochial contents was Shrovetide.

The Derby contest lay between the parishes of St. Peter's and All Saints', the latter having their goals at Nun's Mill and the former theirs at Gallows Balk on the Normanton Road; play was started in the Market Place, the ball being tossed into the air at high noon. The scene which then took place, as described in Glover's History of Derbyshire (1829), is of the usual violent and unrestrained character, the struggle engaged in by a surging mass of humanity being scarcely less brutal than actual fighting.

The Corfe Castle game, already alluded to, in which the Purbeck company of marblers played to preserve an ancient right-of-way, was played annually on Shrove Tuesday and Ash Wednesday, and is authenticated by records as far back as the year 1553.

At Ashbourne in Derbyshire, it was formerly a well-honoured custom to play a rough and unorganised game of Football in the streets every Shrove Tuesday.

At Chester it was the custom, time out of mind, for the Shoemakers yearly, on Shrove Tuesday, to deliver to the drapers in the presence of the Mayor, "at the Cross on the Rodehee," a public open space outside the city, "one ball of leather called a foote-ball, of the value of three shillings and fourpence, to play from thence to the Common Hall in the said city." This proved a practice productive of so much inconvenience that in the year 1540, by consent of the parties concerned, the ball was changed into "six glayves of silver of the same value," which was given as a prize to the best runner that day, upon the aforesaid open space. "This Rood-eye," or "Island of the Cross," is by the side of the Dee, and, from the annual races now held on it, has become a source of revenue to the city.

In Cornwall the game was annually played several miles "across country," two or more villages being pitted against other three or four in a "big-side" match. In these Cornish games there was some sort of tactical arrangement, a player on one side being told off to "mark" a particular player on the other; and well-understood cries of warning were used, as "Ware East!" and "Ware West!" The sport raged over hills and dales, hedges and ditches, through briars and mires, all tugging away in a manner well calculated to induce courage, strength, and endurance.

In like manner Pancake-day was celebrated in Finsbury Fields by the London apprentices; and at Teddington, Nuneaton, and other old towns, careful householders were accustomed to close their shutters and even to protect their windows with hurdles and bushes during these Shrove-Tuesday carnivals.

In these rough-and-tumble contests the game generally commenced soon after noon on a short winter day. If a player got hold of the ball he was allowed to run with it in his hands till overtaken by one of the opposite side; and if he could shake himself loose again, he might still run on, carrying the ball towards the goal aimed at; if not, he was at liberty to throw the ball on, unless it were wrested from him by an opponent.

Beyond these few elementary laws there were no restrictions whatever, no nice laws to balance skill and dexterity in the scale against sheer brute force. As played thus it was essentially a game in which might was right. This rough style of play, in which any strategy to get possession of the ball and force it through the opposite goal was permissible, was undoubtedly the foundation upon which the Rugby School code was framed.

In other parts of England this Shrove-tide sport was played, or else found its counterpart in some similar scrambling contest for rolls, or cakes, or bread and cheese, thrown from the church steeple. In Cumberland the game was often started by the football being tossed into the churchyard.

Besides being one of the sportive fooleries once common to the observance of Pancake-day, Football was often played at other times and seasons. Sir William Davenant, writing in 1634, waxes somewhat sarcastic at the expense of the Londoners who played "this heroic game" in narrow and irregular thoroughfares like Crooked Lane; observing that like their "military pastime of throwing at cocks, it argued their courage"; yet their mettle might be magnified if instead of playing these "two valiant exercises" in the streets, they gave some of their attention to Archery in the open fields at Finsbury.

After the Puritan repression Football was quite two centuries from the date of the Restoration in recovering anything like its former popularity.

In the eighteenth century Football was at one time a Sunday amusement for the Irish element in London, who frequented Copenhagen Fields at Islington for that purpose, both morning and afternoon. In Scotland the game has always been highly popular.

An important match was played on December 4, 1815, on the extensive plain of Catterhaugh, in Scotland, near the junction of the rivers Ettrick and Yarrow. It was contested between the Dale-of-Yarrow men and those of Selkirk, both sides being joined by numerous individuals from other parishes. The Duke of Buccleuch and Queensberry, with his sons, the young Earl of Dalkeith, and Lord John Scott, the Countess of Home, and many

*Drawn by Stephanof*

FOOT BALL.

[*Published, 1816, by Sherwood & Co., Paternoster Row.*]

other persons of rank and respectability, were present; and the armorial banner of the Buccleuch family, a curious and venerable relique, emblazoned with the word "Bellendaine," the ancient war-cry of the clan of Scott, was displayed, as in former times, when the chief took the field in person. The ball was thrown up by the Duke himself, and after a close conflict of an hour and a half the first game was won by the Selkirk men. The second game produced a stubborn struggle of three hours' continuance, during which much agility and strength were exerted by both parties; it was then gained by the Yarrow men. The decisive game could not be played, the waning of the day, and some confusion in arranging the voluntary auxiliaries making it expedient to close the contest; before quitting the ground, however, a challenge was given and accepted for a grand match between one hundred picked men on each side, to be played at a future time, and all lost bets to be paid to the poor of the winning parish. Some idea of this important match may be obtained from the accompanying print.

All the old poets seem to agree that Football was a sport for the rustic and the peasant. Alexander Barclay, in his "Ship of Fools," published in 1509, has these lines :—

> ". . . The sturdy plowman lustie, strong and bold,
> Overcometh the winter with driving the foote-ball,
> Forgetting labour and many a grevious fall."

Edmund Waller, a century later, wrote—

> "As when a sort of lusty shepherds try
> Their force at Football; care of victory
> Makes them salute so rudely breast to breast
> That their encounter seems too rough for jest."

Sometimes the village boys put dried peas and horse-beans inside their blown but uncased bladder, to make it rattle as it was knocked about.

"... And nowe in the winter, when men kill the fat swine,
They get the bladder and blow it great and thin,
With many beans and peason put within.
It ratleth, soundeth, and shineth clere and fayre,
While it is throwen and caste up in the ayre.
Eche one contendeth, and hath a great delite,
With foote and with hande the bladder for to smite;
If it fall to grounde, they lifte it up agayne,
And this waye to labour they count it no payne."

The London apprentices habitually punted a ball about the streets in winter to keep themselves warm. They observed no rules, merely kicking it to and fro. It is on record that during the severe frost of 1665 the London streets were "full of football"; and a French traveller in England (Mission, 1689) speaks of the game as a "charming and useful winter exercise" of the English youth at that period. He remarks that the football is of leather, "about as big as one's Head, fill'd with Wind; this is kicked about from one to t'other in the Streets by him that can get it, and this is all the Art of it."

The poet Gay remarks upon the London crowds playing Football in Covent Garden and the Strand, and hints that the glazier took care to kick the ball at as many windows as he could.

"When lo! from afar
I spy the furies of the Football war;
The prentice quits his shop to join the crew,
Increasing crowds the flying game pursue.

The ball now skims the street, now soars on high;
The dextrous glazier strong returns the bound
And jingling sashes on the pent-house sound."

It has been thought that Football is the same game, though in a modified form, which was denominated CAMP-BALL—"camp," it is suggested, being a contraction of the word campaign—and mentioned in the old seventeenth-century comedy, entitled *The Blind Beggar of Bethnal Green*. One of the characters in the play exclaims—

> "I am Tom Stroud of Hurling. I'll play a gole at camp-ball, or wrassel a fall."

And earlier than this, in fifteenth-century records, are found numerous allusions to "camping fields," and "camping closes"; "Camp field Lane" is a street-name still found on the older maps of Wednesbury; and an old Norfolk couplet ran :—

> "Get campers a ball
> To camp there withal."

In this game the goals are only ten to fifteen yards apart; it was the object of a player, aided by his own side, to force the ball between the opponent's sticks in spite of all opposition. If the match was played with shoes on the feet it was termed a "savage camp."

Football as played by the boys of our old foundation schools differed in rules according to the circumstances of each particular school. The boys of Charterhouse and Westminster adapted their rules to fit the cloisters which at one time formed their only playground. Winchester boys were allowed to play football only on narrow strips of grass round the edge of the cricket piece, a restriction of lateral space which developed shoving and discounted dribbling. At Harrow, with more room on the field of play, a large amount of catching and free kicking was allowed, though running and collaring were disallowed. At Eton there was a "field game" which admitted of long kicking, and the "wall game" which drew its characteristic rules from the space against the wall upon which it was played. It will be thus seen that the public schools adapted this old English game to the necessities of their respective playgrounds.

The Rugby game is too well known to need description here. It has been under the control of the Rugby Football Union since that great central authority was set up for its standardisation in 1871. It is played in most English schools and colleges; there is a representative "fifteen" to uphold the athletic reputation of most large towns in England; and the great Colonies, like New Zealand and South Africa, show their English breeding by the fine display they are capable of making on the football field. Few sports have the same fascination for an Englishman as those with a spice of danger in them.

> "No game was ever yet worth a rap
> For rational man to play,
> Into which no accident, no mishap,
> Could possibly find its way."

Of all the Rugby games ever played, none linger in the memory like that described in "Tom Brown's School Days," as taking place at the old school itself. We seem to see it all as we read that delightful book: Tom, as soon as dinner was over, making his way into the great playground, with its little-side ground, and beyond the trees the big-side ground, where all the great matches are played; and where to-day he is to be allowed to take part in one—his own school-house matched against the rest of the school.

Tom listens with profound respect as his house companion, East, recapitulates the chapter of accidents which have occurred there quite recently—one leg, and two collar-bones broken, and a dozen fellows lamed.

He is informed that the coming match is for the best of three goals; whichever side kicked two goals was to win. After he has been shown the goals, each constructed of two eighteen-foot poles, fourteen feet apart, with a cross-bar ten feet from the ground, East says to him—

"You'll have to stay in goal, to touch the ball when it rolls behind the posts, because if the other side touch it they have a try at goal. Then we fellows in quarters, we play just about in front of the goal here, and have to turn the ball and kick it back, before the big fellows on the other side can follow it up. And in front of us all the big fellows play; and that's where the scrummages are mostly."

A little more instruction in the technicalities of the game, as "place-kicks," "punts," and "places," and the deeper mysteries of "off-side"; and an initiation into the topographical knowledge of "bounds" and "out of bounds"; and then Tom and his friend prepare themselves for the coming struggle by taking an hour's exercise with the "punt about" or practice ball.

Without transcribing Mr. Thomas Hughes' stirring passage verbatim, the substance of it can be given by a slight attempt at abridgment; but it will be discerned by the discriminating reader that the rules of the game at Rugby School in 1856 were not the rules of the present-day Rugby Union.

"'Hold the punt about,' 'To the goals' are the cries, and all stray balls are impounded by the authorities; and the whole mass of boys move up towards the two goals, dividing as they go into three bodies. That little band on the left, consisting of from fifteen to twenty boys, Tom amongst them, who are making for the goal under the School-house wall, are the School-house boys who are not to play up, and have to stay in goal. The larger body moving to the island goal, are the School boys in a like predicament. The great mass in the middle are the players-up, both sides mingled together; they are hanging their jackets, and all who mean real work, their hats, waistcoats, neck handkerchiefs, and braces, on the railings round the small trees; and there they go by twos and threes up to their respective grounds.

"And now that the two sides have fairly sundered, and each occupies its own ground, and we get a good look at them, what absurdity is this? You don't mean to say that those fifty or sixty boys in white trousers, many of them quite small, are going to play that huge mass opposite? Indeed, I do, gentlemen; they're going to try at any rate, and won't make such a bad fight of it, either, mark my word; for hasn't old Brooke won the toss, with his lucky half-penny, and got choice of goals and kick-off? The new ball you may see lies there quite by itself, in the middle, pointing towards the School or island goal; in another minute it will be well on its way there. Use that minute in remarking how the School-house side is drilled. You will see in the first place that the sixth form boy, who has the charge of goal, has spread his force (the goal-keepers) so as to occupy the whole space behind the goal posts, at distances of about five yards apart; a safe and well kept goal is the foundation of all good play.

"But now look, there is a slight move forward of the School-house wings; a shout of 'Are you ready?' and loud affirmative reply. Old Brooke takes half-a-dozen quick steps, and away goes the ball spinning towards the School goal, seventy yards before it touches ground, and at no point above twelve or fifteen feet high, a model kick-off; and the School-house cheer and rush on; the ball is returned, and they meet it and drive it back amongst the masses of the School already in motion.

"Then the two sides close, and you can see nothing for minutes but a swaying crowd of boys, at one point violently agitated. That is where the ball is, and there are the keen players to be met, and the glory and the hard knocks to be got; you hear the dull thud, thud, of the ball, and the shouts of 'Off your side,' 'Down with him,' 'Put him over,' 'Bravo.' This is what we call a scrummage.

"But see! it has broken; the ball is driven out on the School-house side and a rush of the School carries it past the School-house players-up. 'Look out in quarters,' Brooke's and twenty other voices ring out; no need to call though, the School-house captain of quarters has caught it on the bound, dodges the foremost School boys, who are heading the rush, and sends it back with a good drop-kick well into the enemy's country. And then follows rush upon rush, and scrummage upon scrummage.

"You say you don't see much in it all, nothing but a struggling mass of boys, and a leather ball, which seems to excite them all to great fury, as a red rag does a bull. My dear sir, a battle would look much the same to you, except that the boys would be men, and the balls iron. You can't be expected to appreciate the delicate strokes of play, the turns by which a game is lost and won—it takes an old player to do that; but the broad philosophy of football you can understand if you will.

"The ball has just fallen again where the two sides are thickest, and they close rapidly around it in a scrummage; it must be driven through now by force or skill, till it flies out on one side or the other. Look how differently the boys face it. Here come two of the bull-dogs, bursting through the outsiders; in they go, straight to the heart of the scrummage, bent on driving that ball out on the other side. That is what they mean to do.

"Then the boys who are bending and watching on the outside, mark them—they are most useful players, the dodgers; who seize on the ball the moment it rolls out from amongst the chargers, and away with it across to the opposite goal; they seldom go into the scrummage, but must have more coolness than the chargers; as endless as are boys' characters, so are their ways of facing or not facing a scrummage at football. Three-quarters of an hour are gone; first winds are failing, and weight and numbers beginning to tell. Yard by yard the School-house have been driven back, contesting every inch of ground."

Presently there is a vast change in the position of affairs. Then the Homeric game proceeds :—

"The School leaders come up furious, and administer toco to the wretched fags nearest at hand; they may well be angry, for it is all Lombard Street to a China orange that the School-house kick a goal with the ball touched in such a good place. Old Brooke of course will kick it out, but who will catch and place it? Call Crab Jones. Here he comes, sauntering along with a straw in his mouth, the queerest, coolest fish in Rugby; if he were tumbled into the moon this minute, he would just pick himself up without taking his hands out of his pockets or turning a hair.

"But it is a moment when the boldest charger's heart beats quick. Old Brooke stands with the ball under his arm motioning the School back; he will not kick out till they are all in goal, behind the posts; they are all edging forwards, inch by inch, to get nearer for the rush at Crab Jones, who stands there in front of Old Brooke to catch the ball. If they can reach and destroy him before he catches, the danger is over, and with one and the same rush they will carry it right away to the School-house goal. Fond hope! it is kicked out and caught beautifully.

"Crab strikes his heel into the ground to mark the spot where the ball was caught, beyond which the School line may not advance; but there they stand, five deep, ready to rush the moment the ball touches the ground. Take plenty of room! don't give the rush a chance of reaching you! place it true and steady! Trust Crab Jones—he has made a small hole with his heel for the ball to lie on, by which he is resting on one knee, with his eye on old Brooke. 'Now!' Crab places the ball at the word, old Brooke kicks, and it rises slowly and truly as the School rush forward.

"Then a moment's pause, while both sides look up at the spinning ball. There it flies, straight between the two posts, some five feet above the cross-bar, an unquestioned goal; and a shout of real, genuine joy rings out from the School-house players-up, and a faint echo of it comes over the close from the goal-keepers under the Doctor's wall. A goal in the first hour—such a thing hasn't been done in the School-house match these five years.

"'Over!' is the cry: the two sides change goals.

"'Are you ready?' 'Yes!' And away comes the ball, kicked high into the air, to give School time to rush on and catch it as it falls. And here they are amongst us. Meet them like Englishmen, you School-house boys, and charge them home.

"Old Brooke ranges the field like Job's war-horse; the thickest scrummage parts asunder before his rush, like the waves before a clipper's bows; his cheery voice rings over the fields, and his eye is everywhere. And if these miss the ball, and it rolls dangerously in front of our goal, Crab Jones and his men have seized it and sent it away towards the sides with that unerring drop-kick. This is worth living for; the whole sum of schoolboy existence gathered up into one straining, struggling half-hour, a half-hour worth a year of common life!

"The quarter-to-five has struck, and the play slackens for a minute before goal.

"And now the last minutes are come, and the School gather for their last rush, every boy of the hundred and twenty who has a run left in him. Reckless of the defence of their own goal, on they come across the level big-side ground, the ball well down amongst them, straight for our goal, like the column of the Old Guard up the slope at Waterloo! All former charges have been child's play to this. Warner and Hedge have met, but still on they come! The bull-dogs rush in for the last time; they are hurled over or carried back, striving hand, foot, and eyelids.

"Old Brooke comes sweeping round the skirts of the play, and turning short round, picks out the very heart of the scrummage, and plunges in. It wavers for a moment—he has the ball! No, it has passed him, and his voice rings out clear over the advancing tide, 'Look out in goal!' Crab Jones catches it for a moment; but before he can kick, the rush is upon him and passes over him; and he picks himself up behind them with his straw in his mouth, a little dirtier, but as cool as ever.

"The ball rolls slowly in behind the School-house goal, not three yards in front of a dozen of the School players-up.

"There stands the School-house præposter, safest of goal-keepers, and Tom Brown by his side, who has learned his trade by this time Now is your time, Tom! The blood of all the Browns is up, and the two rush in together, and throw themselves on the ball, under the very feet of the advancing column; the præposter on his hands and knees arching his back, and Tom all along on his face. Over them topple the leaders of the rush, shooting over the back of the præposter, but falling flat on Tom, and knocking all the wind out of his small carcase. 'Our ball,' says the præposter, rising with his prize; 'but get up there; there's a little fellow under you.' They are hauled and rolled off him, and Tom is discovered a motionless body.

"Old Brooke picks him up. 'Stand back, give him air,' he says; and then, feeling his limbs, adds, 'No bones broken; how do you feel, young 'un?'

"'Hah-hah,' gasps Tom as his wind comes back, 'pretty well, thank you—all right.'

"'Who is he?' says Brooke. 'Oh, it's Brown; he's a new boy; I know him,' says East, coming up.

"'Well, he is a plucky youngster, and will make a player,' says Brooke.

"And five o'clock strikes. 'No side' is called, and the first day of the School-house match is over."

And this was football on the field of Rugby—one of England's preparatory academies for the battlefields of the world.

The Association game is dubbed, by its supporters, "the civilised game." It is played by smaller teams—eleven aside, instead of fifteen—and the rules forbid much of that which goes to make up the rough element in "Rugger." The ball is round, instead of oval, and must not on any account be touched with the hands, save and except only by the goal-keeper.

Within the last quarter of a century the "Soccer" game has become the most popular sport in England, and in its hold on the masses has far outstripped the Rugby game, tens of thousands flocking to witness the matches on the most inclement days of winter. Says a recent authority, writing in an influential magazine :—

"It is a sign of a nation's decadence when able-bodied men pay others to play their games for them, and it is a pitiful sight to see hundreds of thousands of yelling spectators attending matches—their sole desire being to see their own side win."

Be that as it may, the popularity of football seems strong enough at present to slight this condemnation, as a year or two ago it was unaffected by the contemptuous references of Rudyard Kipling to—

"The flannelled fool at the wicket,
The muddied oaf at the goal."

BOWLS.
[*From Walker's "Games and Sports,"* 1837.]

*To face page* 175

# XI

## BOWLS

A courtier's game—Sedate and dignified—Method of playing—The bowls and their bias—Old English bowling-greens—Historic games—Literary notes and Shakespearean references—The similitude between the game of Bowls and Life—An old Worcestershire bowling club.

BOWLS was a fashionable game among the courtiers of Edward II., and there were few Elizabethan country houses without their bowling-greens. Nor was the game unknown to town life at that period. Lytton informs us that the cool and newly-planted alleys westward of the hamlet of Charing, presented by the Earl of Warwick as a playground to the townsfolk of Westminster, were regularly used in the summer-time by the lordly merchants and wealthy citizens for this their favourite game.

Bowls is a game which can be played without the least loss of dignity; and as a pastime it appeals more perhaps to the sober and sedate than to the superabundant energies of youth.

This game is one of the simplest. Each player bowls two wooden balls across the green, with the intention of getting as near as possible to the Jack, a smaller-sized ball of wood or earthenware, which has been rolled across to "set the mark." Points are scored by nearness to the Jack; and the only other apparatus used is a "footer," a bit of carpet or cloth to stand on when delivering the ball.

The game may be played by two, or four, or six, divided into two equal sides. A player from one side, and one from the other, play alternately, the captain, or "driver," generally playing last.

The size and weight of a bowl varies from about three pounds, according to the taste of the player; but one exceeding 16½ inches in circumference is generally prohibited. In the other direction there is no limit, small bowls being sometimes dubbed "nutmegs." Bowls are made of *lignum vitæ*, or any other hard and heavy wood. They are tested for a length of thirty-two yards. Bowls are made with a bias, the purpose of which is to incline them from rolling in a straight line.

The bias of a bowl is effected in the lathe, the turner making the inner half less than the outer, the effect of which is to give the bowl during its progress along the green a tendency to "draw" or turn gently but steadily towards that part of the green lying on the inner side of it. Formerly the bias was given to a bowl by the insertion of lead, or some other heavy substance, on its inner side; the extra weight thus imposed would draw the bowl to that side. The bias may be denoted by numbers: No. 1 being nearly straight, No. 2 a narrow bias, No. 3 a medium bias, No. 4 a full bias, and No. 5 a wide bias. To "play finger" is to deliver the bowl with the little finger resting on the inner side; to play with "thumb bias" is to deliver it with the thumb resting on that side —whichever side a consideration of the state of the game demands.

A bowling-green has been not inappropriately called "nature's billiard-table."

There is something almost dignified about a well-kept bowling-green, with its smooth, clean-shaven surface, its invariably pleasant and refreshing appearance. Felicitously pertinent is the anecdote told of an American visitor who, having admired the velvet-like turf of the bowling-green of one of our English colleges, asked how the green was kept in such excellent condition, as he wished to have his green in the States made like it.

"Well," replied the old gardener, "first we cuts it, and then we rolls it. Then we cuts it and rolls it again. And we keeps on rolling and cutting of it for three or four hundred years till we gets it like this. That's all we does!"

A quaint entry appears in the Parish Book of St. Mary's Church, Shrewsbury, under the date 1584, relating to this game. It is a complaint that the inhabitants of Astley, an ecclesiastical district of the parish, "played bowls on Sundays." It was therefore ordered by the mother church, says the record, that the Astley people should "adorn and repair their chapel, at their own expense, as a commutation."

And yet into all this we read that Calvin and Knox both played Bowls on Sunday afternoons.

There are few who have not heard of the historic game of Bowls played on Plymouth Hoe, and which has formed the subject of a well-known modern picture. From the elevated ridge of the Hoe there is naturally an extensive view seaward, and the story is told that the captains of the English Navy in 1588 were playing a game of Bowls there when the Spanish Armada hove in sight. When the others would have hurriedly left the game unfinished, their imperturbable leader, Sir Francis Drake, deprecated all hurry and fuss, calmly observing that there would be plenty of time to "finish the game, and beat the dons afterwards."

At the State Trial of Titus Oates in 1685 Sir Edward Southcoat deposed to having been on the bowling-green of Tixall, the seat of Lord Aston in Staffordshire, at a time named in the evidence, when there was present "a particular company."

In the history of London we are informed that bowling-greens were once numerous in the vicinity of Bowling Green Lane, Clerkenwell. About 1675 these were both open and covered, and were laid with turf or gravel. The bowls were either flat, or some were round, but the simple object was always the same—to lay your bowl so many times nearest the Jack, or mark.

The city historian goes on to state that there was also played here a game of ground balls, which were driven through an arch, and that this game was the one which developed into the favourite diversion of Charles II., Pall-mall.

According to Pepys, it was the custom for Londoners to play bowls with their wives; an entry in his Diary dated 1662, is to the effect that he went "to Whitehall garden, where lords and ladies are now at bowles." Ladies seldom play this game nowadays.

Few changes seem to have occurred in the rules of the game, and the methods of playing it, throughout the centuries of its existence. The footer was anciently called the "trig" (a word probably allied to "trigger"), and the old-time "Jacks" were always brown. The name of the Jack is said to be from the Latin *jactus*, "a throw"; but more probably this bowl, used by both sides alike, and smaller in size, owes its name to the old-English propensity of dubbing everybody and everything a "Jack" if used in a common or a subordinate capacity.

Shakespeare gives this game the greatest antiquity possible for this country, making it popular in ancient British times. Thus in *Cymbeline* (Act ii., Scene 1) the game is mentioned with the use of some of its technical terms, Cloten, a royal prince, being made to exclaim—

> "Was there ever man had such luck! When I kissed the jack, upon an upcast to be hit away!"

And any player knows how exasperating it is to bowl a ball so well as to place it touching or "kissing" the mark, and then to be knocked away again by the "cast" of a subsequent player. Hence the chagrin of the royal bowler is easily understood.

The bard would also have us believe that in those early times the sport (like most others to the present day) was the subject of wagering, for the same character presently states his resolve—

> "What I have lost to-day at bowls, I'll win to-night."

The same authority has quite a dozen other allusions to the game, and to the fact that bowls are made with a bias—that is, a weight inserted on one side to turn them from a straight-lined course. The expert bowler never fails to use this bias to curve his ball inwards, from one side or the other, according as he holds it in his hand when delivering his "upcast."

In *King John* (Act ii., Scene 2) the "bias" of a bowl is used as a metaphor for "interest" (or "commodity," as the poet calls it), and the figure of speech is admirably kept up throughout the passage :—

> "Commodity the bias of the world;
> The world, who of itself is peised well, [poised]
> Made to run even, upon even ground;
> Till this advantage, this vile drawing bias,
> This sway of motion, this commodity,
> Makes it head from all indifferency,
> From all direction, purpose, course, intent."

And so on; the world of itself being admittedly well-balanced and fit to run even, were it not for the bias of self-interest which draws men from the straight path of integrity and honour.

The word "bias," used to indicate whatever predisposes the mind in a particular direction, is, in fact, derived from the "two-faced" construction of a bowl which makes it deviate from the straight line. In the game itself, as previously explained, the direction in which a bowl "narrows" towards the Jack is controlled by the player, who, in delivery, holds it in his hand either for "thumb-bias" or for "finger-bias," as the exigency demands. So it has come about that we speak of a man being "unduly biased," or of another having "unconscious bias."

Another term used in common speech and derived from this game is "rub"; as when we say, "Ay, there's the rub." For "he who plays at bowls must look out for rubs"—that is, he must consider the inequalities of the ground, and with careful eye and the exercise of sound judgment make due allowance for them. Indeed, the possibilities of the game of bowls are almost infinite—it calls for so many good qualities that the poet has compared it with the game of Life—

> "Life, like the Game of Bowls, is but an end,
> Which to play well, this moral verse attend.
> Throw not your bowl too rashly from your hand,
> First let its course by reason's eye be plann'd;
> Lest it rolls useless o'er the verdant plain,
> Like heedless Life—that finishes in vain.
> Know well your bias;—here the moral school
> Scarce needs a comment on the bowling rule;
> Play not too wide, with caution eye your cast,
> Use not extent of Green, or Life, to waste:
> Nor yet too straight—in Life observe the same—
> The narrow-minded often miss their aim!
> Bowling too short, you but obstruct the Green,
> Like him who loiters on Life's public scene;
> Whoe'er at bowls, or business causes strife
> Will rubs on Greens receive—and eke in Life;
> One bowling trick avoid in moral play,
> Ah, never, never block your neighbour's way.
> These rules observed, a Man may play his game,
> On Bowling Greens, or through the World, with fame."

Bowling, it has just been said, is the diversion of the urbane middle-aged; and as this is the period of life when men have grown staid and are less inclined to the fickleness of idle changes, it is not surprising to find that many Bowling Clubs have been in existence for a great number of years. There is scarcely a town or village in the country without its bowling-green, and of the clubs in connection therewith quite a respectable percentage can claim a history running over a century or so.

Though not a boisterous form of recreation, bowling has never been divorced from a mild conviviality; hence, perhaps, much of that which has endeared it to the average Englishman of social tastes and sober habits—

> "Quaint joys, brave boys, Harry bring out your bowls,
> But first the bottle to refresh dull sowls."

At Hadley, near Worcester, the Bowling Club boasts of a continuous existence from a date anterior to that of Drake's historic game on Plymouth Hoe. The date assigned is 1575, when Queen Elizabeth visited Worcester, and in the possession of the Club is a large oak panel bearing the names of all the peers of the realm at that date, accompanied by the emblazonry of their seventy-three shields of arms. The historian of the Club has pictured the green animated by the presence of its members at successive periods; by the local worthies in the Golden Age of Elizabeth, treading the turf with stately steps, clad in trunk hose, doublet, and ruff; by the Worcestershire Cavaliers of the Stuart period, in elaborate attire crowned by flowing locks and plumed hats; by the Georgian members in powdered wigs and knee breeches; and so on, down to the Club's still prosperous present.

The bowler's urbanity, beyond leading to that permanence of association which characterises the life of his club, is also conducive to conviviality. Consequently in some Bowling Clubs the possession of a wine cellar is not an unknown concomitance; and the members then assemble not only to rally round the Jack, but to toast each other's prowess in the flowing bowl afterwards.

That the exercise is one which is not only congenial to the average taste, but is invigorating and beneficial to the health, is illustrated by the record of the Hadley Bowling Club. One member, the Rev. George Williams, rector of Martin Hussingtree, designated the "Lion" of the club on account of his long membership of half a century and upwards, was still bowling at the age of eighty-three. His fellow-members, after the manner of all good Englishmen, celebrated his jubilee in 1839, the club specially meeting at the festive board, all with "bias" of good feeling towards their venerable colleague, no man "bowling short" in doing him honour, and every speaker "true to the ground," "bowling home," however "wide" his delivery.

Naturally a club with the respectability of an antiquity like this has (or had) some quaint rules. Rule 22 is to the effect "that if any one kick the bowl or block it, he shall forfeit half the money they are bowling for," from which it is apparent that the game was played for money as well as love. But not the least curious old rule was "that if any breaker-in shall not pay his debts, the servant of the green shall draw him on his breech across the green." Other times, other manners.

# XII

## QUARTER-STAFF, SINGLESTICK, ETC.

Significance of "quarter"—Robin Hood's encounter with the Tanner—Locksley's bouts with the Miller and Little John—A game too rough for the taste of the present day—Single-stick—Cudgel-play.

A QUARTER-STAFF was an old English weapon which got its name from the manner of using it. It consisted simply of a stout pole, usually about 6 feet 6 inches long, or sometimes a little more than that. In using it, a firm grasp was taken by one hand in the middle of the staff, and by the other a looser hold, half-way between the middle and the end, or at a point marking the "quarter."

In the attack, the latter hand was shifted from one quarter to the other (hence the name of the weapon) giving the staff a rapid circular motion, which brought the ends on to the adversary at unexpected points. As an amusement it was rather rough, and yet innocent in comparison with other sports of our forefathers.

A few odd verses excerpted from the old ballad relating Robin Hood's adventure with the tanner, Arthur-a-Bland, will convey a fairly good idea of the game :—

"Then Robin he unbuckled his belt,
And laid down his bow so long;
He took up a staff of another oak graff
That was both stiff and strong.

'But let me measure,' said jolly Robin,
  'Before we begin our fray;
For I'll not have mine to be longer than thine
  For that will be counted foul play.'

'I pass not for length,' bold Arthur replied,
  'My staff is of oak so free;
Eight foot and a half it will knock down a calf,
  And I hope it will knock down thee.'

About and about and about they went,
  Like two wild boars in a chase,
Striving to aim each other to maim
  Leg, arm, or any other place.

And knock for knock they hastily dealt,
  Which held for two hours or more;
That all the wood rang at every bang,
  They plied their work so sore."

There is much more of the ballad, but this will suffice for our present purpose. Also in "Ivanhoe" we have a delectable description of a similar encounter—this time between one of Locksley's sturdy band, "The Miller," and Gurth the Saxon.

"The two champions being alike armed with quarter-staves, stepped forward into the open space in order to have the full benefit of the moonlight. . . . The Miller, holding his quarter-staff by the middle, and making it flourish round his head after the fashion which the French call *faire le moulinet,* exclaimed boastfully, 'Come on, churl, an thou darest; thou shalt feel the strength of a miller's thumb.'

"'If thou be'st a miller,' answered Gurth undauntedly making his weapon play round his head with equal dexterity, 'thou art doubly a thief, and I, as a true man, bid thee defiance.'

"Less obstinate, and even less dangerous combats, have been described in good heroic verse. Yet though Quarter-staff play be out of date, what we can in prose we will do for these bold champions.

"So saying, the two champions closed together, and for a few minutes they displayed great equality in strength, courage, and skill, intercepting and returning the blows of their adversary with the most rapid dexterity, while from the continued clatter of the weapons, a person at a distance might have supposed there were at least six persons engaged on each side.

"Long they fought equally, until the Miller began to lose temper . . . not a frame of mind favourable to the noble game of quarter-staff, in which, as in ordinary cudgel-playing, the utmost coolness is requisite; and it gave Gurth, whose temper was steady though surly, the opportunity of acquiring a decided advantage.

"The Miller pressed furiously forward, dealing blows with either end of his staff alternately, and striving to come to half-staff distance; while Gurth defended himself against the attack, keeping his hands about a yard asunder, and covering himself by shifting his weapon with great celerity, so as to protect his head and body.

"Thus did he maintain the defensive, making his eye, foot and hand keep true time, until observing his antagonist lose wind, he darted the staff at his face with his left hand; and as the Miller endeavoured to parry the thrust, he slid his right hand down to his left, and with the full swing of the weapon struck his opponent on the left side of the head, who instantly measured his length upon the greensward."

Than this passage from Sir Walter Scott, nothing could give a more entertaining or more enlightening description of Quarter-staff play.

In the same work of fiction, which is a veritable store-house of information on the subject of old English sports, we read how the bold Robin Hood, on his first meeting with Little John, disdaining to take advantage of a comparatively unarmed man, laid down his bow, and unbuckling a stout oaken stick at his side, proceeded at once to settle their difference . . . which was the disputed passage of a plank bridge . . . by a bout of quarter-staves.

We are not to doubt that in the old fighting days, when men relied not so much upon the law as upon themselves for personal protection, that with this weapon of the humble—the trusty staff with which the man of low degree habitually defended himself—there were performed as valiant feats of arms as ever were recorded by Froissart or sung by troubador.

But the display of a stout and pliant wrist must ever be at a marked disadvantage with an exhibition of strong and graceful horsemanship; nor can a stick cut from the hedge ever be expected to compare in attractiveness with the gleam of richly fabricated armour. Our indebtedness to Scott, therefore, for his vivid "prose" description, is practically immeasurable.

In Dryden's day, the staff was still carried upon the back, for he writes:—

> "His quarter-staff, which he could ne'er forsake,
> Hung half before and half behind his back."

Nowadays the sport is entirely unknown, having gone out of use many generations ago; nor, do we think, would it ever be likely to come into favour again, being rather too rough for the taste of the present day.

Somewhat analagous games to Quarter-staff are SINGLE-STICK and CUDGEL-PLAYING.

Single-stick Playing is so called to distinguish it from Cudgelling, in which two sticks are used, the Single-stick player having the left-hand tied down and using only one stick both to defend himself and strike his antagonist. The object of each gamester in this play, as in Cudgelling, is to guard himself, and to fetch blood from the other's head—whether by taking a little skin from his pericranium, drawing the crimson stream from his nose, or knocking out a few of his teeth.

In Cudgelling, as the name implies, the weapon of attack is a stout staff, or cudgel, and the player defends himself with another one, having a large hemisphere of basket-work upon it called the "pot."

Bacon speaks of the use of cudgels by the captains of the Roman armies. In the eighteenth century matches with cudgels were quite the vogue, and public subscrip-

Attempt to force the guard. On guard.

SINGLE STICK. SOMERSETSHIRE GAMESTERS.

[*From an engraving by Scott. Publishtd, 1810, by J. Wheble, Warwick Square.*]

*To face page* 186

tion lists were got up to provide prizes. "Chambers' Book of Days" mentions a cudgel match held at Shrivenham, in Berkshire, on April 30, 1748, the patrons of which included Lord Barrington and other members of the aristocracy, when the prize-money distributed amounted to a little over five pounds; the comment upon which is—"We find nowadays Pugilists engage in a much more brutal and less scientific display for a far less sum."

## XIII

### WRESTLING

Almost obsolete—Except as a music-hall "turn"—Or in the form Ju-jitsu—The "Cornish hug"—Cornish rules—An old London pastime—Chaucerian allusion—"Wrastling" in a Robin Hood ballad—Sir Thomas Parkyn, a notable patron—His meetings at Bunny—His rules and style of play—A great wrestling match in 1826, Devon *v.* Cornwall.

WRESTLING had become one of the least practised of our old English sports, till the recent revival of the art as a music-hall "turn"—a use for which it was particularly well adapted, inasmuch as a Wrestling Match never fails to hold the interest of the spectator from first to last by its sustained excitement, which is often of a nerve-straining intensity.

The importation of scientific Ju-jitsu from Japan may also have had something to do with the new-born interest now manifested in the art. But as an unscientific exercise Wrestling has been practised by the least civilised of nations from the very earliest of times; and as is well known, it made a very considerable figure among the old Olympic games.

In England the inhabitants of Devon and Cornwall have from time immemorial been celebrated for their expertness in the pastime. "The Cornish," says old gossip Fuller, "are masters of the art of wrestling, so that if the Olympian games were now in fashion, they would

CORNISH WRESTLING

[*Published, 1800, by J. Wheble, Warwick Court.*]

*To face page* 189

come away with the victory. Their hug is a cunning close with their fellow-combatants, the fruits whereof is their fair fall, or foil at the least." To give a Cornish hug is a proverbial expression. Another old writer on Cornwall says of this characteristic sport:—

> "The beholders then cast or form themselves into a ring, in the empty space whereof the two champions set forth, stripped into their dublets and hosen, and untrussed, that they may so the better command the use of their lymnes; and first shaking hands in token of friendship, they fall presently to the effect of anger: for each striveth how to take hold of the other with the best advantage, and to beare his adverse party downe: wherein, whosoever overthroweth his mate, in such sort, as that either his backe, or the one shoulder, and contrary heele do touch the ground, is accounted to give the fall. If he be only endangered, and makes a narrow escape, it is called a foyle."

Concerning the rules of the game the same writer adds —"This pastime also hath his laws, for instance; of taking hold above the girdle—wearing a girdle to take hold by—playing three pulls for trial of the mastery, the fall-giver to be exempted from playing again with the taker, but bound to answer his successor."

The citizens of London in past times have been expert wrestlers, and there are records of some famous contests among them. In the reign of Henry III. there was a great match between them and the inhabitants of Westminster, held in St. Giles's Fields, at which the Londoners proved victorious. At the return match held shortly after in Westminster a riot broke out through the overbearing attitude assumed by the Bailiff of that city, and the tumult could not be quelled for several days. Stow informs us of a similar outbreak against the Lord Mayor of London, during a wrestling match held at Clerkenwell in 1453. The excitement engendered by Wrestling is evidently of a contagious nature.

The common form of prize given at these old Wrestling Matches, seems to have been a ram. Thus writes Chaucer in the "Rhyme of Sir Thopas":—

"Of wrastling was there none his pere
Where any Ram shulde stonde."

—and again in another passage he says of a miller—

" . . . for over al there he cam
At wrastling he wode have away the Ram."

Other animals were sometimes offered as prizes; as a Cock, a Bull, or a Horse. Thus an old ballad of Robin Hood finding himself in the West Country runs to this effect:—

"As he went, by a bridge was a wrastling,
And there taryed was he,
And there was all the best yemen
Of all the West Countrey.

A full fayre game was set up;
A white bull, up ypyght;
A great courser with sadle and brydle
With gold burnished full bryght.

A payre of gloves, a red gold ringe,
A pipe of wine, good faye.
What man bereth him best, ywis,
The prize shall bear away."

Coming down to much later times, we find it a practice in some parts for the squire of the parish to give a hogshead of ale every year, to encourage the meeting of all local wrestlers, and offering as the prize "a good beaver hat, as a recompence to him who gives the most falls."

The decay of the martial and more spirited exercises, like Archery and Wrestling, said to have set in from the want of places proper for these purposes rather than any lack of inclination on the part of the people—and this points to the wrongful enclosure of village greens and the appropriation of common-lands—was followed by the pursuit of such amusements and "gamings" as could be cultivated at inns, taverns, and common drinking-houses. Stow, in his "Survey of London," complains bitterly that "running is turned into royot" and "our bowes into bowls"; from which it has been inferred that in national popularity Archery was succeeded by the game of Bowls.

In the history of Wrestling mention can never be omitted of the eccentric Sir Thomas Parkyns, Baronet, of Bunny Park, Notts, who died in 1741, and was the author of a curious work entitled, "The Inn Play, or Cornish Hugg Wrestler." Nor was he a mere writer on Wrestling; he was an able and skilful athlete himself, as well as being a ripe scholar and an energetic justice of the peace.

He was educated at Westminster School under the famous Dr. Busby, where it is said his attention was first directed to Wrestling by having to translate a well-known epigram from Martial, a portion of which he rendered thus:—

> "I study next, rouse my poetic vein;
> My body then anoint, and gently strain
> With some meet exercise; exult in mind
> At every turn, myself both free to find
> From crimes and debts; last, I bathe, sup, laugh, drink,
> Jest, sing, rest, and, on all that passes, think."

Afterwards, as a student at Gray's Inn, we find him relieving the dry study of the law by taking lessons in Wrestling, Fencing, and Boxing from the best masters the Metropolis could produce.

Settling on his ancestral estate early in life, and while the vigour of youth was still fresh and buoyant within his robust frame, he established an annual wrestling match in his park, open to all comers. The prize was a gold-laced hat of the value of a guinea; but if the reward was small the glory was great, for Wrestling was then a popular sport.

Sir Thomas was no idle patron of these meetings; he never objected to try a fall with the best man on the ground, and on more than one occasion won and wore the prize hat himself. All his servants were selected for their well-set-up frames, strength, and muscularity; and especially for their approved ability as wrestlers. His favourite footman and coachman, for example, had defeated the baronet in the wrestling ring, throwing him on his back in such a consummate style that, like the generous Robin Hood of old, he immediately took them into his service.

This method of selection was no mere whim—it was sound policy; for he knew, as well as any man could, that a good wrestler was bound to be a sober man.

"Whoever would be a complete wrestler," wrote Sir Thomas, "must avoid being overtaken in drink, which very much enervates;" besides putting a man in a passion, and bereaving him of his senses. Very quaintly does he continue this argument, contending that Bacchus is among the greatest of wrestling masters, having in his school many assistants like Brandy the Frenchman, and Usquebaugh the Irishman, whose great trick is to "teach mostly the trip, which I assure you is no safe and sound play."

In describing the antiquity of Wrestling, he alludes to the episode of Jacob's encounter recorded in Genesis, and slily advises his readers to avoid wrestling with angels in the night; for though the struggle may be maintained till break of day, "yet they will have the fall, and be out of joint with Jacob's thigh."

A good specimen of Sir Thomas's style is found in the following directions for giving an opponent the throw known by adepts as "the flying horse":—

"Take him by the right hand with your left, your palm being upwards as if you designed only to shake him by the hand in a friendly manner in the beginning; and twist it outwards, and lift it upwards to make way for your head, and put your head under his right arm-pit, and hold his hand down to your left side, hold your head stiff backwards, to hold him out of his strength; then put your right arm up to the shoulder between his grainings, and let your hand appear behind past his breech; but if you suspect they will cavil at that arm, as a breeching, lay your arm along his belly, and lift him up as high as your head and in either hold, when so high lean backward, and throw him over your head."

Which instructions were doubtless found very effective—when they could be carried out—by the practitioner.

On his monument in Bunny Church Sir Thomas Parkyns is depicted in his wrestling dress, potent and postured, ready for either "flying horse" or "Cornish hug." His attitude is the first position in Wrestling, and symbolises "the divine and human struggle for the glorious mastery." The moral is further enforced by some Latin verses which have been Englished to commence thus:—

"At length, by conquering Time subdued,
Lo! here Britannia's wrestler lies;
Till now, he still unshaken stood,
Whene'er he strove, and gain'd the prize."

This athletic worthy had never experienced a day's illness "till Death gave him the backfall" in his seventy-eighth year. The Wrestling Matches he instituted were kept up till about 1810.

A description of a Wrestling Match held in 1826 between a Devon man and a representative of Cornwall, on the Green of the Eagle Tavern, City Road, London, discloses the differences in style affected by these two neighbouring shires.

The Devonian was a chubby-faced farmer, all life and activity, holding himself erect, and offering to his opponent in the ring every advantage. His name was Abraham Cann.

The Cornishman, named Warren, was sallow and sharp-featured, all caution and resistance, bending his body in such a way that his legs were inaccessible to his opponent; he waited for the critical instant when he could spring in upon his impatient adversary.

Cann was extremely muscular and of fine athletic proportions; he stood with legs apart, having a hold like a vice, and strength to pinion with ease the arms of any adversary he could come to grips with.

Warren was a miner, and also possessed amazing strength, though it was not so well distributed throughout his frame.

Cann led off by putting out his hand as quietly as if he were going to seize a shy horse; Warren threw off his touch with all the impetuosity of a surprised horse. But there was no escaping Cann's pinch, and when they came to grips he had tripped his opponent in a trice, using his toe in a scientific but ineffectual manner; for though he threw his man clean to the ground, it was not on his back, as required.

In the second bout Warren stooped and crouched more than ever to keep his legs out of Cann's reach, who punished him for it by several kicks below the knee, which would have told more severely if his shoes had been on, according to his county's fashion.

After shaking each other rudely, straining knee to

knee and forcing each other's shoulder down, neither could gain any advantage so long as they but held by the arm and breast-collar, as ordinary wrestlers do. But presently they closed, their legs intertwined, Warren having Cann's back pressed to his breast-bone and lifted from the ground. To pitch him down with his back squarely on the ground required more prowess than he possessed; for when at last the attempt was made, it was Warren who was seen sprawling flat on his back, while Cann, whom he had been forced to liberate to save himself, had been thrown a few yards off on all fours.

The dispute over this fall, which should have been a victory for Cann, eventuated in the appointment of a new referee, the first one having declared that Warren had touched ground with one shoulder only.

Strange to record, the next and final bout proved to be an exact counterpart of the disputed fall. Warren made the same move, only lifting his antagonist higher. Cann turned himself precisely as before, but using a much greater effort, apparently put to it by his opponent's marvellous strength. His share, however, in upsetting his supporter was greater this time, as he relaxed one leg much sooner, and adhered closer to the chest during the fall; for at the end he was seen uppermost, still coiled round his supine adversary, who this time admitted the fall, and, starting up, offered his hand to the victor. It was a termination honourably accepted as satisfactory to both sides.

## XIV

### PRIZE-FIGHTING—PUGILISM

Cuffs and Fisticuffs—Fists *v.* Lethal Weapons—"Gladiators," or prize-fighters with swords—Exhibitions at Hockley-in-the-Hole and Marylebone—The classic "pugilatus"—Boxing—Degrading women-fights—Broughton, "the father of English pugilism" (1742)—Sparring at theatres and in race booths—The patrons of Pugilism, reverend and aristocratic—Sir John Astley's "light play"—The Sayers and Heenan fight (1860)—How Sir John Astley saw the fight—the last classic battle in the P.R. (1863)—Fighting days and amateur Pugilism—The "Merry Mills" arranged for "Saint Mondays"—From amateur to professional pugilist—The cult of Bone-setting—Consulting the witches—Fêting a hero—The pugilist in literature—Anecdotes of fighters and fighting—Boxing as an exercise—The decay of Prize-fighting—How fights were brought off—Boxiana.

CENTURIES before Pugilism had been reduced to a "science," the Englishman had adopted the practice of using his naked, unarmed hand for attack, if not for defence. It was the natural weapon, ready to the resort of a man never reluctant to enter a quarrel; of a man indomitable, but never bloodthirsty.

So long as he used his open hand for cuffing an enemy, it was a weapon of attack only; but when he clenched his fists, and his cuffs became fisticuffs, then he discovered the possibilities of defence as well as of attack; he found that he could not only strike a heavier blow, but could ward off one by the same natural means.

Hereward the Wake may be accepted as the name of

the first Englishman who is recorded to have exhibited a partiality for resorting to the arbitrament of the Court of Cuffs. In obtaining a disguise in which to pry upon the proceedings of the Norman Conqueror, it is related of him that he exchanged buffets with a potter, as part of a bargain. He demanded the potter's outfit; the potter objected; and they settled the difference in the old-fashioned English way—they stood up to each other's blow in turn, and judged the better man by the result.

Another great Englishman of those early times who was not averse to the use of his hands, was King Richard I. In an old romance written round the inspiring subject of Cœur-de-Lion, it is recorded that on his adventurous return from the Holy Land he exchanged fistic favours with the son of his principal warder during his incarceration in a German prison. Naturally the King was the challenger to this barter of buffets; he "stood forth like a true man," says the ancient chronicler, to take the first blow. And he received one that staggered even his stalwart frame. Then in requital, "having previously waxed his hand," the reckless prisoner returned the box on the ear with so much interest as to kill his antagonist on the spot—which was scarcely a wise proceeding on the part of a prisoner.

Sir Walter Scott does not hesitate to accept the truth of this story as a warrant for introducing into "Ivanhoe" the incident of Richard, *incognito*, indulging in an interchange of cuffs with the jolly friar he encountered in the forest.

Without any brawling, and quite as a friendly interchange of courtesies between two brave men, the sturdy priest was allowed to bare his brawny arm up to the elbow, and, putting all his strength into the blow, to give the

King a buffet that might have felled an ox. But his challenger stood firm as a rock ; and then, as promised, proceeded to repay the loan of the cuff with an interest as deep "as usury ever exacted in traffic." Then it was the burly priest's turn to offer his cheek to the smiter. And he received a buffet given with such strength and goodwill, that he rolled head over heels upon the plain —presently to rise sore and dazed, though neither angry nor crestfallen.

From illustrations such as these it at once becomes manifest that hand-fighting had not in those times developed into what its votaries now proudly style "the noble art of self-defence." No defence was offered.

The fighting propensity is said to be strong in every true-born Englishman. But accompanying this natural characteristic, and as a set-off which balances the whole, is the Englishman's well-known love of fair play.

Perhaps it was this more generous element in his character which first gave encouragement to fisticuffs as a national form of fighting. In the earlier centuries, when the arm of the law was not far-reaching enough to afford every man personal security, he was allowed to carry weapons for his own self-defence. Then came a period when the carrying of a sword formed the distinctive mark of the gentleman, and men of inferior social status had to content themselves with a staff or club for their personal protection.

Towards the close of the eighteenth century the carrying of swords or other lethal weapons fell entirely out of fashion, while at the same time proficiency in the art of boxing began to be cultivated ; and in time this accomplishment became popular with all classes of Englishmen. As soon as the Englishman had brought the use of his fists to a "science"—or, perhaps, as he preferred to call it, to "the noble art of self-defence"—

he began to look upon the use of the knife as cowardly, as a practice utterly beneath his contempt. And so it came to pass in due time that among foreign nationalities the fists of the ready Englishman were always more to be dreaded than the murderous knife of the desperado.

> "An Englishman will take his part
> With courage prime and noble heart;
> Either forgive, or resent offence
> And bang-up in his own defence.
> No sword nor dagger, nor deadly list,
> He'll rise or fall but by his fist.
> The battle o'er—all make amends
> By shaking hands—becoming friends."

says the old ballad of *Boxiana.*

Ignoring the duello as a custom lying outside the region of recreative sport, reference will be made only to those displays of swordsmanship which were competitive exercises in the use of lethal weapons for the winning of prize-money. For, long before the institution of the pugilistic Prize Ring, the term Prize-fighting was applied to contests with swords and daggers, and other weapons of that nature. It will therefore be necessary to devote a few paragraphs to this transitional period in the history of Prize-fighting.

As the old-established Bear Gardens of the Tudor period became gradually converted into theatres, exhibitions of Prize-fighting for a long time found equal favour with the dramatic performances and other innovations to the programme of popular amusements.

One of the most notorious quarters of old London for the public exhibition of all sorts of brutalities perpetrated under the name of sport, was Hockley-in-the-Hole. "You must go to Hockley-in-the-Hole and Marybone, child, to learn valour," says Mrs. Peachum to Filch, in *The Beggar's Opera* of the poet Gay.

In 1701 the Middlesex Grand Jury made the following presentment :—

"We having observed the late boldness of a sort of men that stile themselves masters of the noble science of defence, passing through this city with beat of drums, colours displayed, swords drawn, with a numerous company of people following them, dispersing their printed bills thereby inviting persons to be spectators of those inhuman sights which are directly contrary to the practice and profession of the Christian religion, whereby barbarous principles are instilled in the minds of men ; we think ourselves obliged to represent this matter, that some method may be speedily taken to prevent their passage through the city in such a tumultuous manner, on so unwarrantable a design."

The march through the streets consisted of a parade of the bulls or the bears which were to be baited, or of a procession of the swordsmen who were to fight ; and as to the bills which were distributed, the following copy of the printed matter upon one lot will give a very fair idea of their general tenor :—

"A trial of skill to be performed between two profound masters of the noble science of self-defence on Wednesday next, the 13th of July, 1709, at two o'clock precisely.

"I, George Gray, born in the city of Norwich, who has fought in most parts of the West Indies—viz., Jamaica, Barbadoes, and several other parts of the world, in all twenty-five times upon the stage, and was never yet worsted, and am now lately come to London, do invite James Harris to meet and exercise at the following weapons : Back-sword, Sword and Dagger, Sword and Buckler, Single Falchion, and case of Falchions.

"I, James Harris, master of the said noble science of defence, who formerly rid in the Horse Guards, and hath fought 110 prizes and never left a stage to any man, will not fail (God willing) to meet this brave and bold inviter at the time and place appointed, desiring sharp swords, and from him no favour.

"No person to be upon the stage but the seconds.

"Vivat Regina."

Here is a similar announcement extracted from *The Postboy* of July 8, 1701 :—

"At His Majesty's Bear Garden, Hockley-in-the-Hole, a trial of skill is to be performed to-morrow, being the 9th instant (without beat of drum) between these following masters—

"I, John Terrewest, of Oundle, in Northamptonshire, master of the noble science of defence, do invite you, William King, who lately fought Mr. Joseph Thomas, once more to meet me and exercise at the usual weapons.

"I, William King, will not fail to meet this fair inviter, desiring a clear stage, and from him no favour.

"NOTE. — There is lately built a pleasant cool gallery for gentlemen."

This delectable rendezvous was usually known as the Bear Garden ; and as a matter of fact the bears and bulls which were solemnly paraded through the streets were baited there every Monday and Thursday. In 1709 a tragic occurrence took place at the Gardens ; the proprietor of the place was attacked by his own bears, and was almost devoured before any one was aware of his danger. His hurts proved fatal—a result which seldom overtook any of the hireling crew who appeared on his public platform. The results of the encounters between those valiant swordsmen who announced their own prowess in such high-sounding challenges were generally arranged beforehand. The losing man often undertook to receive a number of cuts, provided they were not too many or too deep, for a fixed proportion of the prize-money. The bouts were always fought, however, with the most seeming ferocity ; for it was in this way they gulled the British public, and put money in their own pockets.

Historically, British Boxing is analagous to the *pugilatus* of the Romans. The British are supposed to possess an exceptional length of arm which gives them the material advantage of a "long reach" in pugilistic encounters. This may or may not be a fact; if a fact, it may be the result of evolution; but be it as it may, it is quite certain that a bout at fisticuffs comes to the average Englishman of modern days as the most natural way of settling a dispute when resource must be had to physical force.

The regulated system of fighting with closed fists, which bears the name of Boxing—a sport almost peculiar to England—dates only from the earlier decades of the eighteenth century. The rules, including the important ones regarding rounds, and the interval of half a minute between each, which gave such a marked character to the practice—a touch of humanity which slightly relieved its brutality—were the production of one John Broughton, the first to assume the position of Champion Prize-fighter of England (1742); and of whom more anon.

As previously stated, Prize-fighting was a practice originally performed with swords; and it was on the decline of the sword-combat exhibitions, in the reign of George I., that the comparatively harmless amusement of Boxing arose.

The fighting with swords took place upon a raised platform, to lift the combatants into full view of the assembled crowds who generally thronged these exhibitions. The same arenas seem to have been used, before the advent of Broughton's scientific system of Boxing, for prize-fighting matches with fists between women. The favourite form of this diversion was to set two women pummelling each other, both of them holding a half-crown in each hand; and it is remarkable that well-dressed crowds would pay eagerly to witness these contests, delighting in the climax when one, giving way to the female tendency to scratch or tear an opponent's hair, opened a hand and dropped her coin—a weakness of femininity which of course lost her the match.

An account of a "Tour through Great Britain" in 1725 records in illuminating terms the existence of "a new Bear Garden, called Figg's Theatre, being a stage for the gladiators or prize-fighters," &c. The amusing part of the announcement, however, is the conclusion of it, showing how jealous these gentlemanly gladiators were of their precious reputations; for after informing us of the location of the said theatre in Tyburn Road, it runs—

> "N.B.—The gentlemen of the science taking offence at its being called the Tyburn Road, though it really is so, will have it called the Oxford Road."

Which alteration of name doubtless soothed the susceptibilities of these fine gentlemen. But would it have been so wanton a libel on the "fancy" to have hinted that Prize-fighting ever tended towards Tyburn tree? True is it that if James Figg the Prize-fighter did not exactly die in the odour of sanctity, he lies buried at Marylebone Church in very good company, which includes not only well-known artists, sculptors, and astronomers, but no less a personage than the Rev. Charles Wesley.

On the other hand Figg appears to have been, in his time, a very noted character, for his features have been preserved to us by Hogarth, who gives us his portrait in "The Rake's Progress." Significant as this conjunction is, the tribute of a contemporary rhymster is equally so—

> "Long live the great Figg, by the prize-fighting swains
> Sole monarch acknowledged of Marybone plains."

The truth seems to be that the amusements provided at Figg's Theatre were more varied than select. For his patrons he occasionally got up "sets-to" between women. One advertisement of the period announces that "Mrs. Stokes, the City championess is ready to meet the Hibernian Heroine at Figg's." Numerous records of similar Amazonian challenges might be turned up if the subject were not too disgusting. One or two others must suffice to illustrate the point.

Pugilistic encounters between women sometimes took place in the booths that toured round the country from fair to fair. These, however, were not always fought for prizes, but occasionally as "affairs of honour." The following is the form of two newspaper advertisements of the year 1772—

> "CHALLENGE.—I, Elizabeth Wilkinson, of Clerkenwell, having had some words with Hannah Hyfield, and require satisfaction, do invite her to meet me upon the stage, and box me for three guineas; each woman holding half-a-crown in each hand, and the first woman that drops the money to lose the battle."

> "ANSWER.—I, Hannah Hyfield, of Newgate Market, hearing the resoluteness of Elizabeth Wilkinson, will not fail, God willing, to give her more blows than words, desiring home blows and from her no favour. She may expect a good thumping."

Perhaps it was as well such viragos fought thus with their fists clasped upon coins; it was a condition which most ingeniously precluded the possibility of face-scratching or hair-pulling.

No better gauge of the demoralising effects of Prize-fighting could possibly be produced than these examples of the indulgence of unsexed females in this most unwomanly of pastimes. Here is another newspaper extract, dated 1768—

> "Two women fought for a new shift, valued at half-a-crown, in the Spaw Fields, near Islington. The battle was won by a woman called Bruising Peg, who beat her antagonist in a terrible manner."

In another place we may read that in the summer of the same year "an extraordinary battle was fought in the

*Drawn by J. R. Cruikshank* — *Etched by G. Cruikshank*

A SPARRING MATCH AT THE FIVES COURT.

[*Published, 1813, by George Smeeton, 139 St. Martin's Lane.*]

*To face page 205*

Spa Fields by two women against two taylors, for a guinea a head, which was won by the ladies who beat the taylors in a severe manner."

John Broughton, the first hero of the sparring ring, had his boxing booth in Tottenham Court Road, in 1742, where he enjoyed the patronage of the Duke of Cumberland. He was the first to assume the position of "champion" pugilist, a distinction he retained for eighteen years.

His celebrated London gymnasium went by the name of the "Tottenham Court Nursery." The professor's advertisement setting forth the attractions of this amphitheatre for boxing affords rather amusing reading. It announced "a Lecture on manhood, or Gymnastic Physiology, wherein the whole theory and practice of the Art of Boxing will be fully explained by various Operations on the Animal Œconomy: and the principles of championship illustrated by proper experiments on the Solids and Fluids of the Body: together with the True method of investigating the nature of the Blows, Stops, Cross-buttocks, &c., incident to Combatants. The whole leading to the most successful Method of beating a man deaf, dumb, lame, and blind."

Of John Broughton, the recognised father of English Pugilism, it has been admitted that he possessed constant originality as well as power, in his style of boxing; and that, apart from his profession, he was a man of solid sense and some ability. The Duke of Cumberland, his royal patron, once took him a trip to the Continent, and on showing him the Grenadier Guards at Berlin, asked the pugilist what he thought of those fellows for a "set-to"; to which Broughton replied that he would have no objection to take on the whole regiment, provided he were allowed to have a breakfast between each two battles.

When he had reached the height of his reputation he was unfortunate enough to fall one day into a quarrel with a butcher named Slack. The offended Slack had the temerity to challenge the champion. Broughton and his supporters treated the challenger with contempt, and the betting was ten to one on the champion. But early in the battle Slack contrived to hit his opponent between the eyes so effectively as to blind him; and the poor man, though his strength and agility were undiminished, was never able to see his assailant for the rest of the fight.

With a brutality characteristic of the man, the Duke of Cumberland called out, "Why, Broughton, you can't fight—you are beaten, man!"

And it was perfectly true. The battle was over in fourteen minutes, and the hitherto undefeated champion was completely vanquished. The royal patron of the sport is understood to have lost thousands of pounds on the result, while Slack, by one adroit blow, gained a prize of six hundred. Broughton survived in obscurity, and died in 1789.

The theatre established in London by Broughton for the display of boxing was specially erected in the year 1742. Within the next fifty years numerous schools were opened in the Metropolis, where boxing was taught on scientific principles. In 1791 a well-known fighting man named Mendoza opened the Lyceum in the Strand for boxing.

But public patronage went far beyond that. A writer of a work on the subject, published in 1813, says:—

"Have not our classic theatres within the last twenty-five years—possessing all the advantages of authors the most exalted and refined; actors the most inimitable and chaste, either to exort the tear or provoke a laugh; music the most ravishing; scenes and decorations, in point of magnificence and splendour, unparalleled—

invited Pugilism to their boards? The names of some of the first-rate Boxers have enriched their play-bills; and the audience (of whom no doubt can attach as to respectability) have testified approbation by the loudest of plaudits."

So late as 1830 semi-theatrical entertainments were given at a Chalk Farm rendezvous, where prize-fights and other brutal sports found places in the programmes along with balls, masquerades, and the legitimate drama.

For a quarter of a century or more after this it was quite customary for travelling circuses to include among their marvellous feats of horsemanship a classical exposition of Boxing, generally rendered between two well-known veterans of the Prize Ring.

In these palmy days of the Prize Ring there was published an aquatint which admirably illustrates the popularity of the sport, and copies of which now fetch a good price among collectors. It is inscribed, "To the admirers of British Courage this representation of the great contest between Spring and Langan upon Worcester racecourse, January 7, 1824, for the championship of England, is respectfully dedicated by their obliged servants, James Clements and John Pitman." The grand stand is shown thronged with spectators, and also subsidiary stands erected on either side of the "ring," in which the combatants are facing each other.

And, as to the respectability of the patrons of Pugilism? Was not the "noble art" countenanced and supported by men of undoubted standing in the social scale?

Let us take Thackeray's description of a typical sporting parson, a member of a county family, to boot, who is supposed to have flourished about the Waterloo period, as depicted in that incomparable novel, "Vanity Fair."

"The Reverend Bute Crawley was a tall, stately, jolly, shovel-hatted man, far more popular in his county than the baronet, his brother. At college he pulled stroke-oar in the Christchurch boat, and had thrashed all the best bruisers in the 'town.' He carried his taste for boxing and athletic exercises into private life; there was not a fight within twenty miles at which he was not present."

Illustrative of the fact that a bout at fisticuffs was also once looked upon as a source of amusement, an extract may be given from a recently published volume of reminiscences. The hero of the anecdote is the Marquis of Waterford, and the date of the exploit about 1830—

"His character seems to have been a mixture of the hard-riding sportsman of his generation and the buffoon and practical joker—a type so common in the pages of Lever. In his youth Lord Waterford, with his companions Lord Methuen and the brothers Billy and Ffolliot Duff, were never so happy as when beating the town and challenging draymen and butchers to fisticuffs. Lord Methuen was a man of prodigious physique, and in his day was reputed to have raised a 15-stone man from a table with one hand. Billy Duff, on the other hand, was of light and spare build, but a very capable boxer. He fought a sturdy butcher once in the middle of Pall Mall, when the butcher, deceived by Duff's appearance, was handsomely beaten. For some years London rang with the exploits of this little band."

In the "Tom and Jerry" period a gentleman did not merely patronise the pugilist—he emulated him. It was one of George IV.'s delusions that he had fought, and "polished off," a Brighton butcher of some renown in the local fighting ring.

Sir John Astley in his published Reminiscences, makes this confession :—

"I used now and again to go and see a merry mill, and often found a portion of the battle-money for one side or the other. The fight that I recollect most about, before I went to the Crimea, was the match between Broome and Orme at Mildenhall, in Suffolk."

This fine old sporting baronet was himself a good amateur boxer, and in another part of his autobiography says :—

Drawn & Etched by H Alkin Esq[r]

A PRIVATE TURN-UP, *in the Drawing Room of a Noble Marquis.*

*London Published by Jones & C[o] July 21, 1821.*

"It was during the autumn of 1852 that I gave up a spare hour occasionally to practise the noble art of self-defence—a study I can conscientiously recommend to any young man, as it cannot possibly do him any harm, and it may stand him in good stead sooner or later. Would that all my compatriots could be taught to rely upon their ten digits, and then we should hear less of the use of the knife or revolver, as all differences might be settled with Nature's weapons. I used to take frequent lessons from one Ned Adams, who was as clever as a monkey, and we used to start our boxing bouts with the distinct understanding that we were to 'play light'; but deary me! it is much easier to intend to do so than to carry it out; for I put it to any man—if you get one or two smart taps on your proboscis, just sufficient to make your eyes water, it stands to reason that you must do your level best to give your opponent something just to equalise matters, and, with a vicious lunge, you revel in feeling that you have got well home with your left; but, quicker than thought, in comes his right, and if you only see stars you are pretty lucky, while if you have the audacity to reproach him for his interference with your nasal organ, he meekly replies, 'Well! you see, gov'nor, you 'it me first, and it wasn't altogether playful, neither. Still, I'm sorry as I let go, and I 'opes it ain't 'urt yer!' I soon found out that to box well you must have a wonderful command of your temper."

The popularity of professional pugilism culminated with the historic encounter between Tom Sayers and Heenan. The former, having fought his way up to the championship of England, beating the Tipton Slasher, (the previous holder of that premier position,) in 1857, gained immense notoriety in 1860 by accepting the challenge of Heenan, the American champion. Sayers was comparatively small in stature, whilst Heenan was above the ordinary height; and it is said that when Sayers met his monster opponent for the first time he felt a little daunted. The fight nevertheless came off, and at a very early stage Sayers' right arm was rendered useless; but still, with this disabled limb, he continued the combat for some time, and in the end, if he did not obtain the victory, he made it a drawn battle, and received with Heenan the honour of a double belt.

Sir John Astley, in the Reminiscences already quoted, gives a very racy description of his personal experiences at this notable prize-fight. He tells how he purchased for the sum of five pounds a ticket bearing the vague inscription "There and Back"—for such was the growing vigilance of the police authorities at that time, only the most exalted members of the "fancy," only those who had been admitted to the inner mysteries of the now proscribed cult, could be entrusted with the secret of the proposed rendezvous. Finding himself at a certain railway station in London, on an appointed day, all in accordance with the whispered instructions which accompanied the ticket, he took his place in a first-class carriage, and the train started. The route was anything but direct, and when the train pulled up finally, it was in a lonely spot, the nearest station to which was Farnborough. The favoured passengers got out on to the line, and after scampering across country and clambering over many fences, they eventually found the Ring ready pitched on a good bit of turf in an admirably selected situation. There is no need to follow the description of the battle, which lasted two hours; but the termination was as sudden as it was farcical. All at once the infatuated crowd was startled by cry of "Police! police!" and, although it was a false alarm, instantaneously it became a case of *sauve qui peut*, and Sir John confesses how ignominiously everybody "skedaddled back" to the protection of the waiting train, and steamed away from danger without a moment's delay.

After that Tom Sayers was everywhere greeted as a hero; his doughty deeds became the topic of general conversation; but he did not long survive to wear his blushing honours, as a year or two afterwards he succumbed to pulmonary consumption.

The English championship belt was then left for

competition, and fell afterwards to Jem Mace and afterwards to Tom King, who were succeeded by less known worthies. In fact the glories of the Prize Ring declined very rapidly, and with the advance of popular education the Ring was never again able to raise its head in respectable English society. Englishmen are now content to enjoy a bout with the "mittens" or "pillow-cases," as the old-time Ring patrons disdainfully dub the boxing-gloves. The last of the great classic battles was that for the championship fought between King and Heenan in December, 1863.

Pugilism might conveniently, though perhaps not technically, be divided into the amateurism of the masses and the professionalism of the Prize Ring; although it would sometimes have been difficult to discover the dividing line between the two, when men were found ready and willing to hammer each other round a twelve-foot ring for the trifling "prize" of a gallon of beer. Of Boxing and the use of the gloves no direct cognisance is being taken here; reference is being made solely to the plain, unceremonious fighting with bare knuckles, as practised in the good old times of our dead-and-gone grandsires. Not that Boxing was despised, or even neglected; as a matter of fact, no Fair, Wake, or Race Meeting would have been deemed complete without its sparring booths, to which gentlemen were invited to "Walk up! Walk up!" in order to don the gloves and spar with some light-weight "chicken" who had made himself some sort of a reputation in the Prize Ring, if but a local one, and the mere announcement of whose name would attract a good assemblage round the ropes. It was always a proud boast for any amateur to be able to say he had "had the gloves on" with the "Darlaston Dumpling" or some other well-known Prize Ring celebrity of equal magnitude.

Although kicking, with a dexterous use of the clog, is said to characterise the Lancashire man's method of assault, the generality of Englishmen throughout the length and breadth of the land appeal as naturally to the protective use of their clenched fists as a duck takes to the water.

In the more populous parts of the country, which comprise the great mining and manufacturing centres, this characteristic was always more marked than in the agricultural districts.

A century or so ago, ere the spread of elementary education had made any impression on the moral fibre of the people, and when the preservation of the peace was in the feeble hands of elective parish constables, "merry little mills" were of almost daily occurrence among certain sections of the labouring classes. Not only were all personal disputes settled on this good old plan, but failing a more legitimate call to arms, a fight would often be "got up" for mere amusement. In the old days ere Factory Acts had regulated the hours of labour, every week in the year was honoured by a "Saint Monday"; and to fill up the holiday hours on such days, it took very little to provoke a fight. Challenges were freely given and as readily accepted. The "prize" was mainly the empty honour of a victory which gave an enhanced reputation for manly prowess in a society which, above all things, admired such feats of arms. Of material advantage there was practically nothing to reap; the loser, or his backers, certainly had to pay for the ocean of beer with which the gladiatorial combat was afterwards celebrated.

For such small rewards and on such slight provocations were sturdy miners and hardy ironworkers ever ready and willing to pummel each other into a jelly. They would have scorned to wear padded boxing-gloves, preferring always to use the "raw 'uns"—as they liked to call their case-hardened knuckles. And so, to alter C. S. Calverley a little, very often—

"They met, they planted blows on blows;
They fought as long as they were able;
One chap would get a bottle nose,
T'other's two mortal eyes turn sable."

Be it always remembered that the professional "bruiser" was but an amateur who had shown conspicuous ability in defeating all his fellow-amateurs against whom he had been pitted. Let us see how he was trained to become a professional exponent of the noble art.

When a pugilist went into training, he generally retired to some quiet and secluded village in charge of his trainer, whose system of getting his man "fit" for the fray was to subject him, for the space of five or six weeks, to all manner of austerities. The first week or so was given to treating the patient inwardly, during which period he was "physicked" most unmercifully. Then began the external treatment. The victim was fed on lean beef so underdone that it was difficult to determine whether its "juiciness" was derivable from blood or from gravy. He was exercised, and he was rubbed down; but the most occult portion of his preparation for the ordeal of the Prize Ring was the "pickling" of the skin of his face and hands. This was a process by which it was attempted to prepare those parts of his anatomy to stand the severest usages of battle without abrading. To which end, the skin of the fists and face was frequently and systematically rubbed with a mysterious wash, the concoction of which was one of the most valued trade secrets of a trainer, but the chief ingredients of which were generally understood to be lemon-juice and whisky. All this, be it known, is quoted from the published disclosures of the *cognoscenti.*

In the Black Country, such practices forming part of the pastimes of the people, taken in conjunction with the frequency of colliery accidents when there were no Mines Regulation Acts to protect the lives and limbs of the underground workmen, led to the profession of bone-setting becoming quite an accomplishment among an illiterate set of practitioners. So famous did some of these bone-setters become, that not infrequently their services were sought from afar by the rich and the great; and thus it came to pass that when the great Sir Robert Peel had his ribs broken, he did not disdain to send for the assistance of one of these Black Country specialists.

Hardy of frame and inured to danger as these miners, forgemen, and furnacemen were, it is strange that while they were always able to bear physical pain and bodily discomfort with so much stoical indifference, they should have been so susceptible to the terrors of the imagination. Yet so it was. The boldest among them, one who had fought his hundreds of rounds, or at some pit accident had evinced real heroism, or one whose hardihood made him look upon prize-fighting, dog-fighting, and other barbarous and cruel forms of sport without a single qualm, would blanch in the presence of a feeble old beldame who pretended to powers of divination. They were superstitious to a degree. Their consultations of "wise women" regarding the fortunes of their fighting-cocks and bull-pups, the awe with which they regarded the incantations of these pretenders in the Black Art, and the unmistakable dread they had of the power of the uncanny woman's eye, ill assorted with the boldness with which they always met and freely encountered material dangers. Such, however, was the paradoxical nature of the pachydermatous proletariat of the Midland mining district in the old days.

The highest type of hero among them was an invincible pugilist, a successful cocker, or a leading bullot. Such worthies were in far higher esteem than the parson or his churchwardens. It is on record that a noted cocker of Willenhall, one Tommy Read, having to leave that town, was escorted many miles on his way by faithful followers, dozens of whom took leave of their hero in this exuberant form of admiration; and whenever he afterwards paid the town a visit, his appearance was the signal for every man to throw down his tools, strike work on the instant, and celebrate the visitation by a mighty carouse of unrestrained drunkenness.

At holiday-times and other high festivals special events were arranged, particularly at Christmas-time and at the Wakes. How deeply the sport entered into the lives of the people may be gathered from two entries in the diary kept of a Wednesbury man of the old school. They are worded thus :—

> "1838. November 16. Billy Gramby died. (He was a well-known pugilist.)
>
> 1839. September 9. A man killed in a fight, Wake Monday, in William Corfield's yard. A child killed same week in High Bullen."

David Christie Murray, the novelist, who is a native of West Bromwich, declares himself a lover of the noble art of self-defence, and boasts that his first lesson in the use of the boxing-gloves was received from no less a personage than the Tipton Slasher, once champion prize-fighter of England. In lamenting the abolition of the noble art the novelist says: "So long as it was the fashion to fight with fists the use of the knife, the bludgeon, and the brick-bat was far rarer than it is now."

Not only Christie Murray, but other eminent novelists, from Albert Smith (in "Christopher Tadpole," chap. xl.) to Sir Walter Besant, have quoted the Tipton Slasher as a typical hero of the pugilistic "fancy."

Mr. G. T. Lawley writes in his articles "Old Black Country Methodism" (published in *The Methodist Recorder*, 1902):—

> "Jemmy Butler, a noted pugilist of Darlaston, when he won his fight against Joe Burton, of Bilston, in 1827, was carried on the shoulders of his backers from Cann Lane to Darlaston, a distance of four miles, followed by cheering thousands, who were treated to free drinks by nearly every publican in the town. He was called 'Darlas'un's Glory,' and when he was killed in the following year in a fight with one Joseph Foster, his remains were followed to the grave by nearly all the colliers, gunsmiths, and lock-filers of the district, who mourned his loss as though he had been some great benefactor to his race."

The James Butler here mentioned was killed in a fight at Barebone's Bridge on December 29, 1828—an event which took place as an ordinary portion of the usual Christmas diversions. Possibly this is also the same incident which is alluded to in the following fictional extract, although the names of the parties are reversed for the purposes of the novelist in using up incidents of real life. It is an extract which gives an insight into the fighting propensity which in so marked a manner characterised the men who spent their lives amidst the fighting of dogs and game-cocks, in witnessing almost daily encounters between dogs and bulls, badgers and dogs, and familiarising themselves with other forms of animal pugnacity. The quotation is from the novel entitled "Old Convict Days," by Louis Becke. The hero of the story is a runaway apprentice who began life in the earlier decades of the nineteenth century, and who was put to learn the gun-lock filing at Darlaston. He thus relates in autobiographical style an episode illustrative of our subject :—

"That night my master declared that his son would fight any lad of his age and weight in the town. The challenge was taken up, a match made, and on the next day it was agreed that the fight should come off in the Leasows. Accordingly the lads met, and I, being always forward in such affairs, acted as bottle-holder for my master's son. This battle was a desperate and determined one; after it had lasted a good time, an unlucky blow from my champion stretched the other lad dead. His body was at once carried off by his party, and we went home. Soon after the constable came, and in his usual quiet way told young Butler he was wanted, and would have to go with him. As they were leaving the house I came in with a hod of coals, when the old constable said to me, 'Ah ! Will, you'll have to go too. I'll come for you to-morrow.' I thought to myself, 'You may come for me, but I fancy you won't find me !' Having had a taste of Stafford gaol, and with the horrible feeling of the lash still fresh in my memory, I determined to turn my back on Darlaston. I did not see the place again for fifty years. The day after the fight saw me on my way to Birmingham with my little belongings done up in a bundle."

A vivid picture of the hard life led in the old Black Country is revealed by another passage in Mr. Louis Becke's novel. As the reader may imagine, brutal pleasures were the natural corollary to lives spent in so much sordid toil, ill-paid and unregulated by hygienic principles or moral influences as it was, in the strenuous times of the early nineteenth century. After a striking allusion to the horrible dog-fighting practised among the colliers and gun-lock filers of Darlaston, the writer proceeds in his autobiographical style :—

"Brought up in this school, and having it always dinned into me that the man who keeps a fighting dog must be a fighting man, it is very little wonder that I got some of the nature of those around me —men and dogs alike. Having shown some fighting qualities, I was frequently backed, and forced to take part in what in Darlaston was called 'French and English.' For 'French and English' two boys were matched to 'fight to a finish' in this style: Each boy was perched on the shoulders of a man, who held his (the boy's legs tightly, leaving his arms free. In this position the two boys met in a ding-dong, hammer-and-tongs sort of fashion. Neither of them was able to get away, being kept up to it by his bearer; and after battering and bruising each other for a time one would have to cry for quarter."

Nor was this indulgence in fisticuffian violence at that time confined exclusively to the lower stratum of society. If we are to believe Borrow, it was rife even among the schoolboys of the upper classes. In "Lavengro," contrasting experiences at the Edinburgh High School with schoolboy life in England, he says, "The Scotch, though by no means proficient in boxing (and how should they box, seeing that they have never had a teacher?) are a most pugnacious people." But while school fights in Scotland were productive of nothing more serious than sound whacks, discoloured eyes, and the shedding of a little blood, "in England," says "Lavengro," "where the lads were comparatively mild, gentle, and pacific, I had been present at more than one death caused by blows in boyish combats, in which the oldest of the victors had scarcely reached thirteen years; but these blows were in the jugular, given with the full force of the arm shot out horizontally from the shoulder." If this is a true picture of the times—and George Borrow is supposed to paint from nature—the practice of scientific pugilism as a recognised institution must have been more reprehensible than the duello.

Boxing in itself is an admirable form of physical exercise. It is deserving of all encouragement if it teaches a man to be fearless, self-reliant, and ever ready to face danger in the defence of the innocent.

Of pugilism, pure and simple, no good word can be said. It is brutalising in its effects, as a general resort to physical force must always be. There are, indeed, said to have been many chivalric champions of the Prize Ring, notwithstanding which this characteristically British institution fell rapidly out of favour after the great fight for the championship of the world in 1860, between the renowned Tom Sayers, of England, and the equally famous Heenan, of America. Its supporters of wealth and rank gradually but surely fell away from it. Why? Because they could no longer, as men of honour, identify themselves with those who professed to be "sportsmen," and yet whose self-interest would scarcely ever allow a meeting to proceed as a "fight to finish" if the more heavily backed champion was in danger of losing. The fact was, the very nature of the sport attracted as the bulk of its followers and votaries the very lowest classes of society, coarse in their nature, brutal in their inclinations, and never over-nice in their practices. It was impossible to separate the patronage of the Prize Ring from a too intimate association with bruisers, blacklegs, and riff-raff of every kind.

The erection of a ring and the engaging in a prize-fight had long been an illegal act; as a matter of fact, all battles of this kind took place surreptitiously, and to prevent the interference of the police the place where the stakes and ropes were to be set up for an encounter was a secret divulged only to a select few of the patrons, backers, and recognised votaries. The place selected was generally some quiet and retired spot, from which the principals, their aiders and abettors, could all make a hurried and effective escape should the police get scent of the meeting and put in an appearance to stop it.

Seclusion was not the only consideration in selecting the best site for surreptitiously bringing off a fight. The spot fixed upon was most frequently on the border line between two counties, so that, should the police of one countv appear upon the scene, the disturbed sportsmen took their flight through another county, and quickly put themselves out of the range of arrest. These were the early days of Peel's policemen, and very much bothered was the new force by these elusive tactics. There was one spot near Birmingham, where the three counties of Warwick, Worcester, and Stafford all came together, which was a particularly favourite place with the Midland fraternity, and to which they regularly took the ropes and stakes for an impromptu ring.

In high-class encounters the Ring would usually consist of a carefully selected piece of level turf twenty-four feet square, strongly roped and staked out, each of the combatants at a diagonally opposite corner, where he would tie his colours to the stake, and was assiduously attended by his trainer and bottle-holder.

Dishonest practices, both by the principals and their backers, who were nearly always prepared for a money consideration to sell the victory, gradually lost the Prize Ring its patronage of all respectable supporters. After the days of Tom Sayers the sport fell into decay—as must, indeed, any sport, however innocent it may be, if it is pursued in an unsportsmanlike manner.

While much might be said for Boxing as a means of self-defence—an accomplishment which man, in common with the lower animals, will always be in need of till the millennium arrives—it is equally clear that no argument could ever be advanced which could justify fist-fighting as a recreation, or elevate it into a logical court of appeal.

It is therefore felt that enough has been said here to recall the status which this sport formerly enjoyed and the high estimation in which our fathers once held it. The subject has a literature of its own. One notable work on Pugilism is entitled "Boxiana"; it is embellished with engravings of all the champions and celebrities of the Prize Ring during the eighteenth century and down to the year of publication—1812.

For those readers who require more information on this subject, "Boxiana" will be found to contain a defence of Pugilism, some account of its history and antiquity, the Rules of the Ancient as well of the Modern Prize Ring—to say nothing of laudatory biographical sketches of the heroes whose portraits constitute its leading feature.

Another literary authority which would prove useful to the inquiring reader is "The Handbook of Boxing," by Owen Swift, Professor of Pugilism. This appeared in 1840, and possesses a table of contents similar to that of the former work, to which is added a useful Chronology of all the great events which took place within "ropes and stakes" for the entire century previous—(1740–1840).

## XV

### OLD TAVERN GAMES

Skittles and Nine-pins—Kayle-pins—Loggats—Quoits—Marbles.

THERE is a group of pastimes which not inappropriately might be called tavern games. Before the present-day stringencies of the licensing laws most old inns and taverns provided some form of outdoor amusement for their patrons; till thirty or forty years ago in most tavern-yards and inn-gardens might be found a Skittle Alley, or a Quoit Pitch, or sometimes a Marble Alley. The customers called for their ale, played their games, and, by a well-understood custom, expected the losers "to pay the shot." Gaming on licensed premises is now strictly forbidden, and games of this kind are now less frequently played, for fear of endangering the licence.

SKITTLES, kittle-pins, kettles, and kayle-pins are all nearly allied names for similar pastimes, in which men or wooden pins are set up, to be knocked down by the skill of the players, who from a distance bowl or throw at them.

The game of Skittles differs from that of Nine-pins, though the same number of men are set up in both, namely, three rows of three, forming a square presenting one angle (not one of its sides) towards the player, and the king pin being in the centre.

SKITTLES.

[*Published, 1801, by J. Wheble, Warwick Square.*]

*To face page 222*

In NINE-PINS the player stands away at an agreed distance to bowl at the pins, and the contest is to knock down the whole in the fewest throws. The bowls are often of the size of cheeses, and so heavy as to require a strong man to wield them effectively; from the "take off" they were trundled along a plank laid flush in the ground and leading towards the centre line of pins.

In playing Skittles there is a double exertion, one by bowling and the other by tipping; the first is performed at a given distance, and the second standing close to the frame upon which the pins are placed, and throwing the bowl through in the midst of them; in both cases the number of pins beaten down before the return of the bowl (for it usually passes beyond the frame) are called "fair," and reckoned to the account of the player; but those that fall by the coming back of the bowl are said to be "foul," and of course not counted. One chalk or score is reckoned for every fair pin, and the game of skittles is won by obtaining thirty-one chalks precisely; less loses, or at least gives the opponent a chance of winning the game; and more requires the player to go again for nine, which also must be scored exactly.

KAYLE-PINS, or Keels, was a form of nine-pins or skittles, that class of game which some one has stigmatised as "an idle exercise," perhaps because it was so often the resource of those who neglected their work or preferred the tavern to the workshop. Sometimes six and sometimes eight pins were set up, one of them taller than the rest, in a single row; the players tried to knock them over, not with bowls, but by throwing at them with cudgels or clubs similar to those used in the modern game of Aunt Sally.

The game mentioned in *Hamlet* as LOGGATS was one played by boys and rustics, who substituted bones for wooden pins, throwing at them with another bone—"a sheepes-joynte bone"—instead of bowling. Thus Hamlet, in the graveyard scene, inquires—

> "Did these bones cost no more the breeding, but to play at loggats with them?"

The game of QUOITS is not only a very ancient pastime, but is rather superior to many others of its class in the amount of skill it calls for. The Greeks threw the *discus*, the classical predecessor of the quoit.

The quoit is a circular plate of iron perforated in the middle, and not quite flat, but having the outer circumference turned down to a sharpish edge for cutting into the clay-bed at which it is pitched. Rustics formerly played the game by pitching horse-shoes. These clay-beds are two in number, about eighteen to twenty yards apart, and having the centre point marked by an iron pin called a hob.

The size of the quoits, and the distance apart of the hobs, may vary according to the strength and poise of the players. The game may be played by two, or any equal number divided into two sides, who stand at one of the hobs and pitch an equal number of quoits to the other, and the nearest of them to the mark are counted towards the game. The discrimination is made in this way: If A's quoit lies nearest the hob and B's quoit is second, A can count but one towards the game, though all his other quoits lie nearer to the mark than B's others. B's nearest quoit cuts out all the rest of A's. But if no such quoit had intervened, all A's quoits would have reckoned as one each.

Having cast all their quoits, the players walk to the opposite end to determine the state of the game; and, taking their stand there, pitch back again to the other mark; and so on, alternately playing from end to end.

MARBLES seem to have been used by boys as a substitute for Bowls; and originally nuts, round stones, and other small natural spheres which would roll evenly, were used for marbles. It is recorded of Imperial Augustus that when a young boy he played with little Moorish boys "cum nucibus" (with nuts). Properly made marbles were sometimes called taws; and a variety of games were played, perhaps the best known being Shoot-in-the-Ring. In this game a number of boys put each an equal number of marbles in the ring, to shoot at them in turn with another taw; the one who shot out the most of them, keeping them, and winning the game.

The tavern marble-alley of the old Black Country type was an oblong cement-laid floor, elevated about eighteen inches, measuring about twenty feet by twelve, and having a raised wood rim to prevent the marbles rolling off. The players knelt down to shoot their taws with the thumb, and were expected to "knuckle down" fairly in doing so. The playing of marbles by men belongs to the simple life of forty or fifty years ago; the practice is now obsolete.

## XVI

### COCK-FIGHTING

Its antiquity—Greek, Roman, and prehistoric evidences—A Shrovetide custom *tempo* Henry II.—The diversion of kings and schoolmasters—Early books on the subject—Athenian commendation of the cock's pugnacity—Popularity of the cock-pit after the Restoration—Hoyle's treatise on the game-cock—Game-cocks naturally pugnacious—The points by which to judge a good one—The age for pitting—The dieting and training of the birds—The rules for matching them—Girth indicative of strength—A contrivance for gauging the size of a game-cock—Fighting weights—Scaling for matches—Preparation for the cock-pit—Trimming a game-cock for the fight—The cruelty of the practice—How the operation is performed—The spurs—The trainer—His duties after the battle—The treatment of wounded birds—How competitors were named—Favourite strains—The "Hen-cock," the "Wednesbury Gray," and the "Duck-wing"—The cocker's kit—The bird bag—The Cock-fighting code—The setters-on permitted to handle to prevent ogling too long—And to carry a craven bird ten times to the scratch—"Dying game" though vanquished—The Main—"Catch weights"—The Welsh main—The "battle royal"—Only one battle for each bird—The bye-battle—The cock-pit—Indoor and outdoor pits—Tavern cockings—The arena—The "Welscher's" cage—Popular meetings—Newmarket, Bath, Nottingham, Walsall, Lichfield, Newcastle, Birmingham—Duddeston Hall—Sunday cockings—The "Paradise of Cockers"—A cocking described in detail—Feeding and "walking" cocks—The Gillivers of Polesworth, the last of the great cock-masters—"Cockspur" village—Some of the Gilliver records—Breeders—The mysteries of the cocking cult—The patrons of the sport—Schoolmasters and clerics—A Tipton clergyman reproved—Willenhall's Cock-fighting Parson—Noble patrons—The mixed company at a cock-pit—Rowdyism rampant among cockers—Cockers *v.* "Methodys"—Some Bilston records of the sport—Magisterial cautions issued—A barbarous cock-fight at Shrewsbury—West Country depravity (1703)—The "judgment of God" on a cocker—A fatal quarrel over a cock-fight

—Prohibition of Cock-fighting—*The Field* denies that it is extinct now—How the Act is evaded—Police-court prosecutions—The folk lore of Cock-fighting—St. Peter and the cock—The weathercock—Charming a fighting cock—How to gain a turn of fortune—Consulting the oracle to spot a winner—Casting spells over a competitor's bird—Sacrilegious rites to secure victory in the arena—The literature of the sport—Place-names derived from it—The gambling element—Words and phrases coined from the sport—"That beats cock-fighting"—"Cock-pit" a figurative battle-ground—The terms "cock-master," "cocker," "cocking"—"No cock's eyes out yet"—"Cock-stride"—"Cock-eyed"—The ballad lore of Gallomachia—"Wedgbury Cockin'"—"The Battle of Bilston"—"Wednesfield Wake"—"Tommy Read's Welcome to Willenhall"—The funeral dirge of Maxey Dick—The cock-fighter's epitaph.

FEW sports boast greater antiquity than that of Cock-fighting. Themistocles was a cock-fighter, and from Ancient Greece the practice was carried to Rome. Julius Cæsar was one of its patrons, and through his troops the sport of Cock-fighting is said to have been introduced among the Britons. The learned who have traced the sport back to its origin in Ancient Greece, declare that it began there with the matching and pitting of Quails against each other. However that may be, it is certain that the sport as conducted with game-cocks took a firm root in England. Game-fowl are known to have been found in Ancient Britain before the Roman invasion; among the relics of the prehistoric Lake-dwellers found at Glastonbury are specimens of the spurs used in Cock-fighting.

From William Fitzstephen's Life of Becket we learn that in the reign of Henry II. the sport was regularly practised by the schoolboys of London. The custom was for each boy to attend school on Shrove Tuesday, carrying in his arms a game-cock. The bird was ultimately destined to become a present to the schoolmaster; but before the change of ownership took place, the cocks were fought in pairs on the schoolroom floor, the etiquette and ceremonial of the improvised cock-pit being strictly controlled and regulated by the schoolmaster himself. The sport occupied the whole of the forenoon, after which a half-holiday was usually given.

These academies were usually monastic schools; in that age it was considered no degradation to see one bird peck out the eyes of its gallant antagonist; the blood-stained floor of the academical cock-pit conveyed no reproach to the minds of teacher and taught, though it might meet their gaze for months afterwards.

Throughout the Middle Ages the diversion was followed with more or less zest, from one century to another, although occasionally it came in for the disapproval of our law-makers, and was prohibited 39 Edward III., in whose reign it had become a fashionable amusement; and again in the reign of Henry VI.; as it was, once more, in the year 1569.

Henry VIII., however, was a great patron of the sport, and established a royal cock-pit opposite Whitehall Palace, in a building which was afterwards used as a Government office. In fact it may truthfully be said that long ere horse-racing became "the sport of kings," Cock-fighting was unreservedly honoured as a royal pastime. The Whitehall cock-pit was fitted up with great magnificence; and Misson, a French traveller, writing his impressions of this country in the reign of William III., says in his "Travels in England":—

"Cock-fighting is one of the great English diversions. They build great amphitheatres for this purpose, and persons of quality sometimes appear at them. Great wagers are laid; but I am told that a man may be badly bubbled if he is not very sharp. Their combats between bulls and dogs, and sometimes bulls and bears, are not battels unto death, as are those of cocks."

No longer are mains fought by the boys of grammar

schools, nor is the master's salary made to depend upon the proceeds of cock-fights. There is a clause in the statutes which Bishop Sandys had drafted for Hartlebury Grammar School, and granted by Queen Elizabeth, which provides: "The said scholemaster and usher shall and may have use and take the profitts of all such cockfights and potations as be commonlie used in scholes." Evidently in those days the cock-pit was popular and profitable. Its traditions linger on, but not to the profit or to the honour of those who are caught indulging in this time-dishonoured sport.

Roger Ascham, the famous schoolmaster of Lady Jane Grey, once proposed to write a "Boke of the Cockpitte," to treat with a schoolman's erudition, a recreation which was allowed by the sentiment of the period to be one that was perfectly "fitte for a gentleman."

On the testimony of an English writer of the period ("Anatomy of Abuses," 1583) we have it that the public regularly "flocked thick and threefold" to all exhibitions of Cock-fighting. To the student of bygone manners and customs, and particularly of old sports and pastimes, there is much interesting information to be found in that old work. "The Anatomy of Abuses," by the way, although in the main nothing more than a Puritanical diatribe, throws some strong side-lights on many of the sporting allusions contained in Shakespeare's works.

As evidence of the popularity of the pursuit in the next century, reference may be made to a very rare little volume to which attention has been called by Mr. George T. Lawley, of Wolverhampton, in his interesting newspaper contributions to this subject. It was printed in 1602 under the following curious title: "The Commendation of Cocks and Cock-fighting, wherein is shown that Cock-fighting was before the Coming of Christ. London. Printed for Henry Tomes, and is to be sold at his Shop over against Graie's Inne Gate in Holborne." The work, however, had no bearing on the English side of the subject, but confined itself to a learned proof of the sport's antiquity, giving a number of Greek and Latin quotations to that end.

Under the Commonwealth a law was passed to prohibit the practice of setting cocks to fight; but needless to say the practice was not only resumed after the Restoration, but grew into greater popularity than ever.

It cannot be a matter for wonderment that among those who found amusement at the cock-pit in the eighteenth century was the famous Duke of Marlborough. The spirit of such an ever-victorious general could doubtless always find much that was congenial in the manœuvres of two pugnacious fighting-cocks.

While condemning the moral sentiment of the eighteenth century, which in a period of prevailing ignorance and unbridled licence not only permitted but actively encouraged such brutalising sports, it is well to bear in mind the moral standard of the intellectual and cultured Greeks. We may read that Themistocles, while marching against the Persians, passed on his way two cocks fighting. He commanded a halt that his soldiers might gaze upon the fierce combatants. "Behold," cried the great commander, "these do not fight for their household gods; nor for the monuments of their ancestors; nor yet for glory, nor for liberty, nor for the safety of their children. They fight only because one will not give way to the other." This appeal inspired the soldiers, because they saw they had so much more to fight for than those irrationally pugnacious birds. Needless to say, they gained a victory over their enemies; but more curious is it to learn that thenceforward Cock-fighting was by special law particularly ordained—

> "Where by the Ægean Sea a city rose,
> Built nobly; pure the air and light the soil—
> Athens, the eye of Greece, mother of arts
> And eloquence."

Manifestly the moral fibre of the ancient Athenian was, in respect of this at least, no whit nobler than that of the sporting Englishman of the eighteenth century.

*The London Gazette* of 1684 contained in one of its issues the following notification, inserted practically as a semi-official announcement: "At the Royal Cock-pit at Windsor, on the 27th Instant, begins a great Match of Cock-fighting between Two Persons of Quality, which will continue the Whole Week." This was not the only notice of its kind printed in the Gazette during the reign of Charles II. In 1678 had appeared one notifying a "Cocking to be fought in His Majesties' Cock Pit at Newmarket."

Throughout the eighteenth, and well into the nineteenth century, this brutal sport lost none of its popularity. Cocking was still the sport of kings and princes, and the cock-pit was the place of resort which claimed the very considerable proportion of public support equivalent to that bestowed on the music-halls of the present day. In the parish of Westminster alone there were at one period three noted cock-pits—one on the site of what are now the offices of the Privy Council, which was attached to the Palace of Whitehall, already mentioned; another in Birdcage Walk, at the corner of Dartmouth Street; and a third in Tufton Street. The two first of these were carried on under royal patronage, and were largely resorted to by members of both Houses of Parliament. That well-known work "Hoyle's Games," when published a century or more ago contained a very practical Treatise on Game Cocks. First are given directions for "breeding and managing the birds," with specific instructions as to the "laying out of the breeding walk." From this part of the work we learn that a good cock, "in respect of exterior qualifications, should possess a thin long head, or very taper, if short; large full eyes, stout crooked beak, thick long neck, short compact body, with a round breast, firm stout thighs, placed well up to the shoulders, long strong legs, and if they correspond in colour with the beak, that is esteemed a perfection; broad thin feet and very long claws; an upright easy carriage and stately walk, with wings not lying close to the back, but in some measure extended."

This notable authority on sport then proceeds to demonstrate the technical advantages to be derived from these various physical conformations; how that a long neck gives a long reach in battle, that a cock with thighs placed rather behind cannot maintain a prolonged fight, and so on. But the writer adds that "there are good cocks of all colours, though the feathers should be thin, short & hard, which are signs of good health." Dieting is next dealt with; then the diseases to which Game Fowls are subject, together with "the method of treating a cock after fighting." Next are set out the "General Orders & Rules for Cocking," supplemented by "the rules observed at the Royal Cockpit, Westminster," and a blank form of agreement or "signed articles for a cock match." And if this is not complete enough for the most inveterate sportsman, there are given tables of carefully calculated odds for use in wagering on various numbers of battles, and a key to the weights of the combatants as they are set down on "a match bill."

Such was the height of the niche to which Englishmen then elevated the sport of Cock-fighting. Though fallen from its pedestal in the West, it remains to this

*Howitt*

COCK PIT ROYAL, 1796.

*To face page 222*

day the national sport of the Filipinos, in the Far East.

That game-cocks are naturally prone to antagonise one another, without the interference of any third party to incite them, is a well-known fact. On one occasion General Peel, accompanied by another local magistrate, put the matter to the test at Atherstone. Selecting the morning time, before the birds had received their first meal, a pan of food was placed on the ground, and two hungry game-cocks were turned out to feed. The pugnacious birds ignored the food entirely; but they challenged and engaged each other without a moment's hesitation. Again and again the experiment was tried with other birds, and always with the same result—the fact had to be accepted that game-cocks naturally prefer fighting to feeding.

As sings the poet of the "Pit" respecting the absolute certainty of an engagement "when cock meets cock" (so surely they be of the true game-fowl breed)—

> "When true Game-birds meet (unlike that coward breed,
> The Dunghills)—these would rather fight than feed."

On the same behalf it has also been adduced in evidence that not infrequently when a gallant bird has struck his opponent dead he has instantly jumped upon the prostrate body and given forth a jubilant crow of triumph—as if the achievement had brought unadulterated bliss to the chanticleerian breast.

The various points by which to choose "a cock of the game," the fanciers have duly set out long ago. "The School of Recreation; or, A Guide to the Most Ingenious Exercises," printed in the year 1723, may or may not be the earliest authority on this branch of the subject extant. But the writer gives rules quite worth quoting at length. He says that a game bird is to be judged by the four "characters" following :—

"1st.—The cock must be of a strong shape, proud and upright, and for this the middle-sized, neither too small nor too large, is best, because most matchable, strong, and nimble. The head small like a sparrow-hawk's; his eye large and quick, back strong, crook'd at the setting on, and coloured as the plume of his feathers; the beam of his leg very strong, and coloured as his plume; spurs long, tough, and sharp, hooking inward.

"2nd.—He must be of a good colour, and herein the grey, yellow, or red-pyle, with a black breast, are to be preferred, the pyle rarely good, and the white and dun never. A scarlet head is a demonstration of courage, but a pale and wan of faintness.

"3rd.—He must be of courage true, which you shall observe by his proud, stately, upright standing and walking, and his frequent crowing in his pen.

"4th.—He must be of a sharp and ready heel, which (in the opinion of the best cock-masters) is of high estimation; a sharp heel'd cock, though somewhat false, is better (as despatching his business soonest) than a true cock with a dull heel."

The age at which a cock could best be "pitted," and for the special purposes to which his trainer had prepared him, was two years. At least Lord Derby, who was no mean judge when in the zenith of his fame as a sportsman, and who turned out his 2,000 or 3,000 fighting cocks in a year, always fought them at that age. A properly trained bird at two years of age was found to be in the pink of fighting condition.

After the systematic breeding and the careful selection of the game bird, the next matter of importance which claimed the fancier's attention was the proper dieting and training of the fighting-cock. Here is what the old authority already quoted says upon the subject :—

"Let the cock be full two years old; then in the latter end of August take him up and pen him, and see that he is sound, hard feathered, and full plumed. The first four days after penning, feed him with the crumb of old manchet, cut into square bits, thrice a day, and with the coldest and sweetest spring water that can be had. And after you think by this time he is thoroughly purged of his corn, worms, gravel, and other coarse feeding, take him in the morning out of the pen, and let him spar with another cock some time to heat and chafe their bodies, break fat, and glut; first having covered their spurs with hots of leather to injure their wounding and drawing blood of one another. After they have sufficiently sparr'd that they pant again, take them up and remove their hots and prepare them for a sweating bout, thus: Take butter and rosemary, finely chopped, and white sugar-candy mixed together, and give them the quantity of a walnut, which will scour, strengthen, and prolong breath. Then having (purposely) deep straw baskets, fill them halfway with straw, put in your cock, and cover him with straw to the top, lay the lid close, and let him stove till the evening. At five o'clock take him out, *and lick his head and eyes with your tongue*, then pen him and fill his trough with manchet and hot wine. After this, take a gallon of wheat and oatmeal flour, and with ale, half a score whites of eggs and butter, work it into a stiff paste, bake it into broad cakes, and when four days old cut it into square bits."

So well were these birds fed—as assuredly the foregoing will testify—it became proverbial to say of any person who was both gourmand and gourmet, that he "fed like a fighting-cock."

Proceeding with our quotation from this elaborate "system" for the training of feathered champions:—

"The second day, after sparring, bring your cock into a green close, and show him in your arms a *dunghill* cock; then run after him and allure him to follow, suffering him now and then to strike the dunghill cock, and to chafe him up down for half-an-hour till he pants again, and, thus heated, carry him home and scour him with half-a-pound of fresh butter, beaten with the leaves of the herb of grace, hyssop, and rosemary, to the consistence of a salve, and give him the quarter of a walnut, then stove and feed him as above. And thus for the first fortnight, spar and chafe him every day. The second fortnight, twice a week will be enough to chafe or spar your cock, observing that you stove and scour him proportionately to his heating. The third and last fortnight (for six weeks is long enough) feed him as before, but do not spar him, but chafe him moderately, twice or thrice, as before, then roll his aforesaid scouring in brown sugar-candy, to prevent him being sick; rest him four days and then to the pit."

After these instructions for the training of the bird, the writer of this rare old work proceeds with his detailed directions for the matching of the gallant combatants. As a step towards securing the much-coveted victory this was even more important than all which had previously been done. The writer proceeds:—

"Here, observe the length and strength of cocks. The length is thus known: Gripe the cock by the waist, and make him shoot out his legs, and in this posture compare and have your judgment about you. The strength is known by this maxim: 'The largest in the girth is the strongest cock.' The dimensions of the girth are thus known: Gripe the cock from about the joints of your thumb to the joint of your great finger, and you will find the disadvantage. The weakling cock is the quickest, easiest riser, and the short, strong cock the surest striker."

Dr. Plot's "Natural History of Staffordshire," written in 1686, makes mention of a machine then in use in this county for gauging the size of fighting-cocks. Rightly the writer designates this ingenious contrivance as—

"the nicest piece of art that ever I saw relating to the feathered kingdom, and, indeed, the most curious was an instrument shown me by the Right Worshipful Sir Richard Astley, of Patshull, baronet, of his own invention to match game-cocks, discovering their size, both as to length and girth, to so great an accuracy that there cannot be easily the least mistake."

A century or so later than this, when matches were made, articles were frequently signed which stipulated that no bird should weigh less than 3 lb. 6 oz. or more than 4 lb. 8 oz. As the birds were scaled they were paired; and as a rule the lightest pair of cocks were fought first, then the next in weight, and so on till the heaviest pair were the last to be pitted.

In resuming our extracts from "The School of Recreation," we next read how this learned professor of the whole art and science of Gallomachia would have the bird trimmed for the ordeal of the cock-pit:—

> "Thus being well matched, accoutre him for the pit, clip his mane off close to his neck, from his head to his shoulders. Clip his tail close to his body, the redder it appears the better. His wings sloping with sharp points; scrape smooth and sharpen his spurs; leave no feathers on his crown, then moisten his head with spittle."

The game-cock that had been properly bred, after being highly trained and scientifically trimmed in preparation for the fray, presented an appearance which commanded admiration, for he looked a fine-boned and clean-shaped bird, the most symmetrical of his species.

Only in very recent years has the question been raised as to the cruelty of trimming game-cocks for the Poultry Show. By one party to the controversy the practice was condemned as a vicious and ruthless custom which ought to be forthwith discountenanced by exhibitors at, and by the authorities who control, the various Poultry and Agricultural Shows of the country.

On the other hand, expert opinion was readily forthcoming that there was more character in a trimmed than in an untrimmed bird. The game-cock, even after the suppression of the cock-pit by law, had always been regarded as a fighting bird, for which purposes it was specially bred and trained; and therefore, to show it to its best advantage, its breeders said it ought to be presented in proper fighting trim—just as a pugilist would strip himself for the Prize Ring.

In trimming a game-cock the skilful operator takes off the comb and wattles in a very few snips; and the contention is that the pain is reduced to such a minimum the bird has been known to pick up his own flesh a few minutes afterwards, and even to fight for the cannibalistic morsel. At all times the newly-trimmed cock certainly takes the matter very unconcernedly after the first pangs are over, and it is a matter of further contention that there is no comparison of the pain thus inflicted with that imposed on a poor dog when his ears are clipped.

The judges at Poultry Shows have therefore been induced to accept the theory that although the game-cock will not be called upon to fight, the best fighter would be the one in the best trim for the combat, and they have in consequence adopted a standard of form and symmetry, in preference to one of plumage alone.

In ancient times a fighting-cock was doubtless put to the encounter armed only with his natural spur—the projecting hind toe of his strong "scratching foot." The steel heels with which he was armed for the fray in later times have been attributed to the inventive genius of a Staffordshire sporting miner of the early eighteenth century ; but this theory has been upset by the discoveries at Glastonbury, to which reference has already been made. It is difficult to decide which commands our admiration the more—the ingenuity of the contrivance inspired by the inventors of refinement of cruelty, or the dexterity with which the game-cock learnt to use it. It sometimes needed but one dexterous stroke of this artificial weapon to pierce an antagonist clean through the brain.

So far our attention has been engaged by the preliminaries which led up to the actual encounter. While the contest was proceeding the trainer, whether he were acting as pitter or not, would naturally be a keen and close observer of all the points made by the bird he had so assiduously prepared for this trial of pluck and fitness, discriminating with the eye of an expert between the effects of the cock's native mettle and those attributable to the sportsman's own art.

*Lambert Marshall, Pinx.* *L. Romney, Sculp.*

HECTOR, A HEN-COCK.

[*Published, 1833, by M. A. Pittman, Warwick Square.*]

*To face page* 239

After the battle was over, and supposing the feathered gladiator came out of the arena unconquered, there were other equally important duties required of the conscientious trainer of game-cocks. That calling most urgently for its discharge was certainly neither a delicate nor an inviting one. It is thus set forth by the writer of 1723:—

"The battle done, search and suck your cock's wounds, and wash them well with hot urine, then give him a roll of your best scouring, and stove him for that night. If he be swelled, the next morning suck and bathe his wounds again, and pounce them with the powder of the herb Robert, through a fine bag; give him a handful of bread in warm urine, and stove him till the swelling be down. If he be hurt in the eye, chew a little ground ivy and spit the juice in it, which is good for films, hards, warts, &c. Or if he hath veined himself in his fight, by narrow fighting or other cross blows, when you have found the hurt, binding the soft down of hair to it will cure it. When you visit your wounded cocks a month or so after you have put them to their walks, if you find about their heads any swollen bunches, hard and blackish at one end, then there are unsound cores undoubtedly in them: therefore, open them, and with your thumb crush them out, suck out the corruption, and fill the holes with fresh butter, and that will infallibly cure them."

Competing birds were usually known by their owner's names and the marking of their own plumage, as "Taverner's Gray," for instance, mentioned in the old ballad; and with regard to which particular colouring there was ofttimes a sly advantage for the cock possessing it, of which the initiated were not only cognisant, but of which they seldom failed to avail themselves. It is said that the sober-coloured feathers of such a male bird gave it the general resemblance of a hen, and by reason of this somewhat uncommon plumage it was classed as a variety known under the paradoxical name of Hen-cock. When one of these was placed on the floor of a cock-pit its adversary would sometimes be deceived by the feminine appearance of the new-comer, and instead of showing fight, would commence to make those gallant bows, scrapes, and pirouettes for which amorous chanticleer is so celebrated. Then the Hen-cock, watching its opponent's politest moment, would treacherously deal it a sudden and deadly blow which completely settled the question of sex without any further shadow of a doubt whatever.

Among the *cognoscenti* there were certain strains, with distinctive plumage markings, always in great favour. One strain much sought after were the famous fighting "Wednesbury Grays," which had the reputation of being deadly antagonists in the pit. In addition to the plumage marks characteristic of good birds, mentioned in Instruction No. 2, previously quoted, may be named the redoubtable "duck-wing."

The duck-wings were amongst the most beautiful of their breed, and were so called because they bore similar marking to the bar on the mallard's wing.

During the reign of Henry VIII., some lovers of Cock-fighting being gathered together at Westminster, Sir John Anderton put down the first duck-winged cock ever seen in a cock-pit, crying—

> "There's the jewel of England.
> For a hundred in hand,
> And a hundred in land,
> I'll fight him 'gainst any cock in England."

Brandon, Duke of Suffolk, accepted the challenge, and wagered the tithes of Eccles, bestowed on him by his royal brother-in-law, upon the result. He lost both the battle and the tithes, and duck-winged cocks are to this day known in Lancashire as "Anderton's jewels."

The birds were carried to the cock-pit in bags. The bag was quite a feature in the cocker's equipment.

> "And straight the skilful judges of the play
> Brought forth their sharp heel'd warriors, and they
> Were both in linen bags, as if 'twere meet
> Before they died to have their winding sheet,"

sings the sporting Parson of Aynho.

The bag in which Lord Derby's fighting birds were carried about was made of silk of the finest quality, and on it was painted a game-cock, shown "trimmed" ready for the fray. The comb and wattles are shown cut, and the tail is trimmed wedge-shape. The painting is beautifully done on this notable memento of aristocratic sport, which is still in existence, and allusion to which may excuse a slight digression here.

When, in the early part of the nineteenth century, Cock-fighting fell into disrepute, and Lord Derby had died, the whole of his lordship's cocking kit fell into the hands of Potter, the well-known Feeder, who retired to Hartlebury to keep a tavern, where he died half a century ago at the ripe age of ninety.

This kit, including the silk bag and a collection of silver spurs having the name "Potter" marked on the leather thongs by which they were attached to the bird's legs, passed into the hands of another "fancier." This was a man named Brown, who, till a few decades ago, kept The Globe Tavern in Great Hampton Street, Birmingham. This sportsman of the old school lost his licence through an alleged offence in connection with Cock-fighting, although he seems really to have been guiltless on this particular occasion. A trimmed cock was taken away from his premises, and it was alleged that it had been fought there. As a matter of fact it had not; which, however, could not be proved to the satisfaction of the court.

Just one other reference to the subject of "the bag." Miss Burne, in her Shropshire Folklore Collections, gives a proverbial saying of that county which makes allusion to this particular kind of bag: "There'll come a good cock out of a ragged bag," which, she says, is a good old Cock-fighting simile, lately used to her by a farmer whose buildings were out of repair, but whose stock was in good condition.

Doubtless there were several codes of fighting in vogue at various times and in different places. The following is a set of fighting rules which regulated inter-county and other important matches towards the end of the palmy days, which this old English sport enjoyed in the early nineteenth century :—

Rule I.—The pit shall be circular, twelve feet diameter, and eighteen inches high, the floor to be covered with carpet, and a mark made in the middle of the pit.

Rule II.—The cockers, or pitters, shall each choose a judge, who shall choose another, whose decisions on all questions of fighting and bets shall be final.

Rule III.—All cocks to be weighed before being pitted, unless in a catch-weight fight; and no bird must be handled after fairly delivered unless on the permission of the referee.

Rule IV.—When a cock is fast in his adversary, the owner shall draw the spurs out, but not hold him any longer than is necessary for releasing him.

Rule V.—If, after the cocks have been pitted, they refuse to fight while the pitters count ten times ten, or a hundred, a fresh bird must be pitted, and the owners must toss which bird is to fight, the winner to have choice. The odd bird must be taken up, but not away from the pit. If these two refuse it is a drawn battle, but if one strike he is the winner.

Rule VI.—No pitter shall be permitted during a fight to clean his bird's beak or eyes, or press him against the floor, or squeeze him to make him fight.

Rule VII.—If a cock be disabled by a broken leg or blindness from continuing the fight, the pitters shall place the birds beak to beak, and if the disabled bird does not strike the game is won.

Rule VIII.—The crowing of a cock is not fighting, nor is breaking away from his adversary fighting.

Rule IX.—In all cases of appeal, fighting shall cease until the referee gives his decision, which shall be strictly to the question, and final; the birds not to be taken out of the pit, nor the spurs taken off, until the matter is settled.

Rule X.—Any pitter guilty of using unlawful means to force his bird to fight, such as pinching him or pricking him, shall lose the battle.

Rule XI.—The highest number of battles won to decide the main.

Rule XII.—All bets must stand unless declared off by consent of both parties.

The sport began when, in their natural antagonism, the birds gave full and unrestrained play to their magnificent rage. In their tactics and manœuvring they displayed a cunning which was almost human. At first they flew at each other with the fierceness of two tigers; but presently, to gain breath, they would suspend hostilities, only to resume the attack after deliberately watching each other to catch an unguarded moment, a second of fatal unalertness.

If, however, the cocks ogled each other too long—say longer than the timekeeper could count forty or fifty, or whatever was previously agreed—the setters-on were permitted to handle them in order to place the opponents once more beak to beak.

This was called "setting," and became necessary, as a rule, at a period when the unhappy combatants had spent all but their last remnant of strength, and were practically exhausted by the fury of their repeated onslaughts. Beyond this no handling was ever allowed, or a "foul" was claimed.

A cock might be carried to the scratch thus ten successive times, and if he still refused to fight was then known as a craven, and declared to be beaten. In this connection, however, there was one strange rule of the cock-pit code; for, if a cock who would fight died of his wounds while his craven opponent was being carried to the scratch, the laws of Cock-fighting decided that the survivor was the victor, and not the one who "died game." It was surely by such a code as this that roguery and chicanery found an easy way into the very heart of the sport.

Often both combatants were nearly at their last gasp as they were thus "set" to face each other, their strength ebbing away as fast as the blood from their wounds. The poet of the cock-pit has thus described the pathetic ending to some of these gallinaceous tragedies :—

> "Their wings, which, lately at each blow they clapped,
> (As if they did applaud themselves) now flapped,
> And having lost the advantage of the heel,
> Drunk with each other's blood, they only reel;
> From either eyes such drops of blood let fall
> As if they wept them for their own funeral."

And yet occasionally one final flicker of fast failing strength would sometimes show that all the old gallant spirit of the brave bird remained unconquered, even in death. The dying gladiator, gathering all his remaining strength for one supreme effort—

> "He struggles up, and having taken wind,
> Ventures a blow, and strikes the other blind."

And, even then, the opponent was often found to be a bird "worthy of his steel." Though now perfectly blind, he, too, was still unvanquished ; for, sightless as he was, he would continue to fight around, guided only by his own natural antipathies :—

> "With him (alas!) the proverb holds not true,
> The blows his eyes ne'er saw his heart must rue.
> At length by chance he stumbled on his foe,
> Not having any pow'r to strike a blow;
> He falls upon him with his wounded head,
> And makes his conqu'ror's wings his feather bed."

*L. Marshall, Pinx.* *L. Romney, Sculp.*

GAME COCKS.

[*Published by M. A. Pittman, Warwick Square, 1831.*]

*To face page 244*

Mr. George T. Lawley has called attention to what he considers the inaccuracy of the definition of a "main" as given in Brand's "Popular Antiquities." Mr. Lawley, who may be regarded as an authority on the literary side of the subject, says the term is not derived from the French *main*, "the hand," signifying a battle fought "off-hand," and without due preparation. As is well known, a large amount of preparation was necessary to fight a main of cocks ; besides the terms and the amount of the wagering, there was the weighing and pairing of the birds, which had always to be matched in regard to weight and size with the utmost nicety.

Otherwise, if no such conditions were observed, as demanded the carrying out of these and other necessary preliminaries, then the battles were said to be fought at "catch-weights" ; and such fight became a very plebeian kind of meeting. In fact, it may be said that as a general rule, the pastime as pursued by the poorer people was an ordinary cock-fight, arranged very readily and for small stakes ; while the "main" was the form in which the aristocratic patrons of the pit pursued it, matching one cock-master's birds against another's, or pitting the best birds of one county against those of another, and wagering very large sums on the result.

Other authorities have derived the term *main* as applied to Cock-fighting from the French source, because we may speak of a "main of cocks," as we speak of "a main of dice," or "a hand at cards."

The technical term which preceded the word *main* was "cock-match" ; which seems to have become obsolete after the year 1760.

So that a "main" certainly could not be fought "off-hand." Mr. Lawley says the term *main* in this connection really signifies "on the whole" ; as when we speak of a thing being correct "in the main" ; and was applied in this sense because it was an arrangement whereby the victory went to the side which won the greatest number of single combats—that is, which had the most wins "in the main," or "on the whole." And this is undoubtedly correct, although other notable authorities and writers of eminence have fallen into error on the point.

Lecky's "England in the Eighteenth Century" says :—

> "The Welsh main, which was the most sanguinary form of the amusement, appears to have been exclusively English, and of modern origin. In this game as many as sixteen cocks were matched against each other at each side, and they fought till all on one side were killed. The victors were then divided and fought, and the process was repeated till but a single cock remained."

This is very crudely put, because if all on one side were killed in the first round, the other side were clearly victors at once, and there was no need to proceed to a second round—to say nothing of pitting one's own birds against each other.

Mr. W. Gilliver's account of a Welsh main, as it was conducted at Lichfield half a century ago, shows the conditions of this class of contest to have been similar to those now commonly in force for greyhound coursing. A Welsh main at Lichfield took place annually on Boxing Day, the prize always being a fat pig weighing twenty-five score. There were always sixteen cocks entered, at £1 each for an entrance fee. The winner had to come successfully through four encounters, the successive rounds reducing the competition to 8, 4, 2 and 1 respectively.

Sometimes a Welsh main was arranged to commence with eight cocks; in this case the winner had to conquer three times, the eight being reduced to 4 in the first round, to 2 in the second, and to 1 in the third and final round.

In this method of arriving at one surviving conqueror from among a whole host of competitors, the final duel was known as the Battle Royal—the winner emerging triumphantly from a heap of slaughtered foes.

A monograph on Cock-fighting by Dr. Samuel Pegge, the antiquary, says—

> "Suppose, sixteen pairs of cocks; of these, the sixteen conquerors are pitted a second time; the eight conquerors are pitted a third time, the four a fourth time, and lastly, the two conquerors of these are pitted a fifth time, so that, incredible barbarity, thirty-one of these creatures are sure to be inhumanely destroyed for the sport and pleasure of those who will yet assume the name of Christians."

Here, as Mr. Lawley points out, the learned doctor makes the mistake of supposing that the number of winners in each round would always be the same on both sides. It can easily be seen that the first round was not bound to result in one side winning eight battles and the other winning an equal number; the result might be nine and seven, or fifteen and one, or any similar pair of numbers to account for sixteen battles fought out. A backer did not match two of his own birds against each other.

To obviate the very possible result of each side winning exactly half the battles, and so ending the contest in a "drawn main" (when each side would draw their own stakes), cockers seldom made an "even set" main, say a set of sixteen birds against another sixteen. The usual plan was to match fifteen, or seventeen, or any other odd number against an equal number, comparing each pair of combatants to within an ounce of weight.

As a matter of fact, the procedure in a properly fought (English) main was for each bird to fight only one battle, and victory went to the side which counted a majority of single wins in such bye-battles. Of course, there may have been occasions when the parties interested were so carried away by what they miscalled their love of sport as to pair the conquering birds against each other a second, or even a third, time. But these were very few, and were discountenanced by those who had, or were supposed to have, any weight or influence in fixing the standard of etiquette for the cock-pit.

The only case (at a well-regulated cock-pit) in which a cock would be allowed to fight a second battle on the same day would be where a champion of exceptional prowess had vanquished his opponent by a sort of *coup de main* in a very few seconds from the start; his owner would under such circumstances be allowed, if he chose, to fight this unscathed hero a second time, but always against a bird of his own weight.

The following newspaper report of an important cock-match contains the scoring :—

"March 31, 1824. A main of cocks was fought between Lord Anson and Molyneux for Staffordshire, and Colonel Yates and Edmund Peel, Esq., for Warwickshire, for 25 guineas a battle, and 500 guineas the main. The following is the correct statement of the result of the fighting :—

| Gilliver for Warwickshire. | | | Potter for Staffordshire. | | |
|---|---|---|---|---|---|
| Tuesday ... ... ... ... | 7 | 1 | Tuesday ... ... ... ... | 4 | 3 |
| Wednesday ... ... ... | 3 | 1 | Wednesday ... ... ... | 3 | 1 |
| Thursday ... ... ... ... | 7 | 2 | Thursday ... ... ... | 5 | 4 |
| Friday ... ... ... ... | 4 | 1 | Friday ... ... ... ... | 2 | 2 |
| | 21 | 5 | | 14 | 10 |

This was all one main, running over four days' fighting, and the result being judged by the aggregate made by each side at the conclusion of the fourth day. The double columns indicate, for instance, that on the

Tuesday Gilliver won seven main battles and one bye-battle—a bye-battle being a match battle.

A bye was often fought between young cocks at an age when they were called stags and might be of unequal weight.

As the sport of Cock-fighting is an ancient one, so it may be expected the English word *cock-pit* is an old one, as it named the arena in which the action took place.

A cock-pit was round in shape, and not large in size. Thus an old writer expresses himself :—

> "In roundness such as it a cock-pit were."

And Shakespeare, alluding to its circumscribed area in his Prologue to *Henry V.*, says :—

> "Can this cock-pit hold the vastie fields of France?"

In the seventeenth century there was a London theatre (The Phœnix) called by the name of the "Cock-pit," from the fact that it was standing on the site of an old bird-fighting establishment. That part of a theatre called the "pit" originally derived its name from its similarity of construction to a cock-pit.

There were indoor cock-pits and outdoor cock-pits : the former for select meetings, and the latter for holiday crowds and other popular assemblies.

The permanent buildings were not necessarily large, and only in very populous or much-frequented centres were they specially built. Often they were assembly-rooms at taverns, or any kind of large outbuilding attached to an inn, converted to the purpose. Most large, old-fashioned hostelries possessed cock-pits of some sort, either permanently fitted up or easily adaptable on occasion.

The architectural features of a cock-pit which had been specially erected for the purpose were exclusively utilitarian, and void of all artistic treatment, innocent of all attempts at embellishment. The exterior generally presented the appearance of a low, round tower; the interior that of a dwarfed and unimposing amphitheatre. The centre was occupied by the stage, which was the arena for the display of the birds, and on which no human feet were allowed to tread except those of the setters-on This stage was usually about a foot lower than ordinary table height to those who sat immediately round it on the two rows of highest-priced seats. Behind a low barrier rose two or three other tiers of benches; sometimes the uppermost outward ring of the amphitheatre constituted a standing space or a kind of promenade.

Outdoor cock-pits were as often as not connected with licensed houses, and were enclosed by a wall, or some other kind of a high permanent fence. At Wednesbury the fence was of the zareba kind, strengthened with gorse bushes; as the local ballad says of one who wished to see the sport without paying :—

"Peter Hadley peeped through the gorze."

Many of them were rough-and-ready structures, which could be hastily thrown up on a fair-ground or a race-course. In the Black Country a pit-mound was sometimes utilised as an amphitheatre for impromptu matches.

The open-air cock-pits were found convenient when more profit was to be made out of the prices of admission paid by the crowds of spectators who patronised the exhibitions, than by the entrance fees paid for the birds entered.

The fighting arena itself was comparatively small, the

open-air ring being only some ten or twelve feet in diameter. Its flooring was either the natural greensward, or it was artificially turfed.

The inner rings of spectators were generally seated to allow those standing in the outer rows to see over their heads. In the permanent buildings there were sometimes galleries around. Here the general arrangement was that of a miniature circus; or perhaps of a theatre in which there was no stage, but where the performers occupied the pit—that part of a theatre which derived its name from this fact.

In some cock-pits a part of the equipment was a curious contrivance for circumventing, or rather for punishing, the unprincipled bettor who, having lost, tried to decamp without paying over to the winner the forfeited wager. This contrivance was a cage or basket in which the defaulter (or "welsher") was ignominiously hoisted to the ceiling, and there exposed to the howling derision of the house. In this we seem to see a rude attempt at making the punishment fit the crime; for the instrument both imprisoned and exposed the culprit, whose great aim was to escape notice and get clear away. Doubtless many Black Country cockers were numbered among John Wesley's converts to Methodism; it is certainly a noteworthy and curious fact that in the first Wesleyan Sunday School founded at Wednesbury there was employed a similar cage arrangement for hoisting incorrigible truants to the roof timbers.

Cockings were held frequently enough wherever aristocratic patrons of the sport, with plenty of leisure time on their hands, were in the habit of meeting; as in London, and other large and fashionable centres like Newmarket and Bath.

But the popular cock-pit meetings frequented by men with less leisure at their disposal were held at holiday times, not the least of which were the Wakes, Fairs, Races, and other local festivals.

During the August race meetings at Nottingham the best blood of the country always met at the White Lion Inn, where the early part of each day was regularly spent at the cock-pit, the scene of some of the most important cock-fights in the country. For Nottingham was another famous centre.

Pearce, the historian of WALSALL in 1813, mentions the Cock-pit of that town along with the Theatre, Bowling-greens, Assembly-rooms, and other places of amusement then in existence there; taking care, however, to specify its exact location in this way:—

"Situate on the left-hand side of the entrance into Park-street from Digbeth, at the bottom of a yard belonging to Mr. Fox, known by the sign of the New Inn. It is the property of Mr. Charles Perks, and is spacious and much frequented at the time of the Races, at which period only it is used."

The advent of Walsall Races was publicly announced in this form:—

> "Performances at the theatre by Mrs. Nunn's company of comedians, and cocking in the large pit, which has lately been erected for the purpose."

LICHFIELD was always a great centre of attraction, especially to the noble sportsmen of the Midland district; its holiday gatherings were also highly popular with the plebeian crowd. The Races of 1813 were announced by the following newspaper advertisement:—

> "A main of cocks will be fought at the Swan Pit, for 100 guineas the main, and 10 guineas each battle, between the gentlemen of Staffordshire and the gentlemen of Warwickshire. Gilliver and Gosling, feeders."

For the same year, the neighbouring town of BURTON-ON-TRENT advertised its Races with the announcement: "Assemblies, Plays, and Cockings as usual."

The following advertisement is culled from the *Staffordshire Advertiser* of July 26, 1811:—

"NEWCASTLE-UNDER-LYME."

"A main of cocks will be fought during the races on August 16 between the gentlemen of Shropshire and the gentlemen of Staffordshire, for 5 guineas a battle, and one hundred guineas the main. Feeders—Jones for Shropshire, and Lincoln Shaw for Staffordshire."

A similar notice appeared in the *Wolverhampton Chronicle* of the following year:—

"Newcastle-under-Lyme Races. A main of cocks will be fought during the races between the gentlemen of Shropshire and the gentlemen of Staffordshire for ten guineas a battle, and two hundred the main. Feeders:—Gilliver for Shropshire, and Gosling for Staffordshire."

The following announcement appeared in the same newspaper of the year 1824:—

"March 31. Cocking on Thursday and Friday, 1st and 2nd of April. A main of cocks will be fought at IVETSEY BANK between the gentlemen of Staffordshire and the gentlemen of Shropshire for 5 guineas a battle, and 300 guineas the main. The fighting to commence at 11 o'clock each day. Jones for Staffordshire, Hadley for Salop."

The next newspaper report goes back to the year 1761, and is additionally interesting from the somewhat romantic episode recorded:—

"The second of the 7 years' main subsisting between the gentlemen of Birmingham and Bridgnorth was decided in favour of the Birmingham gentlemen at Duddeston Hall, in the Whitsun week, by 8 battles ahead in the main and 14 in the byes. What was very remarkable, out of 61 cocks weighed 58 were matched. Next year the 3rd main will be fought at the Crown, in Bridgnorth, in Whitsun week. At the above cocking a gay young fellow, of a very good family near Bridgnorth, having lost all his money (which was a considerable sum), apply'd to a recruiting officer, and enlisted himself; but as soon as he had received the advance-money he returned to the cockpit, and again deeply engaged in bets, and being so fortunate as to win between nine and ten pounds more than he had lost, quitted the pit, and immediately repaired to the officer to whom he had enlisted, came to terms with him for a discharge, and then returned home."

The fame of the cock-pit at Duddeston Hall (Birmingham) in the middle of the eighteenth century was sufficient to inspire the Muses. At least the following lines were deemed of sufficient merit to gain admission to the *Gentleman's Magazine* of the year 1747 :—

"Where Duddeston's walks with varied beauty shine,
And some are pleased with bowling, some with wine,
Behold a generous train of cocks repair,
To die for glory in the toils of war.
Each hero burns to conquer or to die;
What mighty hearts in little bosoms lie!

* * * *

Come, Hogarth, thou whose art can best declare
What forms, what features, human passions wear;
Come, with a painter's philosophic flight,
Survey the circling judges of the fight.
Touch'd with the sport of death, while ev'ry heart
Springs to the changing face, exert thy art;
Mix with the smiles of Cruelty at pain
Whate'er looks anxious in the lust of gain;
And say, can ought that's gen'rous, just or kind,
Beneath this aspect, lurk within the mind?
Is lust of blood or treasure vice in all,
Abhorr'd alike on whomsoe'er it fall?
Are mighty states and gamblers still the same?
And war itself a cock-fight, and a game?
Are sieges, battles, triumphs, little things;
And armies only the game-cocks of kings?

Which fight, in Freedom's cause, still blindly bold,
Bye-battles only, and the main for gold?
The crested bird, whose voice awakes the morn,
Whose plumage streaks of radiant gold adorn,
Proud of his birth, on fair Salopia's plain,
Stalks round, and scowls defiance and disdain.
Not fiercer looks the proud Helvetians wear,
Tho' thunder slumbers in the arms they bear:
Nor Thracia's fiercer sons, a warlike race!
Display more prowess, or more martial grace.
But, lo! another comes, renown'd for might,
Renown'd for courage, and provokes the fight.
Yet what, alas! avails his furious mien,
His ruddy neck, and breast of varied green?
Soon thro' his brain the foe's bright weapon flies,
Eternal darkness shades his swimming eyes;
Prostrate he falls, and quiv'ring spurns the ground,
While life indignant issues from the wound.
Unhappy hero, had thy humbler life
Deny'd thee fame by deeds of martial strife,
Still hadst thou crow'd, for future pleasures spar'd,
Th' exulting monarch of a farmer's yard."

The meeting thus celebrated by the poet was evidently one of the most important in the district, as may be gathered from the terms in which it was advertised in *Aris's Gazette* of June 8th, in that year:—

"Birmingham Cock Match.—On Whitsun Monday, the 8th of June, will be shown at Duddeston Hall, near Birmingham, in Warwickshire, 41 cocks on each side, for a match to be fought the three following days betwixt the gentlemen of Warwickshire, Worcestershire, and Shropshire for 10 guineas a battle, and 200 guineas the odd battle; and also 21 cocks on each side for bye-battle, which bye-battles are to be fought for 2 guineas each battle."

For the following year a somewhat similar announcement was made in the same columns:—

"On Monday, April 11, 1748, being Easter Monday, will be a match of cocks, weighed to fight the three following days at

Duddeston Hall, near Birmingham, each party to weight 41 cocks for 10 guineas a battle, and 200 guineas the main, and each party to weight 20 cocks for bye-battles for 5 guineas a battle, each cock to give and take half an ounce. The Gentlemen of Worcestershire and Herefordshire against the Gentlemen of Warwickshire and Staffordshire."

Here is the announcement of another Birmingham meeting at the close of the same century :—

"April 1, 1793. At the new-erected pit in Birmingham will be fought a main of cocks between the gentlemen of Staffordshire and Warwickshire, to show and weigh twenty-one cocks on each side, for four guineas the battle, and fifty the main. Likewise ten cocks on each side, for two guineas the battle, for byes, and to fight the 22 and 23 of April instant.—Rowley, for Staffordshire ; Turner, for Warwickshire ; feeders. Lovers of the sport are requested to be there as early as possible, as they intend to begin precisely at Twelve o'clock."

Twenty years later, namely in 1817, *Aris's Birmingham Gazette* contained the following :—

"March 31. A main of cocks to be fought at the New Cock Pit, Coleshill-street, Birmingham, on Easter Monday and the three following days, between the gentlemen of Warwickshire and the gentlemen of Staffordshire, for one hundred guineas the main and two guineas each battle. Feeders : Gilliver for Warwickshire, and Partridge for Staffordshire."

Similar notifications for 1792, 1809, and 1824 are on permanent record in Langford's "Century of Birmingham Life." In Birmingham and the Black Country low-class meetings often took place on Sundays.

On the authority of Charles Knight, the well-known historical writer, "Wednesbury Cockings" were as celebrated a century ago as the Derby race-meetings are at the present time.

The open-air cock-pit in this town was "nigh unto the

church," as the balladist has left on record ; it was on a field adjoining the Blue Ball Tavern. The indoor cock-pit, largely used for inter-county and other important fixtures, was situated in Meeting Street, where John Wesley, in his attempt to evangelise the town, had erected his first Wesleyan Chapel.

There is available (thanks entirely to the indefatigable researches made into this subject by Mr. G. T. Lawley) the details of a notable fight which became almost historical in the annals of the sport. The preliminaries to the meeting are sufficiently explained in the following:—

" NOTICE.

" There will be a main of cocks on March 17th, 1785, at the cock-pit in Old Meeting-street, Wednesbury, to decide a bet of one hundred guineas between the gentlemen of Birmingham and the gentlemen of Wednesbury and district. Each party to weigh thirteen cocks : seven to decide the main. All lovers of this sport are respectfully invited to attend, as genuine sport is intended. Time, twelve o'clock precisely."

The terms and conditions of the contest are set forth explicitly enough in this notification of the forthcoming great tournament of the Midland chanticleerian champions. A contemporary report of the encounter, preserved by an old cock-fighter of the locality, Mr. Lawley was permitted to copy. It ran thus :—

" Wednesbury is the very paradise of cock-fighters. No lover of this old-fashioned English sport was ever disappointed with his visit to that well-known town ; and nowhere is the sport indulged in more heartily than here. The numerous patrons who assembled on the 17th inst. to witness the long-contemplated match between Birmingham and Wednesbury veteran cockers met with some capital sport, and the money that was betted was unusually large in amount. The odds all along were laid on the Wednesbury birds, and in the end, after a fair fight, they amply compensated their backers, numbering eight battles to five by their opponents :—

18

"Fight I.—This encounter was between two fine red cocks, well matched, and weighing five pounds eight ounces. The battle lasted eleven minutes, during which there was some hard hitting on both sides, both being mauled badly, but in the end the Wednesbury champion sent his opponent to grass, dead.

"Fight II.—In this a black grey did battle for Birmingham, and a pyle did battle for Wednesbury. The former was the heavier bird, and on showing, the betting was five to three on the grey. A game struggle ensued, the pyle fighting like a Spartan, but after some slashing work he received his opponent's steel, and died fighting. Time, nine minutes.

"Fight III.—A red pyle showed for Wednesbury, and was opposed by a blue pyle. The red had it all its own way, and proved the winner in fourteen minutes. Betting on the main, five to four on the Wednesbury birds.

"Fight IV.—This time Birmingham showed a red pyle, and Wednesbury pitted a black red. Both birds were very fine, and a furious fight ensued, going in flap for flap, and hit for hit in true style. The black-red lost an eye, and was floored, but came up again to time, evidently bent on revenge. At it they went again like tigers, and a brain blow from the black-red secured the victory for Wednesbury. Time, ten minutes.

"Fight V.—These birds were a black red for Wednesbury and a light red for Birmingham. A good fight, but the Wednesbury bird got blinded and ran away. Time, seven minutes.

"Fight VI. Another black for Wednesbury was opposed by a grey pyle, but the latter proved little better than a dunghill bird, and, after a flap or two, bolted. Time, two minutes.

"Fight VII.—A duck-winged grey for Wednesbury, and a dark red for Birmingham next toed the scratch, and another determined struggle ensued. Both the birds knew how to hold, and the feathers flew about the pit like snowflakes. First one and then the other had the advantage, until the grey was floored, but not before the red had lost an eye, and was cut almost to mincemeat. Time, nineteen minutes.

"Fight VIII.—There was much excitement here, the game standing at four to three, but betting was slightly in favour of Wednesbury. Two fine birds were pitted—a black for Wednesbury and a brown for Birmingham. The latter proved victor in twenty minutes, bringing the game four to four.

"Fight IX.—Two fine reds were now shown, and showed rare mettle. Money was betted freely on this fight, terms being about equal, but after some hard and bloody work the Birmingham bird was fit for cooking, the winner giving a loud "cock-a-doodle-doo." Time, seven-and-a-half minutes.

"Fight X.—This time the Wednesbury gentlemen sent in a black of fine plumage and as upright as a Grenadier ; and it was evident their birds got no worse as the game continued. A pyle showed for Birmingham. A good battle ensued, but the latter was overmatched in fighting capacity, and was soon kicking. Time, fifteen minutes.

"Fight XI.—The main was looking bad for Birmingham, and odds against it went begging, but in this battle, in which a brass-back fought for Wednesbury and a dark red for Birmingham, the fortune changed, and the latter scored a victory, after a tough struggle which lasted twenty-six minutes.

"Fight XII.—The duellists in this affair were a red pyle for Birmingham, and a blue pyle for Wednesbury, and on showing the former had the call of the betting. A sharp struggle, however, proved the game qualities of the blue, and after some uphill work the latter proved the victor. Time, eleven minutes.

"Fight XIII.—This fight was soon over, for the Wednesbury men sent in one of the finest birds of the match, having been kept back for any necessity, and, being opposed by one much inferior, had it all its own way. Time, fourteen minutes.

"This brought the affair to a termination, amid the ringing cheers of the Wednesbury patrons, and a corresponding depression on the part of the Birmingham. The settling after was a heavy one ; and several disturbances occurred during the day, in which one or two men were roughly handled."

Among the most notable of the aristrocratic patrons of the cock-pit in its later days was the Earl of Derby. When Cock-fighting was yet numbered amongst the favourite pastimes of the highest in the land, and the cock-pits were frequented as the theatres are now, Lord Derby had as many as three thousand cocks "walked" on his estate, and leases thereon usually contained clauses that the tenant should "walk" cocks and breed puppies for the landlord.

A mysterious cult was that of the Cocker. In training the birds so much depended on two things—breed and exercise. Exercise consisted of being well walked.

Good water was also an essential : in fact the motto of trainers was "Good water and good walking."

The Earl's "feeder," or chief official in the sport, was named Potter, a man who was in his service for a whole lifetime, and well known throughout England in this connection. As a feeder it was his duty to turn the cocks into the pit and to keep the fights going.

The men who faced each other in the pit were the "setters-on" ; these officials were waited on by the feeders or trainers who brought the birds in proper order, after scaling them and arranging the pairs according to their graduated weights.

Among the most famous cockers in England were the Gillivers of Polesworth. Indeed, the modern Mecca of the cocking cult seems to be this north Warwickshire village, where the old home of the Gillivers is almost a museum of Cock-fighting relics.

Joseph Gilliver used to fight cocks for George III. and George IV. at the royal cock-pit at Westminster. He was, indeed, the most celebrated cock-feeder England has produced, and was remarkable for his strict integrity and sterling honesty—qualities which he bestowed upon his descendants who followed him in the profession of cock-masters. On one occasion he went to Westminster to take part in a week's fighting in the royal cock-pit, and a sportsman of the name of Crutch Robinson took a large bet that Joe Gilliver would win all the battles in one day. Naturally there were great odds against this achievement, but on the Thursday the event came off, and Crutch Robinson pocketed a large sum of money.

The Gillivers have had their home at Polesworth for many generations and always as exponents of the once popular pastime of Cock-fighting. So great was their renown in this particular line of activity that the old

*W. Webb, Pinx.* *P. Roberts, Sculp.*

JOSEPH GILLIVER.

[*Published, 1834, by M. A. Pittman, Warwick Square.*]

*To face page 260*

name of the hamlet of Birchmoor in which they resided has been dropped from the Postal Directory in favour of the name Cockspur, substituted as more descriptive of the place's historical associations. Indeed a letter from abroad found the last official representative of the family although it was simply addressed to Mr. Bill Gilliver, Cock Fighter, England. The family cottage is still full of the old "trophies of the sod"; among them are family portraits of bygone sportsmen, as well as pictures of many of their favourite spurred heroes.

Of one portrait-picture of a fighting-cock hanging on its walls, the Gillivers tell a curious story, which accounts for a number of indentations plainly noticeable on the canvas. The Game-cock represented was a favourite bird with which the last of the cock-fighting Gillivers once won a great match for £1,000, at Manley Hall, near Chester, fought in the presence of a very select company of ladies and gentlemen. Of the fifteen battles, this champion gained the eighth for his side, and so won the main. The cock was then sent to the portrait-painter in honour of this notable victory. When the artist had nearly completed the bird's counterfeit presentment, he had occasion to go out of the studio, whereupon the winged warrior evidently took the opportunity to strut round the room till his eye caught sight of what he thought was "a foeman worthy of his steel"—and without a moment's hesitation he made an onslaught on the canvas with the result to its surface already mentioned.

In the ancestral cottage may be seen many other interesting trophies of the past, some of them personal tributes from admiring patrons, suitably inscribed; there are a pair of silver spurs, once the property of the Earl of Leconfield; and a communication from another famous sportsman of the old school, Sir John Astley, which is always proudly exhibited for the manner in which it is addressed—Mr. William Gilliver, Champion Cock-fighter, Golden Lion, Newmarket.

When interviewed a year or two ago, Mr. William Gilliver—perhaps the only surviving past-master in the whole art of Cock-fighting—naturally bewailed the fact that the ancient glories of the sport had departed, never to return—so far as England is concerned. As the Cock-pit still flourishes in France and a few other countries, however, his practised hand has been occasionally called into requisition abroad on great occasions. He boasted that within quite recent years he had challenged all America, through the medium of the sporting papers, to fight a main on French soil of "11 or 13 set battles, from 4 lb. 8 oz. to 6 lb., or give in weights of 17 cocks each side, from 4 lb. 8 oz. or 4 lb. 10 oz. up to 6 lb., and fight all that catch to one oi two ounces of each other." As this old link with the sporting past—he was born in 1827—could not fight his birds in this country, consolation was found by him in breeding them. In this innocent pursuit also he was highly successful, his specimens often taking prizes at the best shows in the country. The breeds chiefly cultivated for exhibition were those which the old sporting Earl of Derby most favoured, white-legged reds, and brown-breasted reds.

In the old days many breeders were men of substance. As large owners and trainers of valuable birds they were sometimes able to amass little fortunes; and as befitted men of substance their demeanour was always staid, their conduct always circumspect. In fact the grave and serious aspect of these eminently respectable gentlemen who appeared at a cock-pit carrying a bag, was in striking contrast with the behaviour of the generality of folk who patronised such places. From their bags these grave, sober-looking gentry produced their best and most saleable game-cocks; they fought them, and they sold them. The cock-pit was to them as an exchange is to a merchant; it was a place where they made their money. A quietness of dress and a reserved manner seemed always to be part of the stock-in-trade of men who obtained their livelihood by dealing in game birds, whose sole occupation was to breed and train them. Their business was one that was full of secrets; and they all looked like men who could keep their own counsel. It was only by long experience and close observation that one acquired a full knowledge of their occult craft.

The keen and ardent sportsman who made himself thorough in all the mysteries of Cock-fighting had to learn many secrets: how to breed the birds by the selection of sire and hen; how to feed the chicks and develop their fighting proclivities; how to trim their feathers and fix their spurs for the encounter; how to weigh and match the birds, noting their marks and their age as well as their weight; and how, in fighting out a main, to take care that only those birds were matched which fell within an ounce of each other in weight. All these were important points, and all of them were liable to attack from the trickery and cheating inseparable from those sports which the gamester can make the subject of his bets, or the results of which can be manipulated in the gambling interests of the unscrupulous patron.

Other times, other manners. It must not be lost sight of that the schoolmasters of olden times, if not always clerics or divines, were all learned and reputable men; and yet they never hesitated or disdained to preside in their own schools over the customary Shrove-tide celebrations of this barbarous sport. Nor, with a real knowledge of their necessitous circumstances, can we blame them too severely if they complacently accepted as their due, as part of their regular perquisites, the gift of all craven and runaway cocks. Anyway, it has been pleaded in extenuation of these old-time pedagogues that in all ages the teaching profession has been too poorly paid; even with all the enlightenment of the present day, education is the one profession in which a man may work with no reward but the wages of an artisan and the conscience of a missionary.

Of clerical delinquents it would not be difficult to find a number of examples. There was the Rev. Robert Wild, a Presbyterian divine, holding the rectory of Aynho, Northamptonshire, in the seventeenth century, whose poem entitled "A Copy of Verses on Two Cocks Fighting" has furnished us with not a few rhyming extracts in graphic language with which to embellish the plain prose of this historical *résumé.*

So late as 1831 a clergyman at Tipton flatly refused a request to preach against the cruelty to animals, which then entered so largely into most of the people's pastimes. He based his refusal on the national expediency of encouraging all sport—which apparently was to be done at the cost of humanity. His conduct was felt to be shockingly reprehensible by the better-thinking part of the community, who unfortunately were in a powerless minority at that time; however, the local poetaster was inspired to vindicate the cause of humanity on that occasion, and he hurled at the erring shepherd his lines of burning scorn, which must have seared that cleric's very soul:—

> "No more be seen to mount the sacred place,
> But in deep mines conceal and black your face,
> Herd with bull-baiters, and their deeds commend
> Make him who fights a cock your bosom friend.
> Dash from your sight God's precious rule of good,
> And congregate with men 'who build with blood,'
> From Cruelty and Hell a pattern take
> And head the Devil's crew at Tipton Wake."

No more notorious cocker existed during the early decades of the nineteenth century than the Parson of Willenhall. Of this worthy—who was said to have royal blood in his veins—Mr. G. T. Lawley relates a most amusing anecdote. It is to the effect that on one occasion he had a cock matched to fight on a Sunday morning. The match lasted longer than he had expected, and he was consequently fetched by the beadle to conduct the service in church. He went reluctantly, but left his feeder in charge of the bird to see the fight properly conducted. After a hard-fought battle the parson's champion was beaten, whereupon some bird of ill-omen, anxious to convey the news, rushed off to church, and putting his head in at the door (probably for the only time in his life, except when he was married), said in an audible whisper, "Parson, yo're cock's lost." This so disturbed the godly minister that he seized hold of the hymn-book from the desk and threw it at the intruder's head, much to the amusement of some of the congregation.

At the Westminster cock-pit, and at a few others of the select and exclusive class, such as were regularly frequented by noble lords and patronised by royal princes, the proceedings were invariably conducted with decency and decorum. Indeed, during the eighteenth century the stately demeanour of the patrons lent quite an air of frigidity to the sport in these aristocratic resorts; even the betting there was conducted in a dull and spiritless manner. At one period it was considered bad form to betray the least emotion; the display of feeling, and, more so, any signs of enthusiasm, would have been deemed intensely vulgar. Noblemen who were squandering their substance, who were actually engaged in gambling away their hereditary estates at the cock-pit, sat perfectly impassive, and to all outward appearance unconcerned spectators of the combats by which their patrimonial acres were passing from them and their children for ever. And yet with all this assumed indifference their infatuation was so deeply rooted, they failed to resist the attractions of the cock-pit to the end of their days.

At all provincial establishments, and even at some of the London resorts, like the famous cock-pits in Tothill Fields and at Gray's Inn, the company was generally of a character best described as "mixed." Assembled with one common object, and rubbing shoulders almost, might be seen the merchant and the tradesman, the lawyer and the sporting parson, the sailor-man and the military officer who had perhaps seen English game-cocks pitted against each other in distant colonies. In the same heterogeneous crowd the more regular *habitués* included decayed gentlemen who had run through their estates; footpads, and known thieves; young bloods, horny-handed workmen, and specimens drawn from all the lower strata of society. This mixed and motley multitude deteriorated into a rabble that became the more noisy the further it was removed from the centre of interest in the arena.

Among these frequenters of the baser sort rowdyism was rampant; they laid and took the odds at the top of their voices; they demanded instant payment when a bet was won; they caught and instantly thrashed any rogue who attempted to slink away without paying when he had lost; and they had no compunction about cracking his skull or breaking his ribs; they bawled and they brawled, they cursed and they fought, and they gave vent without restraint to every passion that animated their brutal natures.

It is beyond dispute that rowdyism was rampant among the regular *habitués* of the cock-pit; nay, it is certain that downright villainy prevailed among those who frequented its meetings. An authority already

Drawn & Engd. by I.R. & G. Cruickshank.

Tom, Jerry and Logic, backing Tommy, the Sweep, at the Royal Cockpit.

Publd. by Sherwood, Neely & Jones April 1821

quoted, writing in the early eighteenth century, winds up his code of rules for those who followed the "fancy" at that time, in a paragraph which in all conscience is painfully characteristic of this degrading sport. His words imply that a sporting loss, with its usual accompaniment of lost wagers, was not always the worst misfortune which might overtake the unfortunate cocker; for it would seem there were always plenty of chances of receiving chastisement, even to the extent of losing an eye or being maimed for life. His concluding words are unmistakably ominous, either for swindling welshers or for any man of craven spirit :—

> "And now I have one word of advice to him that is a lover (or would be so) of this *Royal sport;* and then I have done. *Come not to the pit without money in your breeches,* and a judgment of matches. 'Done and done' is cockpit law, and if you venture beyond your pocket you must look well to it, or you may lose an eye by the battle."

That free fights not infrequently followed the encounters of the feathered champions in the Midland locality is manifest not only from the contemporary record just quoted, but the well-known ballad, "Wedgbury Cockin'," testifies to the fact in that elegant language which alone befits the subject :—

> "The company then fell to discord,
> A bold fight did ensue;
> Kick, pinch, and bite was the word
> Till the Walsall men all were subdued.
> Ralph Moody bit off a man's nose,
> And wished he could have him slain;
> So they trampled both cocks to death,
> And made a draw of the main."

If any further testimony were needed to prove that ruffianism was the invariable accompaniment of these meetings, the concluding two lines of the same ballad should suffice. Indeed, the spirit of bullying terrorism which pervaded all local sport at that time was perpetuated in the form of a proverb which was remembered long afterwards, when football first became popular in the district—it was often the reproach of the Black Country football teams that they set out with the avowed intention of ending the match in "a win, tie, or a wrangle!" The closing lines referred to are—

> "Jack Baker he whacked his own father,
> And so ended Wedgbury Cockin'."

This "Jack Backer," as his name is rendered in the vernacular, is a sort of semi-historical personage, named in the Wesley records of the notorious Wednesbury riots got up against the "Methodys" in the year 1743. On that memorable occasion he is mentioned more than once as a ringleader of the mob, rushing about the streets of the town with an oak bough in his cap; for it seems he was conspicuous both as a Jacobite partisan as well as an Anti-Methodist.

Mr. George T. Lawley quotes the full text of an old paper, which he says was destroyed among a number of other old documents belonging to the parish of Bilston :—

"In 1690 there was a cock-fyght neare unto Wednesbury, in a fielde called ye Holloway, between a certain red cock belonginge to John Tomkys, of Bilston, and a black-red birde belonginge to Thomas Horobin, of Wednesbury, for five pounds a-side. There was a greate assemblinge of people from round about, and much money was betted by ye friends of each birde. Ye fighte lasted some time, but in ye ende ye cock belonginge to Tomkys was killed by ye other, whereat ye owner was so enrayged that he seized hold of ye other bird and wrung off his head, before Horobin could stop him. This causede a great commocion and a general fighte between ye backers, which was not ended till manie persons had received much injurie and detriment in property and bodie, and John Tomkys had payd ye vallie of ye cock. After which they all went peacably together to Joe Willett's house, ye Swann, in Bilston, where ye rest of ye day was spent in feastinge and drinkinge and another match was made."

Another parochial document, of a date nearly a century later, reveals little improvement in the state of Bilston society; it runs :—

"March, 1768. At a vestry meeting held at the house of Benjamin Willetts, by adjournment from the church, after public notice, it was agreed to build a strong room to put persons in that have been guilty of riotous misbehaviours in this parish, and that the expense shall be defrayed by a poor levy."

About four years previous to this the authorities had been constrained to issue the following warning :—

"WHEREAS serious riots and villainies of various kinds have frequently been committed within the Liberty of Bilston, much to the discredit of the people and the scandal of our most holy religion, now we, whose names are subscribed assembled in vestry, pursuant to public notice thereof legally given in the chapel at Bilston, after morning service, on this 10th day of March, do agree that for the future the author of all and every kind of riot and villainies that shall be committed within the Liberty of Bilston, when committed by the justices, shall be prosecuted at the expense of the township.

"(Signed), "EDWARD BEST, *Minister.*

Although this was signed by the clergyman of the parish, who was a county magistrate, and a number of others in authority, it had clearly had no effect. The riotous assemblings complained of never failed to accompany a cock-fight or a bull-bait.

The researches of Mr. Lawley have resulted in unearthing similar parochial notices issued by the magistrates to the parish constables and churchwardens of the surrounding towns :—

WEDNESBURY.—"1750. Notice, that on account of the many disorders and furious riots which occur in the alehouses of this town after cock-fights, all such persons who shall in future aid, encourage, or abet in any way whatever or whomsoever in carrying on cock-fighting, or any such sports, shall have their licenses withdrawn ; and all cockers who shall be caught stirring up or inciting any assembly to riot shall be whipped at the common whipping-post."

DARLASTON.—"1756. This is to certify whom it may concern that all riotts, fellones, and other disorders and misdemeanours at cock-fights and other asscmblies, shall be persecuted at ye parish charge, as witness our hands this 20th day of August."

The next one is interesting from its allusion to the licensing of the taverns where these disorderly meetings took place :—

WALSALL.—"1789. Notice is hereby given, that on account of so many riots taking place at bull-baits, all publicans who shall in future encourage or shall aid or abet other persons in the brutal pastime, or shall aid or abet in any way whatsoever *cock-fighting, or assist cockers*, shall have their licenses withheld, by order of the magistrates."

As a crowning instance of the depravity to which the votaries of this "old English sport" could descend, the following item culled from *Aris's Birmingham Gazette*, of November 12, 1792, would be difficult to beat :—

"COCK-FIGHTING. This barbarous amusement, we are concerned to say, holds its rank among the vulgar sports that disgrace the country. Gentlemen still countenance the barbarity, and are seldom more elated than when they witness a bloody and hard fought battle. For the credit of humanity, we trust that the report is not true, that a gentleman, near Shrewsbury, betted a wager that his breed of cocks would fight, though set on fire. The bet was accepted, and the cock's feathers, which were covered with turpentine, set on fire. The animal, it is said, though roasting alive, fought and killed his adversary in the midst of the flames."

If this was the conduct of one who is described as a "gentleman," what must have been the standard of morality among the working classes at that time? The criminal records of the period disclose a shocking state of society as it then existed; and there can be no question that before the establishment of the common schools at the commencement of the nineteenth century, the labouring classes were sunk in the very depths of depravity—a moral degradation which was glaringly reflected in all the popular sports and pastimes of the day. The saturating of the plumage of two fighting cocks with oil, and the firing of the inflammable material as the birds became absorbed in their natural antagonism, was but one other manifestation of the fiendish spirit which animated the rougher element of Englishmen a century ago.

How little the sportsmen of those days cultivated that true sporting spirit, which enables the worshipper of Dame Fortune to bear his losses with the same equanimity with which he takes his gains, is revealed by Crabbe. The poet truthfully mirrors the times in his work entitled, "The Parish Register":—

"Here his poor bird th' inhuman cocker brings,
Arms his hard heels and clips his golden wings;
With spicy food the impatient spirit feeds,
And shouts and curses as the battle bleeds.
Struck through the brain, deprived of both his eyes,
The vanquished bird must combat till he dies—
Must faintly peck at his victorious foe,
And reel and stagger at each feeble blow.

> When fallen, the savage grasps his dappled plumes,
> His bloodstained arms for other deaths assumes
> And damns the craven fool that lost his stake,
> And only bled and perished for his sake."

A volume, the contents of which were somewhat akin to "The Anatomy of Abuses," already quoted, was written by a West Country Quaker named Hingeston, and published at Exeter in 1703. The following extract will show that this writer's reprobation of Cock-fighting was enforced by the employment of no unfaltering terms of denunciation :—

> "I have been mightily Griev'd and deeply Affected, and that very often, when I have heard of any publick Cock-Matches . . . to see and consider that these Cock-Masters are in this Action undoubtedly treading their Steps to Hell. . . . How methinks can any Man, that is a Man, take delight to see two poor Dumb Creatures Cut and Wound one another. . . . Nay, if at any time they Fight not stoutly, but endeavour to shun the Battle, then with that bitter Spight and Cruelty doth the Owner or his Assistant break the Neck of him. . . . And because God in his creating Wisdom hath not furnish'd these Creatures with Weapons to answer their Devilish Expectation, they will make up that Deficiency by Metal Spurs, in order to make short work and kill them the faster, that the Sport may go on with speed."

The writer who most daringly "improves the occasion" is a Tipton mentor of morals of a century later, one Abraham Smith, whose published work received the gracious approval of our late Queen when she was but a child of fourteen (1833).

He tells of one old cock-fighter who, being brought to a bed of sickness and almost to death's door, cried out to his offended God, and promised most fervently that if he were only restored to health he would for ever forsake his wicked practices. His prayer was answered ; yet the first time he went abroad it was to enter a cock-pit. There, rising to his feet in the midst of the wicked crew, he was just calling out a bet of five shillings, "when at that moment God withheld his breath and he instantly expired."

Another "gentleman," says the same moralist, possessed a game-cock on which he had won many sums of money, but which at last betrayed his confidence when the stake had been raised to an unusually heavy amount. The loss so enraged the owner that he seized the poor bird, bound it alive to a spit, and commenced to roast it in front of a large fire. On some of the bystanders attempting to interfere with his cruel purpose, the infuriated "gentleman" took up a poker and threatened to knock out the brains of any man who went near the unfortunate fowl. "Instantly an awful judgment from heaven finished his career of iniquity"—he was struck dead!

And so the writer points his morals wherewith to adorn his marvellous tales.

But here is a record of actual fact which vividly illustrates the brutalising effects of the pursuit, and the urgent need there was for legislative interference.

> "On Whit Monday evening, May 19, 1834, about 11 o'clock, Joseph Garrington and his uncle, Daniel Foster, both of Darlaston, began to quarrel concerning a cock-fight. From words they proceeded to blows, when Garrington struck Foster with an iron instrument upon the head, which almost instantly killed him."

Cock-fighting was made illegal in 1849, by an Act of 12 and 13 Victoria. One of the most prominent reformers in obtaining this enactment was an Irishman named Martin; yet the sport was pursued in Ireland without any particular vigilance on the part of the police to suppress it for many years afterwards. The ardent cocker of the English school tried to mollify the popular asperities with which the custom was regarded by continuing the practice—surreptitiously, of course—under the name of "a rural sport"; as this it had been euphemistically classified in one of the last books published on the subject in 1840.

A recent magazine article on this subject contained the following :—

"It is the belief of most people that cock-fighting is now perfectly extinct in England, although game-cocks at large are wicked enough to follow their natural instinct and kill each other if they had the opportunity. Cock-fighting, they will say, has been abolished by Act of Parliament, and consequently can no longer exist, 'and,' says that usually well-informed paper *The Field*, 'the bits of pointed steel wire, with the ring of metal and a small piece of leather by which they are attached to the leg of the bird, were purchased the other day for large sums as mere curiosities to be placed in cabinets. But those who are behind the scenes know that a very large number of fighting-cocks are bred in this country yearly, for the same old purpose.'"

*The Field* is here referring to a recent sale by public auction (1903) of a very unique collection of sporting relics, included in which were a spur cabinet made of coromandel wood, an oil painting depicting the "death-blow" in cock-fighting, which was executed for George IV. when Prince of Wales, and a pair of steel spurs with silver sheaths, which were used at Cheltenham at the end of the eighteenth century. With regard to the use of the last-named it had been arranged that the contest should be fought with silver spurs, and it was only at the last moment that the sheaths were slipped off.

Sir John Astley in his biographical reminiscences, which he calls "Fifty Years of my Life," makes allusion to the cock-pits in Lucknow and in several other cities of India, as they existed in 1880. In one place he states that the eggs of certain Indian game-fowl fetched as much as £20 each.

Sir John also records his experiences of the sport in England; how on one occasion he barely escaped from a police raid made on a cock-pit at Manchester; and how on another the police were successfully hoodwinked when a cock-fight was brought off somewhere in the eastern counties—both within recent times

After the passing of the Act of 1849 for the suppression of Cock-fighting, its provisions were sought to be evaded by the plea that the places where encounters were surreptitiously brought off were not "regularly" kept and used for that specific purpose. But the plea was not allowed. In one particular case a man issued invitations to witness a cock-fight in a barn, and his purpose to commit an offence was made abundantly manifest by the finding there of a number of fighting-birds in bags, some alive and some dead, and all with their natural spurs cut back close to the leg so that artificial spurs might be fitted on them. The barn floor was covered with blood, and the mutilated condition of the dead birds proved conclusively the "cruelty" to which they had been subjected.

In another prosecution under the Act some twelve or thirteen men were charged with "aiding and abetting" two others who were brought up as the principals on a charge of "cruelty," in inciting two cocks to fight on a high-road between Huddersfield and Rochdale. Although there were no ropes or stanchions to form a proper ring or cock-pit, the birds were spurred, and they were "played" in the customary manner. A square of four yards had been simply marked out with a stick, and the crowd of about a hundred men surrounded this space; an inner ring of spectators kneeling in front, and an outer ring standing behind them and looking over their heads, formed the "audience." It was contended that the accused were merely present as witnesses; but the fact of their mere presence in a crowd of excited spectators, all shouting to the principals suggestions or instructions as to the mode of setting on the cocks, was deemed quite sufficient to constitute them "aiders and abettors."

But perhaps the most amusing case of this kind was one in which Captain Fitzhardinge Berkeley, a scion of the noble house of that name, and about seventy others were charged at one of the London police-courts. From the evidence it appeared that Jemmy Shaw, a well-known sporting character who kept a tavern near the Haymarket, was engaged on the day of the offence in bringing off an important main for the delectation of a number of gentlemen and the usual following of the Rag-Tag-and-Bobtail class who foregather on such occasions. The police, having got wind of the affair, surrounded the house with a body of constables, made a sudden entry, and arrested the lot. Next morning they were all brought up before the magistrate, together with the cocks, files, and other implements used in Cock-fighting, produced as part of the evidence against them. At the hearing it was most amusing to watch how the gentlemen defendants endeavoured to separate themselves from their uncouth and vulgar-looking companions of the previous evening. They manœuvred till they had formed themselves into a select circle, apart from the others; upon observing which the learned magistrate promptly ordered them to be mixed among their co-defendants, of whose company they were now so ashamed, remarking that distinctions could not be made in a police-court between one cock-fighter and another. Each gentleman was thereupon placed between two roughs, and, the case proceeding, every prisoner was fined impartially the same amount, namely, £5 and costs.

The Folk-lore of Cock-fighting, though not extensive,

is interesting. Mr. George T. Lawley has preserved on record the old Bilston superstition that, to release one from the influence of a witch's spell, it was only necessary to break the neck of a fighting-cock and suck the victim's blood while it was warm. Another superstition of the locality regarded the fighting-cock when he crowed under certain conditions as a bird of evil omen, especially with regard to the bets made on the coming events of the cock-pit, the origin of which latter piece of nonsense is undoubtedly connected with St. Peter's betrayal of Christ. But is not the cock the only creature which ancient superstition supposed to be capable of successfully encountering the arch-enemy and all his evil spirits—and hence its adoption as a vane, otherwise a weather-cock? And does it not in that figurative form always turn round so as to face undauntedly the quarter from which the wind or any other adverse influence may come? Truly, so great is the courage of the cock, it has won the recognition of all ages and commanded the admiration of all nationalities.

There is a well-known Black Country yarn descriptive of the rivalry which once existed between the cockers of the adjoining towns of Darlaston and Willenhall. It tells of the deadly insult—always intended and always accepted as such—offered by one party holding up a game-cock, with which pretence was made to challenge the weather-cock on the church steeple of the rival parish, and desperate were the fights which ensued upon this humorous form of provocation.

Years ago in the Black Country adult cock-fighters and children at play followed a practice in which both alike kept up the traditions of ancient magic. Two boys might be playing at marbles, when a third would approach and offer for some childish consideration, or for mere love of one of the players, "to conjure for him." By this he meant he would throw a spell over the marbles, and so charm them that the game should not fail to go in favour of his friend. He would pretend to work the charm by muttering a lot of cabbalistic gibberish, or sometimes by drawing crosses on the ground over which the marbles had to travel.

In this practice the children were but imitating the superstitious follies of their elders. A cocker of those benighted times would take his bird to be charmed by a "wise woman," or by some male charlatan pretending to supernatural powers and possessing a special reputation for the charming of fighting-cocks.

Followers of the cult, like most other classes of society in those days, were susceptible to their own particular forms of superstition. At almost any cock-pit in the country, as the fortunes of some eventful day wore on, there might nearly always be seen towards the close of a main one or two men sitting with coats turned inside out. Fondly these votaries of Dame Fortune hoped their change of coat would bring them a change of the ill-luck which had persistently pursued them in the earlier stages of the contest; it was thought, perhaps, the fickle Dame, being always more or less blind, would fail to recognise them in this readily effected disguise!

Let the professor of magic be male or female, the deliverance made on such occasions was always couched in that oracular language which could be interpreted either way. In his researches Mr. Lawley was fortunate enough to rescue from oblivion the following cryptic charm. It was a sort of incantation used over any fighting-cock for which its anxious owner wished to obtain the favour of the spirit world:—

"For a reader, a reader of mystic signs
When the night's dark, and when the sun shines—
Strangers may come, I tell them their dreams,
The maid's, the mother's, the goodman's dreams—

I can tell where the thief his wealth has hid,
I can tell what a maid for a husband did.
All round the house and all round the lane
Now tell me, ye imps, what I want for to gain.
'Tis Red will win!
They say, they say!
Here's your bird again—
Away! Away!"

The weird prophet who could command fees on an utterance as indefinite as this must naturally have had very credulous clients. The assurance that "Red" would win must have been as vague as language could possibly have made it, inasmuch as the majority of birds pitted very frequently bore red markings of some kind upon their handsome plumage.

Miss Burne, an authority on Folk-lore, gives particulars of one of these fortune-tellers who lived at Walton, near High Ercall, and to whom fighting-cocks were brought from all parts of Salop, from Cheshire, and from more distant parts in Wales. Over all of them he cast his spells with the utmost disregard to their origin or ownership so long as he was paid his fees. Other wizards equally in favour with the Cock-fighting fraternity of Salop were to be found at Ketley and at Preston-on-the-Weald Moors.

Another Shropshire practice was to hatch a clutch of game-fowl's eggs in the appropriated nest of a magpie. The cocks thus brought to life under the influence of the "devil's bird" were believed to be unconquerable, if not invulnerable.

Other charms, perhaps but little less unholy, consisted in feeding the cock with bread which had been surreptitiously obtained from the communion table; or fortune's favours might be compelled to fall upon a devotee who rose early in the morning, collected the dust on the communion table, and sprinkled it on the cock-pit floor;

or, if this were not obtainable, dust from the churchyard might be substituted with an equally happy augury.

Such were the gross ignorance and the degrading superstition which accompanied the sport of Cock-fighting in our grandfathers' days.

Owing to the prevalence and popularity of this sport, traces of its all-pervading influence may be found permanently fixed for all future time in certain specimens of Black Country place-names. In not a few old towns may be found thoroughfares bearing the name Cock Street. Inns much resorted to by the fraternity were often known as "The Cock," or, better still, sometimes as "The Fighting Cocks"; by this latter name were known old-fashioned hostelries in Birmingham (Moseley), and in Wolverhampton (Goldthorn Hill), which have since lent the name to a whole district. In the same way lands were known by such names as Cock Heath (Wednesbury), Cock-croft (Wolverhampton), and Cock-pit Piece (Wightwick).

Shaw's *History of Staffordshire* (1799), contains the following anecdotes illustrative of the same part of the subject:—

"'Walter Rotton, being a man of many extravagances, such as cock-fighting, &c., soon put an end to his estate, the place being sold to William Normansel, mercer, of Wolverhampton.' A place known as 'Fighting Cocks Hall,' near Wednesfield, and more recently and better known as the 'Twenty Trees,' was sold to pay the cock-fighting debts of one of its owners, and until a few years ago two stone fighting-cocks stood on the pillars of the entrance gates as reminders of the fact. On some of these fights not only hundreds, but thousands of pounds were betted.

"Bearing upon this is a curious story, related of a Wednesbury cock-fight, which is amply vouched for. The story runs that a noble lord who had a habit of stammering was a frequent visitor to the cock-pit of that town. On one occasion, being present at a main, he laid very recklessly on the issue of the last battle of the main, offering (in his stammering way) to-to-to lay f-f-f-£5,000 to-to-to a

£100 that the W-W-Wedgbury b-b-bird would win. 'Done!' cried the sportsman to whom the offer was made. The nobleman, more than usually excited, began to stammer 'D-D-D-D-Done,' but before the word would come which would have completed the bet, the Wednesbury bird was slain outright, and his lordship was thus saved from loss. Squire Stone, of Walsall, who was present, said with a burst of laughter, 'My lord, your want of plain speaking has for once served you in good stead, for it has prevented you being ruined.'"

Among the phrases which the sport has added to our language is the vulgar colloquialism, "That beats cock-fighting!"—by which exclamatory comparison it is meant to convey that the thing under notice surpasses everything else; just as in the opinion of its votaries the sport of Cock-fighting surpassed every other.

Cock-master was the term formerly applied to one who reared game-cocks for the arena. Thus we have a certain John Beest named as "his Majesties Cock-master" to James I. in 1610.

Later we find the term "Cocker" employed for one who regularly followed the sport of Cock-fighting. In 1814 W. Sketchley wrote the "Cocker," published at Burton-on-Trent, which contained a variety of useful information for the instruction of those who were either employed about or occupied as attendants at the cock-pit.

It must not be lost sight of that the regular pursuit of this pastime provided employment for quite a large number of people; so many individuals were engaged in the breeding, rearing, and training of fighting-cocks as almost to constitute a distinct industry.

The term "Cocking" appears in the *London Gazette* of 1678. More than a century earlier, however, this word was in use. In the *Plumpton Correspondence,* dated 1546, we read, "Ye shall se all our good coxs fight if it plese you & see the maner of our Cocking."

In naval architecture the after-part of the orlop deck on

board a man-of-war, ordinarily the quarters of the junior officers, but in action used to receive the wounded, is called the Cock-pit. This name was probably bestowed because the quarters were confined for space, as was the mimic gladiatorial arena which originally bore that name.

Similarly, the term is employed figuratively for a place in which contests are fought out; thus Belgium has been called the Cock-pit of Europe, the destinies of that continent having been largely decided there from the days of Cæsar to those of Wellington.

From the nature of its surroundings and the impurity of its moral atmosphere, two other phrases were obtained which were once in common use. Thus the ill-spirit engendered by interested partisanship was known as "cock-pit animus"; and persons who gave revengeful advice were called "cock-pit counsellors."

From the attitude of the pugnacious bird who struts so defiantly around, we obtain the phrase "cocksure," standing for a "pert self-confidence." Allied terms are the vulgarisms "cocky," and "cocksy," and the substantive "cocksiness," which is the schoolboy synonym for pertness.

That the loss of an eye was a disaster of the first magnitude, foreboding almost certain defeat, was recognised by the coining of a phrase, once much used throughout the Black Country, for comforting one who had met with a misfortune which was not altogether irreparable; as when the comforter would seek to minimise the trouble by soothingly observing, "No cock's eyes out yet!"

Here we may note the frequency with which the wretched cocks gouged out each other's eyes. The natural habit of all their tribe is to "scratch" for food; but with the game-cock this use of the strong scratching claw is supplemented by the use of the spur as a lethal weapon.

> "They scorn the dunghill; 'tis their only prize,
> To dig for pearls within each other's eyes."

Now the skill and measured deliberation of the attack; the equal wariness of the defence with which it was met; the form of finesse, and the strategy exhibited in the preliminary sparring; all demanded the possession, on the part of these feathered fencers, of the most perfect vision possible. Did, therefore, the duellists realise this when they almost invariably seemed to concentrate their whole efforts on striking out each other's eyes?

Sometimes birds were pitted that had previously lost one eye in battle; they were called "Blinkers," and were allowed certain advantages which were supposed to counterbalance their defective vision. There was one strain of birds which was credited with showing a better form of fight after the loss of the eyesight!

The term "cockstride," was once in vogue to denote a small but perceptible space; it was probably derived by observing the very small amount of progress made by a strutting cock. Thus the folk-lore rhyme had it—

> "At the darksome New Year's tide,
> Days outspin by a short cockstride."

One other derivative of this class must bring our selection to a close.

In the colloquial language of the same Doric region from which so many of these slang expressions have been gleaned, an individual with a squint eye, or with one eye so injured as to compel him to "cock" his head on one side in order to eke out the range of his one optic vision, was always said to be "cock-eyed."

Although Gallomachia (which is but a name for Cock-fighting under a classical guise) was a national sport, practised throughout the length and breadth of England, it nowhere took a firmer hold upon the taste of the public than in this oft-quoted region of the Birmingham Black Country. Nay, the pursuit of Gallomachia was rooted here long before the consumption of mineral fuel had earned for this great Midland industrial area its uninviting nickname. And, as already intimated, the town which in the eighteenth century held the supreme distinction for rendering a whole-souled devotion to this ancient sport, with its usual concomitants of gambling, ruffianism, and all-round depravity, was Wednesbury.

The local reputation of this place was celebrated by the ballad-monger of the time in an effusion of some note, entitled "Wedgbury Cockin'," to which passing allusion has already been made. The incidents therein sung by the poet were eminently characteristic of the time and place ; but the rhyme was not only doggerel of the most wretched description, but was so disfigured by the profanities and indecencies of language, then in common use among nearly all classes of society, as to be quite unquotable here.

Although the good folk of Wednesbury were at first proud of the distinction conferred upon their town by the local minstrel, and no convivial meeting throughout the countryside was ever allowed to pass without the roaring forth of its rollicking verses, there came a time when even the most prejudiced patriot of the place was heartily ashamed of it.

Mrs. Loudon, the well-known authoress, in her novel entitled, "The Mummy," quotes as much of this effusion as she dare, and treats it in a very amusing manner—it is supposed in this delectable piece of fiction to be a newly discovered work of antiquity, and severe comments are made on the vagaries of the ancients from whom it is pretended to have been handed down.

That the reader may judge how worthy of Antediluvian or Troglodyte ideas the composition was, here is an excerpt from this notorious ballad, purporting to describe the feasting which followed upon the encounters of that renowned Wednesbury meeting:—

"The beef, too, was old and so tough—
  Of a bull that was baited to death—
That Barney Hyde got a lump in his throat
  As almost stopped his last breath.

The company fell into confusion
  To see poor Barney Hyde choke,
And they took him away to the kitchen
  To hold his head over the smoke.

They held him so close to the fire
  He frizzled just like a beef-steak;
They then throw'd him down on to the floor
  And almost broke his poor neck.

One gi'd him a kick in the stomach,
  Another a kick on the brow;
His wife said 'Throw him into the stable
  The fool will be better just now!'

Some people may think all this strange
  Who Wedgbury old town never knew;
Though those who have ever been there
  Won't have the least doubt it's all true."

Other productions of the ballad-monger sing the cocking fame of some of the surrounding townships, though none of them ever attained the celebrity of "Wedgbury Cockin'," which has always been regarded as a classic.

Mr. G. T. Lawley quotes two. The first is entitled "The Battle of Bilston"; it recounts the varying fortunes of the fight in the usual strain, and how the Bilston bird eventually won, even after its eye had been struck out by its Darlaston antagonist, whose plumage is graphically described as "red as a soldier's coat." Then follows a description of the pandemonium with which such scenes were accustomed to conclude, and of the intervention of the officers of justice always necessary to restore a rowdy crew of disappointed cockers to some semblance of order :—

> " Bill Purslow and Hodgetts the Crier
> Got drunk and forgot for to pay,
> So the Landlord he sent out for Old Tonks,
> Who to the stocks took 'em both right away.
>
> Then their legs he put into the vice,
> When their hard fate they did loudly bewail,
> Till their friends came to pay up their shot,
> And the Constable got to give 'em leg bail."

The second ballad seeks to immortalise the neighbouring parish of Wednesfield. It begins—

> "At Wednesfield on one village Wake
> The cockers all did meet
> At Billy Lane's, the cock-fighter's,
> To have a sporting treat."

Although of a more recent date than many similar productions, that the traditions of the sport were kept up may be judged by the concluding verse—

> "They beat the men from Will'nall town
> Back to their town again,
> And long will they remember
> This Wedgfield Wake and Main."

The song of welcome which always greeted Tommy Read, an eminently successful cocker of Willenhall, whenever he visited his native town, contained this choice bit of hero-worship—

"Tommy Read has come whoam
To O'd Will'nall, by gum.
There'll be some rare 'aten' and drinkin'.
There'll be many a match
Brought up to the scratch
Afore he goos back, I've been thinkin'."

An effusion produced in the adjoining counties, and given by Miss Burne in her collections of "Shropshire Folk Lore," scarcely reaches this standard of literary composition, poor doggerel as it is. The ballad is said to have been sung at the funeral of Maxey Dick (a cocker who was so dubbed because he hailed from Macclesfield), which took place at Horton, near Wem. A great cock-fight had taken place on Easter Monday, 1799, between the gentlemen of Salop and those of Cheshire, for two guineas a battle and twenty guineas on the main.

"You cock-masters all, both far and near,
I will tell you of a cocking, when and where,
At Lea Bridge, as I have heard them say,
Old Pell Head beat the Bonny Gray."

The lines then become so incoherent and the language so vague that it is scarcely comprehensible till we read—

"Then Martin took Maxey off the ground,
And away he went for Wem town
To the Pack Horse Inn; but the mob was too strong,
Poor Martin could not stop there long.
The night being then most dreadful dark,
Away he went for Clemley Park,
And Martin went crying the whole of the way,
And he swore that Maxey had not fair play.
At last poor Martin reached his home,—
Lord! how he then did sigh and groan!
He called for a candle to light him to bed,
And he told them all Maxey Dick was dead."

Whether the narrative itself, or the versification of it, is the less intelligible it would be difficult to decide.

Mr. Lawley quotes the concluding stanzas of a dirge-like piece which mourns the death of a Tettenhall cock-fighter—

"At length the day of all arrived,
  The day when he must die;
He called his children round his bed,
  While a tear bedimmed his eye.
Says he to Charlotte, Poll, and Bett,
  ''Tis now no use to cry;
Yo' mun share the birds among you
  So I wish yer all good-bye.'

His funeral was ushered in
  With more than common gloom,
Each little bird sat on its perch,
  And clucked a mournful tune;
Each little bird who did as much
  As little bird could do,
While the old game cock fluttered o'er the grave,
  A cock-a-doodle-do."

Finally, here is an epitaph, said also to be a Staffordshire composition, on the body of a good fighting bird "killed in action"—

"Imprimis:—First of all, let it not be forgot
My body freely I bequeath to th' pot,
Decently to be boiled, and for its tomb
Let it be buried in some hungry womb.
Item.—Executors I will have none,
But he that on my side laid seven to one,
And like a gentleman that he may live
To him and to his heirs my comb I give."

## XVII

### THROWING AT COCKS

Another Shrovetide sport—The birds trained to avoid the missile or "cock-shy"—A religious origin claimed—Or an expression of national antipathy suggested—Both a parochial and a Court diversion—Hogarth's satire—A churchyard sport—A Quaker's condemnation—A newspaper protest—Allusions in church-wardens' accounts—And in town regulations—Recent prosecutions—"Threshing the Fat Hen."

IT will be noted that the earliest reference to Cock-fighting in this country names Shrove Tuesday as the day for its special celebration. The same day of the year is connected with another ancient sport, which also involved gross cruelty towards fowls. This was known as "Throwing at Cocks," a Shrove Tuesday pastime which seems to have been popular in every quarter of Old England.

For some weeks prior to the day young and active cocks were specially trained for the game by being tied to a stake and thrown at with sticks not heavy enough to maim or materially hurt the bird, but sufficiently so to make it try to evade the missile by fluttering as far as the tether would permit—the cord would usually give the bird nearly a yard's play around the stake.

In the course of a couple of weeks' training the birds became quite agile in escaping the sticks thrown at them. On Shrove Tuesday the competitors who threw in earnest used sticks heavy enough to knock over the bird, and sometimes to kill it; the distance thrown ranging from twenty to thirty yards. The charge made for entering the contest was generally a penny each "cock-shy"; and any competitor who, from the set mark, could knock over the bird, and then run and secure it before it could recover its feet, might claim the bird as his prize.

In the north this annual offering of a bird became commuted by custom into a coin of the realm, which was known as a "cock penny," with which every schoolboy presented his schoolmaster on Shrove Tuesday—a contribution which went towards the much-needed augmentation of the pedagogue's stipend.

This form of mediæval cruelty is said to have had a "religious" origin; to have been devised, in fact, to make the cock suffer in punishment for St. Peter's cowardly offence of denying his Master. Nothing has been suggested of its more probable origin in unregenerate man's deriving amusement from such barbarous practices; and the proposition of vicarious penance implied by the theory given is illogical. Anyhow, we have Sir Charles Sedley's authority for it in the following couplet:—

> "Mayst thou be punished for St. Peter's crime,
> And on Shrove Tuesday perish in thy prime."

Another, and a very far-fetched origin of this Old English pastime has been given in the *Gentleman's Magazine*. A writer in that old storehouse of half-forgotten lore says that the "warrior bird" would have been in much greater favour as a tavern sign if it had not been considered as an emblem of France, and as such opposed to the Lion of Britain. "To this circumstance, arising from the ambiguity of the Latin word *gallus*, which equally denotes a 'Gaul' (or 'Frenchman') and a 'cock,' may probably be attributed the barbarous custom of throwing at cocks on Shrove Tuesday."

To back up this fanciful conceit the writer adduces two illustrations more or less to the point. He says :—

"At Blenheim House, that magnificent memorial of a nation's gratitude, its architect, Sir John Vanbrugh, has placed on a conspicuous situation, the figure of a Cock writhing in a Lion's paw, which being deemed a puerile device, was the subject of this epigram—

> "Had Marlborough's troops in Gaul no better fought,
> Than Van to grace his fame in marble wrought;
> No more in arms than he in emblems skill'd
> The Cock had drove the Lion from the field."

The second argumentative illustration is even less to the point :—

> "The form of a cock which appears on our church steeples by the name of *weather-cock* was perhaps originally placed in these situations in ridicule of the notorious instability of the French. Thus Shakespeare (1 *Henry VI.*) makes Joan of Arc, speaking of the defection of the Duke of Burgundy, say :
>
> "'Done like a Frenchman, turn and turn again.'"

Cock-throwing at Shrovetide was both a parochial custom and a Court diversion. In witness of the latter statement may be quoted an entry from the Royal Household Accounts of 1492 (Ord family MSS.) :—

> "*March 2. 7 Henry VII.* Item, to Master Bray for rewards to them that brought cokkes at Shrovetide, at Westminster............XXs."

In evidence of the first statement extracts may be given from the Parish Accounts of Pinner, Middlesex, where the annual celebration was made the occasion of publicly collecting money in aid of the poor :—

| | | |
|---|---|---|
| "1622. | Received for cocks at Shrovetide | 12s. od. |
| 1628. | Received for cocks in towne...... | 19s. 10d. |
| | Out of towne........................... | os. 6d." |

The method of conducting this sport at Heston in Middlesex has been described in Brand's "Antiquities." (1791). Here for weeks previous to Shrove Tuesday the cock was trained by its owner to "dodge," that is, to evade, any missiles which might be thrown at it; it was taught to watch for the threatened danger, and to jump aside to avoid the blow. Then on the day of the sports, in strict accordance with the usual method of conducting this pastime, the owner would permit three shies for twopence, from a distance of twenty-two yards; the competitor who could knock the cock over and run up and catch it before it had recovered its legs winning the unfortunate bird as a prize. Broomsticks were generally used for missiles, and the diversion took place near the church.

Needless to say, the wretched rooster was sometimes knocked almost to a jelly. The barbarity of this pastime has been satirised by Hogarth in the first of his pictures called "The Four Stages of Cruelty."

During the eighteenth century Cock Throwing was carried on in the village churchyards, even while divine service was proceeding on Sundays; and the scandal was perpetrated "in spite of the Justice, the Minister, the Parish Officers, and the Constables"—if we are to credit the parochial records of Hayes. One entry made in the Parish Registers there, by the Rev. C. Manning, runs in this wise:—

"Feby. 27, 1754. Being Shrove Tuesday, divine service was performed in the afternoon, and no care was taken to prevent the throwing at cocks, rioting, and swearing in the churchyard at the same time; though I gave notice to the churchwardens and the magistrate, and desired that it might be prevented for the honour of God and Public good; but his answer was this—I know no law against throwing at cocks, even in the churchyard."

An Exeter Quaker, one "Friend" Hingeston, already

quoted, writing in 1703, complains that this Shrovetide practice is "Devilish Sport," and describes it as "setting a Cock to a stake and throwing Cubits to him till they kill him, spoiling his Flesh by Bruises and what not. But, above all, after they have tormented him, and in a sense killed him, then they endeavour to bring him to life again by thrusting a Finger down his Throat in order to torment him a second time."

In Staffordshire the cock-fighter of old time pursued a similar custom for the purpose of using up his game-cocks which had been defeated in the pit without being killed. A disgraced cock was tied to a stake and thrown at till killed. This custom had the recommendation of combining amusement with retributory vengeance; there is about it that spirit of praiseworthy economy which recalls the Scottish anecdote anent a row in the gallery of an Edinburgh theatre, when the gods being about to throw a man overboard into the pit, a thrifty soul called out in anxious tones, "Dinna waste him! dinna waste him! Kill a fiddler wi' him!"

In *Aris's Birmingham Gazette* for March 5, 1764, the following significant paragraph appeared:—

"As the barbarous custom of throwing at cocks too much prevails yet upon Shrove Tuesday, to the disgrace of real Christianity, true humanity, and a good police, in a civilised county, all the magistrates in the kingdom should prohibit it, and punish all offenders, for their own and the national credit, being a cruel diversion to kill innocent animals in that wanton manner."

Towards the end of the eighteenth century a better tone began to pervade public opinion, and we find in the issue of *Aris's Birmingham Gazette* for February 10, 1777, a correspondent inveighing against the wanton cruelty of this pastime. The writer appeals to the better nature of a brave and generous people to forego pleasures so flagrantly cruel, and to abandon pursuits as dishonouring to their country, as contrary to the professions of Christianity.

Unfortunately the Church had not as yet thought it part of its duty to exercise a restraining influence in the direction of regulating the people's sports. A quarter of a century later, however, the Rev. Richard Amner preached a sermon at Tipton (1800), in which he uttered his solemn protests against the cruelty of the prevailing sports of the district (and of Cock Throwing in particular) in no uncertain language. And how striking a word-picture of numberless barbarities of the most inhuman character that well - deserved denunciation proved to be!

So prevalent was this Shrovetide pastime, its chronicles have repeatedly entered into public documents such as Churchwardens' Accounts. The cocks were sometimes purchased with money belonging to the church funds, and the profit arising from the public patronage of the sport was expended for the benefit of the parish, and duly accounted for in the Churchwardens' books. In an Improvement Act obtained for Burton-on-Trent in 1779, providing for the better regulation of the town and the cleansing and lighting of its streets, one clause introduced had relation to this very common custom. It provided, "That if any person shall throw at, or set up any cock or fowl to be thrown at, in the manner called Cock Throwing, or shall make or assist in making any fire or fires, called Bonfires, they shall be fined 5s."

But little over twenty years ago the Society for the Prevention of Cruelty to Animals had to prosecute a number of persons at Wakefield for throwing at cocks at one of the local festivals there. It was regarded as quite a legitimate "sport"—a sort of North of England "Aunt Sally," for which a charge of "three sticks a penny" was made; just as if the target were a dolly or other inanimate object. It is satisfactory to know that a fine of £2 and costs was imposed in every case.

But what appears to be a variant of this ancient pastime was unearthed a little later at Rushall, near Walsall. In this case the target consisted of a duck placed in a hole in the ground, with its wings tied, and so fastened down that it could only raise its head and neck just above the surface. The proprietor of this wretched "duck in the hole," was offering it as a prize to any competitor who was successful in killing it by throwing, from a fixed mark, short round sticks, which he was providing at "a halfpenny a shy." The injuries to the poor creature testified to the "cruelty" of the practice, and in the prosecution all the defendants were very deservedly fined.

It may not be out of place to add here an account, as given by an old writer, of another Shrovetide sport, now happily long forgotten. It was called "Threshing the Fat Hen," and was one of those popular diversions, beloved of our ancestors, of the nature of a practical joke, played as follows:—

> "The hen is hung at a fellow's back, who has also some horse-bells about him; the rest of the fellows are blindfolded, and have boughs in their hands, with which they chase the fellow and his hen about some large court or small enclosure. The fellow with his hen and bells shifting as well as he can, they follow the sound, and sometimes hit him and his hen; other times, if he can get behind one of them, they thresh one another well favouredly; but the jest is, the maids are to blind the fellows, which they do with their aprons, and the cunning baggages will indulge their sweethearts with a peeping hole, while the others look out as sharp to hinder it. After this the hen is boiled with bacon, and store of pancakes is made. She that is noted for lying abed long hath the first pancake presented to her, but most commonly it falleth to the dog's share, for no one will own it her due."

# XVIII

## BULL-BAITING

Antiquity of the sport—Mastiffs or ban-dogs used—The first use of the bulldog—A manorial custom to give a bull—The tenure of "bull pieces"—A public-house custom—Method of procedure—Preparing the bull and entering the dogs—Catching the tossed dogs as they fell—Bulldog tenacity—The cry of "Lane!" when the bull broke loose—Baited beef as a food—Illustrations and incidents from Midland records—Sedgley—Tipton—Wednesbury—Handsworth—West Bromwich—Walsall—Jack Willetts, a bullot who was a ballad hero—Bilston's famous Wake of 1743—Willenhall—Birmingham—Sambourn—Mimic bull-baiting played by children—Shropshire—Place-names derived from the sport—Metropolitan bull-baitings at Hockley-in-the-Hole—The "professionalism" of loafers—A reported incident at Lichfield Wake, 1828—"Town bulls"—Parish rivalry leads to bull-stealing—The gross barbarities on record—Old wounds aggravated, forehoofs cut off—A bull baited by a man in place of a dog—Plague and pestilence no deterrent—Prophetic warnings and public protests—Early efforts at suppression—Societies formed—The Bill of 1802 thrown out—An Act of 1822 purposely excepts the bull from protection—A new Act in 1835 forbids the practice—Which, however, dies hard.

BULL-BAITING and bear-baiting and the baiting of badgers were all Old English pastimes, which dated from the twelfth century. It is recorded that on several occasions Queen Elizabeth, at the reception of notable ambassadors, gave entertainments which included a grand dinner, fine music, and the baiting of bears and bulls with sturdy "English dogs."

The dogs which at that period were commonly pitted against the strength of the bull or the cunning of the

*P. Reinagle, A.R.A., Pinx.* *J. Scott, Sculp.*

BULL DOG.

[*Published, 1820, by Sherwood, Neely & Jones, Paternoster Row.*]

*To face page 297*

bear were a formidable variety of the English mastiff breed.

Under James I. this kind of sport was forbidden on Sundays; and under the Commonwealth it was, of course, prohibited altogether. After the Restoration the old national sports were all revived, and the bull-dog then came into high favour.

The bulldog is supposed to have been first used by the butchers for catching and throwing down refractory cattle. By the massive formation of the head, and more particularly the projection of the lower jaw, this breed of dog was capable of seizing an ox by the nose, holding it perfectly still, or at its master's command throwing the heavy beast over on to its side with apparent ease. Says O. Wendell Holmes—

> "The mongrel's hold will slip,
> But only crowbars loose the bulldog's grip;
> Small though he looks, the jaw that never yields
> Drags down the bellowing monarch of the fields."

Not all bulldogs possessed the approved mettle for baiting the noble bull; but the exceptions were very few.

So fixed had Bull-baiting become as a national sport, it was customary in some manors for the lord to make a gift to his tenants, at certain specified times, of a bull to be baited. In numbers of parishes a piece of land was sometimes held by the tenure of providing a bull for the same purpose. In either case the custom was a tribute to the astuteness of the lord who by such manorial grant had contrived to reap some advantage over his tenants—simple fools ever eager to barter away their rights and privileges to any one who would thus pander to their degraded tastes in the matter of popular amusement.

The rolls of the manor of Northwich, in Cheshire

show that between 1729 and 1738 a number of fines were imposed and paid for such offences as "not baiting bulls," and "killing bulls unbaited." It is evident from this that the tenants of certain "bull pieces" had not fulfilled the conditions of the tenure by which they held their land.

The forfeiture of "a white bull with a red nose and ears of the same colour," for non-payment of "wroth-money" at Knightlow, in Warwickshire, every Martinmas, is an ancient feudal tenure, not altogether unconnected with the practice of bull-baiting.

Although Bull-baiting had been a courtly entertainment under Elizabeth, her successor on the throne did all in his power to discourage it. James I. tried to regulate what one writer has called "the national jollity," by publishing his well-known "Book of Sports"; but at the same time (1620) he issued his royal warrant for licensing houses for the playing of tennis, bowls, dice, cards, and suchlike games—bull-baiting, however, being tabooed.

Notwithstanding this, it was a regular custom throughout the following century for "Masters of Publick Houses to keep or procure Bulls to baiten on certaine Holidays, so call'd, as well as other days, on purpose to draw Company to their houses."

In every part of England, in the capital and in the country, the practice of bull-baiting was universally followed with more or less zest; though perhaps it nowhere attained a greater popularity than in the Birmingham Midland district.

As to the method of procedure, we have a vivid description from the pen of the French Advocate, Misson, who lived in England during William III.'s reign, of the manner of "these bull-baitings, which are so much talked of."

"They tie a rope," he says, "to the root of the horns of the bull, and fasten the other end of the cord to an iron ring fixed to a stake driven into the ground; so that with this cord, being about fifteen feet long, the bull is confined to a space of about thirty feet diameter.

"Several butchers, *or other gentlemen*, that are desirous to exercise their dogs, stand round about, each holding his own by the ears; and when the sport begins, they let loose one of the dogs. The dog runs at the bull; the bull, immovable, looks down upon the dog with an eye of scorn, and only turns a horn to him, to hinder him from coming near. The dog is not daunted at this; he runs round him, and tries to get beneath his belly.

"The bull then puts himself into a posture of defence; he beats the ground with his feet, which he joins together as closely as possible, and his chief aim is not to gore the dog with the point of his horn (which, when too sharp, is put into a kind of wooden sheath), but to slide one of them under the dog's belly, who creeps close to the ground, to hinder it, and to throw him so high in the air that he may break his neck in the fall.

"To avoid this danger, the dog's friends are ready beneath him, some with their backs, to give him a soft reception; and others with long poles, which they offer him slantways, to the intent that, sliding down them, it may break the force of his fall.

"Notwithstanding all this care, a toss generally makes him sing to a very scurvy tune, and draw his phiz into a pitiful grimace. But unless he is totally stunned with the fall, he is sure to crawl again towards the bull, come on't what will.

"Sometimes a second frisk into the air disables him for ever; but sometimes, too, he fastens upon his enemy, and when once he has seized him with his eye-teeth, he sticks to him like a leech, and would sooner die than leave his hold. Then the bull bellows and bounds and kicks, all to shake off the dog.

"In the end, either the dog tears out the piece he has laid hold of, and falls, or else remains fixed to him with an obstinacy that would never end, did they not pull him off. To call him away would be in vain; to give him a hundred blows would be as much so; you might cut him to pieces, joint by joint, before he would let him loose. What is to be done, then? While some hold the bull, others thrust staves into the dog's mouth, and open it by main force."

Sir Richard Blackmore, the author of "King Arthur," early in the eighteenth century wrote the following description of a country bull-bait, which is so vivid in its details that it deserves to be reproduced here. This is the passage—

> "So when a generous bull for clowns' delight
> Stands, with his tine restrained, prepared for fight,
> Hearing the mob's loud clamour, and the rage
> Of barking mastiffs eager to engage,
> He snuffs the air, and paws the trembling ground,
> Views all the ring, and proudly walks it round,
> Defiance tow'ring on his brindled brows,
> Around disdainful look the grisly warrior throws
> His haughty head inclined with easy scorn,
> Th' invading foe high in the air is borne,
> Tossed from the combatant's victorious horn.
> Raised to the clouds the sprawling mastiffs fly
> And add new monsters to the frighted sky.
> With disproportioned numbers pressed, at length
> He breaks his chain, collecting all his strength.
> Thus dogs and masters scared promiscuous fly,
> And fall'n in heaps the pale spectators lie.
> He walks in triumph, nods his conquering head,
> And proudly views the spoils about him spread."

Sometimes the horns of the brute were tipped with metal buttons, in the same way that fencing foils are blunted. This was done when the tines were too sharp, or when the bull was one regularly kept for repeated periodical baitings. The knobs prevented the dog's being gored; it was the bull's business to toss the dog, not to gore it.

In the earlier days of the sport, however, we have ample evidence that Sunday was the usual day upon which it was indulged, though it was by no means exceptional for the bull to be baited on the Saturday night for a short time, in order that the keepers might judge of his demeanour, and that those responsible for the proceedings could form an idea whether the succeeding day's sport would be answerable to the expectations of the mob. When the bull proved to be cowardly or mean-spirited it was sometimes changed for another, or else was subjected to torture in order to goad it into madness.

The sportsmen entered their dogs for the contest by the payment of a small fee for each "run," generally about sixpence or a shilling, but on special occasions a higher figure might be charged. Only one dog at a time was let loose on the tethered bull.

At first the dignified beast would merely turn down a threatening horn at the dog; but when the undaunted dog would avoid the danger by trying to get round his antagonist, then the bull would assume a posture of active defence.

The aim of the bull, as it was expected of him by the cognoscenti, would be not so much to gore the dog as to slide one of his horns beneath his belly to "hike" him (as it was expressed in the vernacular); that is, to toss him so high into the air that the fall to the ground would break his back, or in some way disable him.

The dog's owner, friends, and backers, however, had several methods of coming to the "hiked" one's rescue. The readiest was for the man to run and bend down his own broad back, offering it as a cushion to his canine pet.

> "The clamorous youth to aid each other call
> On their broad backs to break their favourite's fall."

The other method, as recorded by the observant foreigner previously quoted, was to present a long, smooth pole slantwise, on which to receive the falling dog in such a way as to permit of him sliding to the ground gently. But the favourite method followed by the gunsmiths of Birmingham, and by the lock-filers of the neighbouring Nineveh (this part of Handsworth was so designated because the Methodists declared that its barbarous sports and other iniquities equalled those of the Biblical city of Nineveh) and also of Wednesbury and Darlaston, was to catch the dog in an apron. The gunlock-filers were invariably "sure catches" with their working aprons.

If the force of the fall were not broken for the poor dog he was stunned, at the least; and not infrequently the "hiked" dog would crawl away completely cowed.

A good dog, on the other hand, would show his mettle by fastening on the bull—on to the nostril for choice. With the eye-teeth of the dog's undershut jaw the bull would be pinned as in a living vice. No matter how much the bull might rage and roar, bellow and bound, it would be impossible to shake off the bulldog. Blows, force, and violence of any kind would be unavailing—the well-bred bulldog would die rather than relinquish his hold. Sometimes the dog's mouth was forced open by the use of a cudgel as a lever; sometimes the dog was only to be parted from his foe by the piece of flesh held in his teeth being torn out.

Occasionally the tortured brute would break loose; then the outcry was for "A lane! A lane!"—that is, for an opening out of the cowardly crew to allow the infuriated bull to pass along. Such an episode is described in the ballad previously quoted:—

> "With disproportioned numbers pressed, at length
> He breaks his chain, collecting all his strength;
> Thus dogs and masters scared, promiscuous fly
> And fall'n in heaps the pale spectators lie."

In such incidents were found plenty of excitement, and not a few serious casualties.

It must not be forgotten that the promoters of the sport made a profit, in the end, by the sale of the bull beef, when noble Taurus, being no longer fit for the

*Howitt, i. et e.*

BULL-BAITING. THE BULL BROKEN LOOSE.

Ring, was relegated to the Shambles. The meat was eagerly bought up by the devotees of the Bull Ring; in fact such meat was highly esteemed. Is not a character in a seventeenth-century play, entitled *A Rogue well Basted*, made to say—

"Trust me, I have a conscience as tender as a steak from a baited bull"?

On the other hand, however, it has been asserted on the authority of the famous Wednesbury ballad that—

"The beef it was old and tough
Of a bull that was baited to death."

But this, perhaps, was the flesh meat of a veteran beast which had toured the various Wake carnivals for a number of years.

Of the immorality of the pastime; of the cruelties incidental to both species of beasts; of dogs disembowelled; of bulls with horns horribly uprooted by their own madness, or with tongues torn out by the relentless dog; of men gored or trampled to death; of the thousand and one horrors and accidents incident to the pursuit of such a pastime, it is here impossible to write exhaustively. It must suffice to give a number of selected illustrations, culled from the local records of Birmingham, and the mining district of South Staffordshire immediately adjacent.

Here is a specimen of the way announcements of the sport were sometimes made:—

"NOTICE!

"On Monday next there will be a bull baited at the Bull Ring in Sedgley when a £5 wager will be laid on Mr. Wilkes's dog Teazer of Wednesbury that he pins the bull's nose within an hour. Entries of dogs can be made at Mr. Perry's on or before Saturday. Fee, 5s."

Briefly it may be added, that Teazer won this wager for his backers; and, holding on to his victim, so infuriated the bull that he broke loose, and ran as far as Coseley, only obtaining release from his enemy's fangs when the flesh of his nostrils gave way; upon which the dog fell off, to meet retribution by being trampled to death by the bull's hoofs. The wretched bull was then turned back by the yelling mob, and eventually sank exhausted in the porch of Sedgley Church, where it was beaten to death by the cudgels of its brutalised pursuers.

Tipton Green has been fertilised by the blood of hundreds of bovine martyrs. For, says the ballad—

"The life blood of a hundred bulls
Has flowed on Tipton Green."

An old document of 1635 describes a parcel of land in that parish as "adjoining to the Town Green, near to where the Bull Stake was fixed."

In the same reign (Charles I.) a number of Tipton men were prosecuted, at the instance of the church-wardens, and heavily fined by the sheriff, for holding a bull-bait on a Sunday.

A Birmingham man (Mr. John Crook) has recounted his experiences at what he mistakenly claims to have been the last exhibition of the kind in the Black Country—the Wednesbury Wake bull-baiting of 1829. He says that on that occasion a great concourse attended, and all, "with the exception of the poor bull," seemed to thoroughly enjoy the proceedings; but that the authorities interfered, confiscated the bull, and committed the two ringleaders to Stafford gaol.

"Hundreds of bulldogs were around the inner ring (with their owners) all trying to break from their chains to get at the bull. The owners of the bull charged eightpence for each dog that baited the bull, about four or five minutes being allowed for the dog to run at him. When money got scarce with the owners of the dogs, and no baiting was going on, a few of them would go round the ring with their hats collecting pence until they had got sufficient to pay for the dogs to run at the bull. When they could not collect enough the stake was taken up and removed to another part of the town. There were three places in Wednesbury for them to pitch the stake—one in the Wednesbury Market Place, one at High Bullen, and the other at Bull Hole, near Wednesbury Church. By the time the Wake week was over the poor bull's face was a complete running mass, the wounds of the previous days being torn open and fresh ones made."

The same authority speaks of another bull being baited at the top of a lane fronting the "Queen's Head," at Handsworth, on the main road to West Bromwich, at which the stage-coach stopped so that the passengers might witness it. These sights happened every year during the four years the writer lived at Handsworth, which ended in 1822. In a more recent note he added a reminiscence which was truly characteristic of the time and place :—

"I have read somewhere that for the entertainment of the Rev. W. Gordon, the first minister at Christ Church, West Bromwich, it was intended either at the opening or consecration of the church (1829) to bait a bull. The animal was present, but the wise minister declined to support the event even by his presence. I am not sure, but I am under the impression that the bull was not baited."

As we shall see presently, it was quite in accordance with the sentiment of the time to associate a bull-baiting with a church celebration of this special nature.

Walsall, according to Mr. J. C. Tildesley, a local historian, had its sporting prowess celebrated in song :—

"There, in the jovial days of yore,
The mad bull weltered in his gore,
And 'bullots' trembled at his roar,
In the old days of Walsall.

A cock, a bull, a surly bear,
A cur tossed yelping in the air,
These were the frolics of the fair,
In the old days of Walsall."

The same writer goes on to speak of the sport as it was practised in the district, and says—

"In olden time it had its full share of bull-baiting, and in this neighbourhood it was that the renouned Jack Willets, the 'bullot,' who went over to Spain to finish his education in the art, used to lead forth to torture huge specimens of Taurus, gaily decked with coloured ribbons, amid the ringing cheers of an excited mob. Here, doubtless, too, as at Bilston, might be heard snatches of the rude ballad—

"Old 'Fancy Dick' from Wedgbury,
Came with his good dog 'Shot,'
But 'Billy Ball' didn't come at all,
For he had quite forgot."

This Jack Willets, the "bullot," was a notorious character who had served as a soldier in the Low Countries, and on his return to his native place had set about teaching his neighbours how to improve their methods in the ancient art of Bull-baiting. In a roving life, some of it spent in Spain, his experiences had led him to see how deficient the English were in appreciating the picturesque side of things; and he therefore determined to introduce into local Bull-baiting some of that display, some of that artistic colouring, which characterised Spanish bull-fighting.

After haranguing the people, and making active converts among his own cronies and personal associates, it was arranged to make the forthcoming Wake at Bilston, in the year of grace 1743, a red-letter festival that should long be remembered throughout the whole countryside.

Every accessory the parish possessed was pressed into

service. The town crier, dressed in a new uniform, which included a well-powdered wig and a silver-laced coat, led the procession which escorted the bull, gaily decked with ribbons and garlands, to the sacrificial stake. Then, leading the noble bull, was the redoubtable Jack himself, in the remnants of his old military uniform, and begirt with a formidable Spanish sword, as marshal, master of the ceremonies, and general manager of the whole proceedings. The band consisted of a wooden-legged fiddler and an asthmatical piper, supported by the clattering staves of the village Morrice-dancers ; the rear being brought up by all the rag-tag-and-bobtail attracted from the country for miles around.

According to the local historian the scene presented to the eye was of a striking character. In the centre of the circle stood the bovine gladiator looking sulkily around him at the host of circling faces, and especially at the savage owners of scarcely more savage bulldogs, who were stationed at intervals inside the ring ready to let loose their dogs on the signal for the onslaught being given. At the entrance to the ring stood Willets with his weapon drawn, which he flourished ever and anon to keep back the spectators from intruding inside the enclosure. Round about crowded the spectators, who, from the favourable nature of the ground, rose tier above tier, giving the scene somewhat the appearance of a Spanish arena. The preliminaries being completed, a man with a stentorian voice stepped into the centre of the ring, and gave the following notice: "All persons having dogs to enter must pay a fee of five shillings for such dog. Likewise, when the dogs are withdrawn, any person armed with this club (here the 'crier' flourishes a cudgel) may enter the ring, and whoever brings the bull on his knees will be entitled to a quarter of the animal."

The signal for the release of two of the dogs was then

given. The bull met them with his horns, and, at the first rush, threw one of them into the air, with his bowels torn out. Another dog took his place, and the two continued to lacerate the animal until one of them met the same fate. The people eagerly caught him as he fell, as though he were a child. Willets then stepped between the combatants, and pricked the bull with the point of the sword, which infuriated the animal until the foam streamed from his nostrils. One after another the dogs were disabled until "Shot," a dog whose fame is mentioned in local ballads of the time, was loosed, and in a few moments he had caught the bull by the nostrils. Willets, knowing that nothing would induce the dog to quit his hold, and fearful lest the sport should be too speedily ended, coolly severed the flesh with his sword, when the dog fell to the ground, still retaining between his teeth the trophy of his skill.

At this juncture the "crier" ordered the dogs to be withdrawn, and they were replaced by a noble specimen of humanity, armed with the club. Advancing towards the bull, who had regained some of his strength during the interval, the man hesitated for a time, as if undecided how to act. At last he raised his club deliberately, and then struck at the bull suddenly, in the hope of stunning him ; but the animal, fully alive to his danger, swerved quickly aside and returned as quickly, and thereby escaped the blow intended for him. Before the man could recover from the force of the effort, the bull caught him with one of his horns and threw him violently against the barriers. Another man now grasped the weapon, and at a blow broke off one of the animal's horns. He fell to the ground bellowing with pain, but rising again, gave one mighty tug in his desperate agony, which released him from the stake, and away he went, pell-mell through the crowd.

Then the air was rent by the shouts from a thousand throats.

> "'A lane! A lane!' was all the cry,
> As fast they ran away,
> Leaving Jack Willets there to die,
> Or live, as best he may."

The scene was now fearful in the extreme. Men trampled on women, women on children, and children on each other, in their frantic efforts to escape. The shouts and screams were loud and hideous; deep curses mingling freely with despairing cries. Jack Willets, of all the mob, remained cool. He leaped the barriers and waited his opportunity. The bull, however, faint with loss of blood, that streamed over his head and body, after making a few faint efforts to escape, fell to the earth, where he was soon despatched by Willets.

What need to describe the closing scenes of that day's events? The sale of the beef provided funds for the final revelries, an orgie of eating and drinking, such as even Bilston Wake never experienced before or has known since.

In the year 1802 a beautiful black bull was baited in Bilston, and was then sold to the Darlastonians, who, having baited it for the other days of the week, actually sold it to the Wednesbury sportsmen, who tortured it to death after a display of courage which should have earned for it a better fate.

In the neighbouring parish of Willenhall they have boasted a poetaster, one William Saunders, who has sung of the bovine battles waged there in the days of yore. The words of the ballad, it may be explained, are supposed to be those of the weathercock on the top of the church steeple, and run in this strain—

"Tho' Willnull then was fair to see
Her beauty but hid deformity;
Sensual lust and brutal spleen,
The harmony marr'd of that fair scene.
The sun one morning fair did rise
Turning the gray into golden skies.
The tip of my tail she turned to gold,
And burnished it bright for men to behold.
Beneath me lay a rabble crowd,
Of the hopeful young, and the aged bowed;
A stake is driven in the greensward fast,
And the bull is tied secure at last.
Shouts of men, and the bull's fierce roar,
The groans of the dog as he dies in his gore;
The shrieks of women, and the curses of men,
Beggars description by mortal pen.
What means that shriek so loud and shrill,
Turning the heart-blood cold and chill?
Why is the crowd fast flying away?
'The bull is loose!'—did I hear them say?
Yes, mad with passion, away he flies,
And with lightning speed in the air he hies
One of the men who had that day
Foremost been in the fierce melee.
As he falls to the earth with a sullen sound,
Shrieks, groans, and cries are heard around;
Then gathered they round with moisten'd eye,
Silently watching their comrade die.
Gently, gently, close the scene,
Men's natures are alike, I ween."

At Birmingham a notable bull-baiting took place in 1798 at the rear of the Salutation Inn, Snow Hill. This was the Chapel Wake held in commemoration of the building of St. Bartholomew's Chapel. The event was made memorable by the capture of the bull by the Birmingham Association—a voluntary militia formed of the respectable trading class during the Napoleonic scare —who marched to the attack with flags flying and drums beating. It was not till the bull had been pursued to Birmingham Heath that it was captured and brought back in triumph by the champions of law and order.

A plaintive ballad written in memory of this day's event had for its refrain :—

> "They broke up the Wake
> They stole the stake
> And they put the bull in the dungeon!"

—or "dunghill," as it was sung in the vernacular.

A remarkable incident is recorded as having occurred at a village on the other side of Birmingham. Whilst a bull-baiting was in progress at Sambourne, in Warwickshire, the bull, by some means or other, contrived to escape from the stake to which it was customary to chain the animal. Having been infuriated by the dogs, it charged furiously amongst the crowd of spectators, in which stood an elderly woman, who for many years had walked on crutches, owing to some complaint affecting her legs. In fear of injury and possible death, the people scattered in all directions, and the cripple, sharing the common terror, dropped her crutches and unconsciously joined in the flight. It was not until she had reached a place of safety that the woman realised that, by the shock, she had recovered the use of her legs. She lived for years afterwards, but never used the crutches again.

In 1828 two men were convicted at Birmingham by Mr. R. Spooner, under the Town Improvement Act, for celebrating Handsworth Wake by a bull-baiting at Little Hockley Pool. Although these culprits were sent to gaol for six weeks, no less than three bulls were at the same Wake baited in Handsworth, which was just outside the jurisdiction of the Birmingham authorities.

It is curious to note that the name of Mr. Spooner in this connection was preserved for half a century afterwards in a boys' game which was popular throughout the Black Country till about 1870. One boy played at being a bull, another at being his master, and all the rest were baiters. The first-named knelt down on the ground, taking care to tuck in his head and all tender parts of his body beneath the protection of his clothing; he held one end of a rope, and his master the other. The fun was to buffet the poor bull with caps and knotted kerchiefs, while the master, standing close to the bull, recited a child-rhyme, and then ran the length of the rope three times; after which any one of the baiters he could manage to touch had to become the bull. Of course, while he was trying to catch one within the length of his tether, the others would run up on the unguarded side and continue to baste the poor bull. The child-rhyme in question ran thus:—

"Hooner, hooner, hooner.
My name's Dick Spooner!
I've got a bull
Named John Bull—
If you won't bait him—
Why, I wull!"

Then with right good will he set the baiters a vigorous example of how they ought to defy his own authority.

It was thus the ancient pastime died away in the Black Country—reluctantly, as it were—with a mimic imitation of it as a sort of memorial to keep up the traditions of the fathers among the children.

Doubtless the practice was just as prevalent in other parts of the kingdom; the illustrations are drawn from this particular region in the Midlands simply because the local records here have been better kept. For example, in "Shropshire Folk Lore" it is related that many savage bull-baitings took place at Madeley Wakes, which were latterly celebrated chiefly at Ironbridge, the busy little town in the parish of Madeley, named from the proud achievement of the Quaker ironmasters of Colebrook Dale, who in 1799 spanned the Severn with a single arch of iron. This Wake was also held in October—viz., five weeks before Broseley Wakes (St. Leonard, November 6th), which again fell seven weeks before Christmas. The bull was baited three times on each of the three days, Monday, Tuesday, and Wednesday—first at the Horse Inn, Lincoln Hill; then in front of the Tontine Inn, at Ironbridge; and thirdly at Madeley Wood Green.

Reminders of its universal popularity are still to be met with in the tell-tale names of certain streets in a number of the older towns, as The Bull Ring, The Bull Stake, The High Bullen, The Bull Hole, The Bull Pit, and so on; even the historic Hoe at Plymouth had its Bull-hill.

Of bull-baitings in the Metropolis the chronicles which have been preserved of them alone would fill a volume. One of the most notorious spots was Hockley-in-the-Hole, in the unsavoury region of Clerkenwell, the frequenters of which are said to have been particularly nimble, when their favourite dogs were tossed into the air, in catching them on their shoulders, although after each encounter—

"Some stretched out in field lie dead; and some,
Dragging their entrails on, run howling home."

This is the public resort of which we read in Hudibras:—

"Just as it is in Hockley Hole
When Rose and Brindle fought the bull,
Some on the dogs will set their heart,
Some take the horrid champion's part.

When thus disposed, the rabble rout
Soon find occasion to fall out,
Thus fools and dogs, and bulls and bears,
Fall all together by the ears,
Whilst wiser men securely sit
And overlook the wrangling pit,
Keep silent tongues, no party take,
But view the sport the puppies make."

In those days there were certain individuals of the loafer type who followed up the baiting of bulls almost as a profession, going round from town to town with a bull, and taking care at least to miss no Monday or Tuesday—always "play days" in the good old times prior to the era of Factory Acts—without holding an exhibition in some Bull Ring or other.

Before quoting the contemporary record of this feature it may be necessary by way of preface to note, first, that Lichfield Greenhill Wake was one of the most popular and largely patronised institutions of its class; secondly, that Luke Saint was a well-known Wednesbury "character"—a sort of recognised semi-official parish jester; and thirdly, that although the ringleaders were convicted and punished, that very fact merely had the effect of elevating them into the position of heroes and martyrs, so low was the moral tone of the time. In fact the whole incident was worked up into a "ballad," the burden of which was—

"Success unto you, Wedgbury lads,
Wherever you may be,
Who took a Bull to Greenhill Wake
To stir up mirth and glee."

But here is the contemporary account of the affair as contained in the *Lichfield Mercury* of October, 1828 :—

"The cruel and disgraceful scenes at Greenhill Wakes on Monday and Tuesday nights, were the subject of investigation at the Town Hall of this city yesterday; and among the gentlemen who evinced their disapprobation of these barbarities, by attending to support by their presence the enactment of the Legislatures, were the Very Rev. the Dean of Lichfield, the Rev. the Chancellor of the diocese, the Rev. B. J. Proby, the Rev. H. White, the Rev. T. G. Parr, and others of the first consideration in the city. As we stated last week, the principal promoters of this brutal exhibition were strangers to this city. They belong, as we are informed, to a gang of wretches who purchase bulls and take them from place to place to be baited, and obtain considerable sums by their inhuman vocation. Their leader is a man of respectable appearance, named John Field. The plan appears to be for him to purchase a bull, and then nominally to give the ownership to one of his infamous followers, who are paid out of the money collected from the mob. In the present case a wretched-looking object called Luke Saint, who possessed scarcely a decent covering, stood forward as the ostensible owner of the animal. Sufficient evidence, however, was fortunately at hand for the conviction of his employer. These individuals, with Thomas Marsh, Joseph Love, Cornelius Foster, and Joseph Horton, all residents of Wednesbury and its neighbourhood, were clearly proved to have taken an active share in the disgusting amusement, and were fined 30s. each, with the cost of their apprehension, making the total penalty about £2 10s. each. George Bates, a woeful sample of humanity, who distinguished himself by a cool, unblushing confession of his cruelty, was fined 40s. and costs. John Wright, Henry Webb Davis, and Joseph Bird, were fined 20s. each and costs. As none of the defendants paid the fines, or offered sureties, they were all ordered into confinement until returns could be made to distress warrants; and in case of non-payment they will have to undergo three months' imprisonment. The Act under which the convictions took place is the General Turnpike Act 3, George IV. c. 126 by the 121st section, of which, persons baiting, or running for the purpose of baiting, any bull, &c., near the side of any highway, or in any exposed situation near thereto, to the annoyance of any passengers, &c., are liable to a penalty of not more than 40s. and costs.

It would almost appear that the parish—or at least some coterie of representative parishioners—sometimes had a proprietary interest in a bull, which would then be known as the "town bull." Darlaston once possessed a "town bull." An allusion to this parochial institution will be found in John Ford's play of *A Lady's Trial,* in which one of the characters named Benatzi says: "A soldier is in peace a mockery, a very town bull for laughter."

An anecdote is told of a famous black bull kept near Tettenhall, and which travelled a wide circuit in the Black Country. This was in the declining days of the sport, and it is said that after a tour of baiting, the canal around Wednesfield and Willenhall has been dotted for miles with dead dogs, the trophies of his prowess.

This same fierce brute was one Easter Monday announced for a baiting at Tettenhall; but the authorities seized the bull and locked it up in a stable.

In the darkness of the night, however, the owners lifted the stable door from its hinges, took the bull into Wolverhampton, intending to bait it there. Again the authorities intervened; whereupon a well-known lawyer of the town, usually known as "Tommy Wood," discovered that though it was illegal (under the Turnpike Act previously mentioned) to bait a bull in a street or public place, it was no offence at law to bait a bull on private property.

Acting on this knowledge, the use of a field was obtained at Cann Lane, and there the bull was baited in the presence of a great concourse of people. Among those accidentally present was the late Sir Rupert Kettle, who afterwards described the exhibition as "a loathsome and disgusting spectacle."

The practice of bull stealing was not unfrequently incidental to the following of this old pastime—such was the zest with which it was followed, such was the rivalry in it between neighbouring parishes. Mr. G. T. Lawley relates a good story of the Bloxwich bull being stolen on the eve of Bloxwich Wake by a gang of Bilston "bullots." When the Wake morning dawned there was no bull at Bloxwich; and the day was well worn away ere the place of its captivity was discovered. But by that time the Bilston men had had a day's sport out of it; whereupon the Bloxwich men in their resentment and the bitter rage of their disappointment, fell upon the Bilstonians, and a desperate encounter ensued.

In 1804 the Walsall bull-baiters made a raid on the Wednesbury bull which was awaiting torture in the stables of an inn near the Wake ground. However, the design was discovered by a belated reveller going home in the early hours of the morning; a band of defenders was rapidly collected from all the night taverns; the would-be thieves were trapped, and well cudgelled for their pains. But to add to the vexation of defeat the Walsall men were handed over to the Wednesbury constable, and had the mortification of sitting in the stocks all next day, and being jeered at by the stream of holiday-makers passing gaily along on their way to the bull-bait.

Thus the practice grew up in more recent times for two of the bullots to keep careful watch and guard over the bull all the night preceding the day appointed for the baiting—a precaution rendered necessary by the many attempts at bull stealing between rival townships.

Mention must be made of a famous town bull once possessed by Darlaston. It was blind; but so acute was its hearing, that by listening intently it could manage to escape the onslaught of a dog time after time.

As will have been gathered, this typical Old English sport was conducive to innumerable cruelties. Among the many barbarities of Bull-baiting which have not only been perpetrated but placed on permanent record, the tearing out of the bull's tongue, and the devouring of it by his canine tormentors, is but a small thing; the horrible laceration of the victim's mouth, nose, and neck into one bloody mass of pulped flesh was of too frequent occurrence to excite any particular notice.

It was an ordinary torment for the dogs to tear open and aggravate old and half-healed wounds; and it was no rare thing to attempt to liven up, to try to irritate to fitful fury, a bull already weakened and half-cowed by previous worryings. This was sought to be effected in a variety of brutal ways. Into the suffering creature's wounds might be poured salt, or pepper, or aquafortis; sometimes a number of "men" might be set to goad at him with sharp instruments, while a host of dogs were let loose upon him at the same time; he might be surrounded by a heap of straw which was set on fire to madden him with the flame and the smoke; or sometimes—this was invented as an ingenious novelty for one Oakengates Wake—boiling water might be poured into the ears of the wretched brute.

As examples of other and inconceivable cruelties which, though perhaps no less wanton, never received the sanction of custom, may be mentioned—the cutting off of the two fore hoofs to compel the bull to defend himself on the mangled stumps; and the hacking off of both horns in order to rivet on to the bleeding stumps an iron prong of a special form and dimension to satisfy the terms of a big wager. This last refinement of cruelty was devised to mark the celebration of one Rowley Regis Wake.

A case is on record which shows the depths of degradation into which frail humanity can descend when all the restraints, all the refining influences of education are virtually as absent as in an uncivilised community—which was practically the case among the lower orders in England prior to the establishment of the public elementary schools. A bull was to be baited at Toll End, a neglected region between Tipton and Wednesbury, and to add an element of novelty to the performance, either for a wager or by way of advertising the entertainment, one man undertook to "bait" and "pin" the bull himself; that is, to take the part of a dog, attack the bull, and seize the bovine muzzle between his teeth. Accordingly, he presented himself at the baiting, and faced his tethered antagonist with an undaunted front; but when this human monster rushed forward with exposed fangs to the attack, the nobler brute quickly lowered his head and gored him right through the neck. With his life's blood streaming forth, the man could only stagger away to fall dead a few yards off. Authentication is given to this story by adding the name of an eye-witness—Mr. Richard Stanton, of Horsley Heath.

As the men of ancient Lystra would have offered up "oxen with garlands" to St. Paul and St. Barnabas, so we may easily believe were the men of unregenerate Sedgley and Tipton ever prepared to sacrifice their lordly bulls to the sport they loved so well. In their devotion to this form of zoolatry, there were no lengths to which they were not prepared to go.

The fetishism of the bull-baiting cult in these two places was painfully in evidence during the cholera visitation of 1832. Though the pestilence was raging throughout the Black Country, devastating whole parishes at a time, the bull-baiters defied all the restraints of religion, all the dictates of right sentiment and good feeling; they everywhere with one consent positively declined to forego the annual Wake ceremonials at the bull-stake.

Local tradition tells how these rabid enthusiasts outraged the feelings of the bereaved and mourning inhabitants by leading through the death-haunted and half-deserted streets of a plague-stricken parish the bull they intended for the sacrificial dogs; the noble brute being decked out with ribbons and rosettes, accompanied by blaring and profane music, hailed by the wild and extravagant plaudits of half-drunken devotees. That these Bacchanalian processions were most frequently paraded on the Sabbath-day, and in one instance on the day specially set apart for prayer and humiliation, and while hundreds of other parishioners were prostrating themselves in the various places of worship, made the public indignation none the less intense.

Bearing these disgraceful facts in mind, due allowance will be made for the strong Sunday-school flavour which attaches to some of the anecdotes which have come down to us from that dire period of plague and pestilence.

It is said, for instance, that the Town Crier of Tipton, having been sent round to announce that the usual Wake carnival would not be abandoned, the cholera which had begun to subside in the parish, broke out again with redoubled virulence; and that the ringleader who had distinguished himself most in the bull-baiting orgie of the Saturday evening previous to the Wake Sunday, "before the Sabbath-day's sun was set was in eternity." The Rev. John Howells, in a sermon preached on the day appointed for prayer and fasting in Tipton, stated that "a man being informed that there would be no bull-baiting at Darlaston Wake, swore that he would have a bull-baiting in spite of God or the devil; but before the Wake arrived the cholera hurried him to the judgment-bar of that God whom he had so blasphemously defied. Then a party of bull-baiters, five in number, combined together to have a baiting in opposition to the measures that had been taken to prevent it. But God frustrated their designs; the cholera attacked the whole party, and not one remained to execute their wicked purpose." And similar tales of "judgments" falling on the principal promoters of the bloody sport in Bilston and other places have also been put into circulation for "the warning of other evil-doers."

About 1833 a protest against the brutal sports which amused our grandparents was made in a book, the object of which is unmistakably declared by the lengthy inscription on its title-page :—

"A SCRIPTURAL and MORAL CATECHISM designed chiefly to lead the minds of the Rising Generation to the LOVE and PRACTICE OF MERCY, and to expose the horrid nature and exceeding sinfulness of CRUELTY TO DUMB CREATURES. Illustrated by examples. With an Address to Ministers of Religion, Parents, Instructors of Youth, and Christians in General. Second Edition. Inscribed by Permission to Her Royal Highness the Princess Victoria by Abraham Smith, Master of St. Bartholomew's National School, Birmingham."

The work was published in Birmingham but Mr. Smith lived at Tipton at the time, and all his "glaring examples" of the prevalent cruelties are taken from Tipton, Sedgley, Willenhall, Rowley, and the neighbouring parishes of the South Staffordshire colliery district. Truly all of them must have been hateful towns to live in when their public streets, their most central thoroughfares, were regularly used for bull-baitings; exhibitions of demoniacal behaviour on the part of a shouting, cursing, violent rabble, to whose din and confusion must always be added the accompaniment of the yelping of a pack of dogs, the bellowing of an infuriated bull. The imagination almost fails to paint this kind of parochial pandemonium.

It really seems that these outrages against public sentiment in 1832, when the whole countryside was writhing under the Cholera scourge, had something to do with bringing to a successful termination all the efforts at suppression which had been going steadily forwards for years previously.

One of the earliest local efforts to put down the sport occurred in Wolverhampton, for when the Bill for lighting, cleaning, and paving the town was introduced into Parliament in the year 1777, a clause was inserted imposing a penalty of £5 upon all persons found guilty of bull- or bear-baiting. A second Bill for abolishing bull-baiting was introduced into the House of Commons in the year 1802, but this shared the fate of the former one. Still the friends of humanity agitated and tried by local means to put down the sport. In 1811 the Attorney-General was consulted, and he gave as his opinion that bull-baiting in the public highway, to the hindrance of business, was not at all tolerated by law, and that persons concerned therein were liable to indictment for a nuisance. The editor of the *Birmingham Gazette*, commenting upon this opinion, said: "The friends of humanity will rejoice at this decision, which we hope may operate as a check to the continuance of this barbarous and brutal sport."

The *Wolverhampton Chronicle* in December, 1827, stated—

> "An association has been lately formed (November 3, 1824) called 'The South Stafford Association for the Suppression of Bull-baiting,' the object of which is to put in force the existing laws against the cruel and unchristian practice within 12 miles of the town of Wednesbury. The clergy and principal inhabitants of West Bromwich and adjoining parishes are active members of the society, and we trust their exertions in an endeavour so praiseworthy may be attended with success."

But as yet the law was too weak to cope with the evil—in fact the Commons had, in 1802, thrown out a bill for the suppression of this degrading pastime, through the influence of Mr. William Windham. Mr. Windham, who moved the rejection of the Bill, said he thought the poor laboured under too many restraints in their amusements. In France and other countries they might dance at will, and see plays all night; but here, if a hop or a pantomime were announced, the magistrates were instantly in arms. It was, he contended, politic and prudent to encourage athletic exercises among the lower classes; and *if heads were occasionally broken in these contests, that was their affair.* There was a species of glory in these conflicts, as acceptable, perhaps, to the individual as that which was courted in the higher walks of life; and it was to be remembered, in the words of the poet, "that he who subdued the world might, under different circumstances, have been only the first wrestler on the green." He should be sorry if the breed of bulldogs were extinct—since the days of Augustus they were the symbol of the national character. There was no more cruelty in bull-baiting than in hare-hunting or the shooting of game. Mr. Canning supported Mr. Windham's arguments, and thought bull-baiting was a matter which should not be dealt with by the Legislature. Sir W. Pultenay, the author of the Bill, said the object of the Bill was to promote humanity. In Shropshire, to his knowledge, persons would assemble at a bull-baiting to the number of between 1,200 and 1,400, and the scenes were disgraceful and brutal. Sir Richard Hill confirmed this statement, and added that in Staffordshire the practice was a source of perpetual disturbance and of regret to the friends of humanity. Mr. Sheridan, the celebrated statesman and M.P. for Stafford, also supported the Bill, and alluded to Mr. Canning's remarks about bull-baiting in Spain, to which practice, he slily added, no doubt it was to be attributed that the valour of the Spaniards shone so eminently conspicuous above that of our British sailors. But there was an essential point of distinction between the bull-fights of Madrid and the bull-baiting in this country. In the former case it was the men who fought, not dogs—men who partook of the danger as well as the sport. In England the case was directly the reverse. Here the animal was fastened to a stake, and a pack of ferocious dogs let loose upon him; the human savages were only spectators, not actors. As to Mr. Windham's anxiety for preserving the amiable race of bulldogs, we must tell him, said Sheridan, that the bulldog was not an animal of an open and courageous nature. It was a sly, sulky animal, that bore a strong resemblance to certain political characters in this respect, that when once he fastens never lets go his hold, no more than certain placemen would let go their place while they could stick to it. After a lengthy debate the Bill was rejected. It was on this occasion that the following *jeu d'esprit* was written :—

"For dogs and hares
And bulls and bears
Let Pultenay still make laws,
For sure I be
That none but he
So well can plead their cause.

Of all the House,
Of man and mouse,
No one stands him before,
To represent
In Parliament
The brutes, for he's a boar (bore)."

In 1827 six men were convicted under Mr. Martin's Act—a piece of legislation for the prevention of cruelty to certain animals (1822)—in penalties of £5 each, for baiting a bull at West Bromwich in November of that year; they were committed to Stafford gaol for non-payment of the fines. Upon the advice of Counsel a writ of *Habeas Corpus* was applied for in the case of John Hill, one of the prisoners, and a rule was granted by Lord Tenterden and Mr. Justice Bayley. The rule was argued in December, 1827, before Mr. Justice Bayley; and after conferring with Mr. Justice Littledale, this rule was made absolute on the ground that the omission of the bull in this Act was an intentional omission!

In 1835 Parliament at last passed an effective Act to put a stop to Bull-baiting. This enactment distinctly forbade the keeping of any "house, pit, or other place for baiting or fighting any bull, bear, dog, or other animal."

But the practice died hard, and bull-baitings were held subsequent to this enactment; notably at Brierley Hill Wake (1835), Willenhall Wake (1836), Tipton Wake (1837), and at Bilston in 1838—for of such were the Saturnalian celebrations that for centuries had marked the annual recurrence of these local carnivals, to the utter demoralisation of the populace, and the blunting of the public conscience.

# XIX

## BULL-RUNNING

The Tutbury Celebration—A bull mutilated at the Abbey gate—To be taken before it escape across the river Dove—And afterwards baited—The Court of Minstrelsy—Concerned in this feudal fine—Custom altered to a contest between the youths of Staffordshire and Derbyshire—And finally abolished, 1778—The Stamford Celebration—Municipally managed—But also originated in a feudal grant—Spanish influences at Tutbury Castle—Little affinity between Bull-fighting and Bull-baiting—An English "bullot" who became a Bull-fighter—Attempted introduction of Bull-fighting into England—Smithfield Market "Bullock-hunting."

As Cock-throwing was a mediæval variant of Cock-fighting, so Bull-baiting had a mediæval counterpart in a sport known as Bull-running. It cannot be said that the pursuit of the last-named frolic was widely spread, Tutbury in Staffordshire having possessed an almost exclusive monopoly of it.

A description of the Minstrels' Bull-running at Tutbury may be fittingly given in the quaint language employed by an old county historian. It appears that in monastic times it was the custom "on the morrow of the Assumption"—that is to say, on the 16th of August—for the Prior of Tutbury to turn out a bull at the Abbey gate for the amusement of the minstrels who appear at one period to have formed a kind of Guild in that part of the country.

"As soon as the bull's horns are cut off, his ears cropt, his taile cut by the stumple, all his body smeared over with soap, and his nose blown full of beaten pepper—in short, being made as mad as 'tis possible for him to be—after solemn proclamation made by the Steward that all manner of persons give way to the bull, none being to come near him by forty foot, anyway to hinder the Minstrells, but to attend his or their own safeties, every one, at his perill; he is then forthwith turned out to them (anciently by the Prior, now by the Lord Devonshire or his Deputy) to be taken by them, and none other, within the county of Stafford between the time of his being turned out to them and the setting of the sun on the same day; which if they cannot doe, but the Bull escapes from them untaken, and gets over the river [Dove] into Derbyshire, he remains still my Lord Devonshire's Bull; but if the said Minstrells can take him, and hold him so long as to cut off but some small matter of his hair, and bring the same to the Mercat Cross in token they have taken him, the said Bull is then brought to the Bailiff's house in Tutbury, and there collar'd and roap'd and so brought to the Bull-ring in the high-street, and there baited with doggs, the first course being allotted for the King; the second for the honour of the town; and the third for the 'King of the Minstrells.' Which, after it is done, the said Minstrells are to have him for their owne, and may sell, or kill, and divide amongst them, according as they shal think good."

Here it will be observed there were the double barbarities of maddening the bull at the outset, added to the cruelty of baiting him at the finish.

The frame of mind which could mutilate a noble bull by cutting off its horns and its ears, and its tail to the very stump, and then fill its nostrils with pepper, all for what was termed "amusement," is not one to be envied. Of course the object was to make the creature "mad" —but the people who perpetrated such abominable cruelties could have been little short of mad themselves.

The actual "madness" of the scenes which characterised these barbarous celebrations has been described in an old ballad—

> "Before we came to it, we heard a strange shouting,
> And all that were in it looked madly!
> For some were a-bullback, and some dancing a morrice,
> And some singing 'Arthur O'Bradley.'"

The observance of the custom was connected with the privileges belonging to the ancient Guild of Minstrells, "legally founded and governed by laws," whose members were bound to be such "as fear God, are of good life and conversation, and have knowledge and skill in the practice of their art"—for it was recognised that among wandering musicians at that period there were to be found not a few "vagabonds and rogues."

The Guild, or "trade society," at Tutbury evidently became somewhat too powerful; so in the reign of Richard II. it had to be "constrained" by John of Gaunt (who was then feudal Lord of Tutbury) in Letters Patent "to do their services and minstrelsies in manner as belongs to them."

A court was anciently established to hear controversies, settle disputes, and at which defaulting minstrels were amerced; to elect officers, the chief of whom was called "the king of the minstrels." There was also held a "dyner," or feast, towards the charges of which the Prior had to contribute "XXXs."—and at which the Guild made merry with their "noise" or concert; and after the closing of the court the Prior delivered the bull as aforesaid, or gave the sum of "XVIIIs." in money. There were other ceremonies, including a procession on horseback of the "woodmaster" and all the keepers of Needwood Forest, with the minstrels two and two going on foot; a service in the church at which the minstrels played "duringe the offeringe tyme," the official contribution being a "bukk's head mayd in silver." The whole proceedings seem to have originated in some feudal tenure or privilege, and the resultant rendering of a service or payment of a fine in acknowledgment thereof.

This was the old-world method of observing the said custom; but in the course of time many alterations crept into the form of it. Thus in later times, after enjoying the indispensable dinner, the Minstrels went to the Abbey gate for the bull to be turned out to them, as of old.

Young men of Staffordshire and Derbyshire then contended, with cudgels a yard long, to drive the bull into their respective counties—a form of diversion scarcely less lacking in humanity than that of older times. The Bailiff of the Manor at this later period compounded with the king of the minstrels, giving the head of the Guild five nobles in money in lieu of his right to the bull; which animal was afterwards fattened at Hardwick to be given to the poor at Christmastide. Ultimately the custom was totally abolished (1778) by the Duke of Devonshire, at the special request of the inhabitants of Tutbury, on account of the outrages commonly committed on these occasions.

A practice so brutal in essence could not fail to deteriorate and to degrade those who kept it up. In course of time it came to pass that all the young men of the neighbourhood flocked to this festival in such numbers that the minstrels and their ancient privileges were practically lost sight of, and it was then that the day's function became a fierce contest between two contending mobs, representing Staffordshire and Derbyshire respectively.

But even in the earlier stages of its existence it is easy to see how the harmony of the minstrels gave way in the afternoon to the discord of a brutal sport; and how the white wands of sober officialdom were exchanged too readily for the murderous bludgeons of an infuriated faction.

An old play written in 1696, by William Sampson, and entitled *The Faire Maide of Clifton*, makes this allusion to the cruel sport for which Tutbury was so long famous—or infamous:—

> "He'll keep more stir with the Hobby Horse than
> He did with the pipers at Tedbury Bull-running."

The custom of Bull-running was also observed at Stamford, in Lincolnshire, but with a different origin and object. Six weeks before Christmas it was customary for the butchers of that town to provide the wildest bull they could find.

This animal was kept overnight by an alderman in an official stable, and early next morning proclamation was made by the Town Crier "that each one shut up their shop doores and gates, and that none upon payne of imprisonment offer to do any violence to strangers, for the preventing whereof a gard is appointed for the passing of travellers through the thoroughfare without hurt. That none have any iron upon their bull-clubs, or other staffe which they pursue the bull with."

Proclamation made, and all shutters being put up, the bull was turned loose by its official aldermanic custodian. "And then hivie-skivie, tag and rag, men and children, with all the dogs in the town" set upon the unfortunate beast like so many furies.

The origin of this Bull-running dated from the reign of John, when a butcher of the town having one day set his mastiff upon a bull, which also belonged to himself, the encounter of the two brutes so delighted the Earl

Warren, feudal lord of the town, who happened to be standing upon his castle walls overlooking the scene, that he afterwards gave the grazing meadows where the delectable fight occurred to be a common-land in perpetuity for the use and behoof of the butchers of the town, and in which they might keep their cattle till the time of slaughter. The only considerable condition imposed was that the butchers should provide a mad bull annually for the continuance of the sport which had been so much to the founder's taste.

An old ballad, called the "Stamford Bullard's Song," commenced :—

"Come all you bonny boys
  Who love to bait the bonny bull,
Who take delight in noise,
  And you shall have your belly-full,
On Stamford town's Bull-running Day
We'll show you such right gallant play, &c., &c."

As to the origin of the custom so far as Tutbury is concerned, it is believed to have been introduced there direct from Spain; for the practice dates from the time John of Gaunt held his Court at the Castle there, after his marriage with Constance, daughter of the King of Castile and Leon.

As to Bull-fighting, there is really little or no affinity or practical connection between the English custom of baiting the bull with dogs and the Spanish national sport of fighting that noble animal by armed men—as some writers have set themselves laboriously to prove.

There were certainly two well-known Black Country "bullots" who went to Spain and became bull-fighters there. The portrait (in oils) of one was on view at a small exhibition held at Wednesbury in 1899. This was one Henry Brittain, son of an inn-keeper in that town, who flourished in the first half of the nineteenth century.

This worthy was a well-known sportsman in the palmy days of the old Wednesbury bull-baitings; in the course of following his trade he was sent out to Spain to carry out some engineering work. While there he developed into a famous bull-fighter. There was nothing particularly new in this development. It is by no means improbable that Brittain was inspired to an emulation of the mighty deeds that local tradition had long ascribed to another Wednesbury man, who had flourished in Spain long before his days; for it is on trustworthy record that about the year 1743 one Jack Willets (said to have been born at Moxley, near Wednesbury, and whose name has been previously mentioned) after making a great reputation in British Bull-baiting circles, went to Spain for the set purpose of matching himself instead of his dogs to fight the bellicose bulls of Andalusia. In this enterprise he speedily made himself a name of great renown as the "English Bull-fighter," and as such was welcomed by the plaudits of every crowd that surrounded the arenas of Spain. Apparently Brittain was the legitimate successor of this Wednesbury bull-fighter—the second and last of his kind. The portrait exhibited was painted in London for his Black Country kinsmen during one of his few visits to England.

When it was sought to introduce an exhibition of bull-fighting at the Islington Agricultural Hall some years ago, the attempt was very quickly quashed. A matador and six other Spanish bull-fighters were charged with cruelty to a bull; the evidence showed that they not only teased the animal by means of scarlet cloaks, but approached the excited brute with darts in their hands, on the ends of which were fastened rosettes, which it was the object of the performer to place upon the animal, the surface of the rosette being covered with glue for that purpose. It was proved that the animal winced when thus probed with the point of the dart, and that in terror it tried to escape from the arena. The offenders being foreigners were, with characteristic British magnanimity, let off with a nominal fine; a promise being exacted that the offence should not be repeated.

Mention may not be omitted of an old custom formerly followed at Smithfield Market, and known as BULLOCK-HUNTING. This was evidently an imitation of a practice which once prevailed at Kingsbridge and other market towns in Devon, where the inhabitants frequently indulged themselves in the amusement of driving the bulls brought to market up and down the streets with dogs, "much" (as a local writer says) "to the disadvantage and against the will of the owners." However this may have been, it is also recorded that the choicest joints of bull beef when exhibited for sale were always recommended by the butchers as having been cut from the carcase of a baited beast.

# XX

## DOG-FIGHTING

The Black Country apprentice brought up with the dogs—When fighting was the order of the day—Cruelties of dog-breaking—Tasting the bitter aloes—A dog killed in a fight—Accorded funeral honours—Prevalence of Dog-fighting in Lancashire and Yorkshire—Recent police prosecutions—The dog-pit—Sir Horace Rumbold's dog—The Dudley breed—"Madman," the celebrated fighting dog—Dog mutilations to improve on nature—How a bull-terrier's ears are cropped—Cruelty of the process—Cutting out the hooked denx claw—Docking dogs' tails.

MR. LOUIS BECKE, the Australian novelist, has made use of the experiences of a Darlaston apprentice, in one of his novels entitled "Old Convict Days." From this it may be gathered that after Bull-baiting and Cock-fighting, the sport which ranked third in popular favour in those degenerate days was that of Dog-fighting.

The verisimilitude of the novelist's description points to a narrative of facts. The spelling of unfamiliar place-names and other discrepancies of the kind, indicate most palpably that the hero of the various incidents described in the novel was a real personage whose life's story had been taken down from dictation by the novelist.

The hero, who apparently was afterwards known in Australia as Bill Day, says he was born in the year 1819 at King's Norton, between the Maypole and the Pack Horse Inns. He goes on to say:—

"I was apprenticed early to one Toby Duffell, a gun-lock filer, and also a publican, living on the Leas, near the Ranter's Chapel, in Darlaston. Here my teaching was so varied that my attention to my proper work was much hindered. My master was an inveterate fancier and breeder of bull-dogs and game cocks. Bull-baiting on Monday and Cock-fighting on Tuesday was the order of the week."

The spelling of "Leas" should be "Leys," which is a Darlaston street-name to this day. Discrepancies of this kind are only confirmatory evidence. The public-house has been identified as the existing Dog Inn in Bilston Street.

The Darlaston apprentice continues to relate his experiences in this strain :—

"Young as I was—having to stand on a box at the vyce (*sic*) while using the file—these sports had a great attraction for me. I lost no opportunity of making myself acquainted with some of my master's 'dog-breaking' tricks. The old story is true that, to prove the tenacity and courage of a bull slut, first one front paw and then the other would be lopped off, and after each operation the unfortunate beast would be tried to see whether it would face the charge of a bull. This barbarity was practised upon beasts incapacitated from active service by loss of teeth. If they stood the test they were nursed and tended so as to be fit for breeding purposes. The most promising of a litter of pups had more care than their owner's children. As the pups grew up they were confined in a darkened place, and were not allowed to see anyone but my master or myself, or to be handled by any other person. So keen was Duffell about dog-fighting that before a match I have seen him run his tongue all over his opponent's animal to make sure that no bitter aloes, or other drug, had been applied to prevent his dog seizing and holding."

In a work published (1835) by the Birmingham schoolmaster who has been quoted previously, is to be found an anecdote which shows to what lengths the dog-fanciers of those days would go in their devotion to—their positive idolatry of—a canine hero that could prove himself invincible. The tale begins with a characteristic prelude which has nothing to do with the main story, and states that a man named Foster, of Darlaston, was killed in a quarrel over a cock-fight on the Whit Monday of 1834. Then it proceeds to say that on the following Wednesday a dog-fight took place for five pounds. After fighting an hour and a half one of the dogs dropped down dead. The other combatant survived his antagonist only half an hour, but of course that was sufficient to accredit him as the conqueror. His owner, it appears, proceeded at once to bury his lost champion in his garden, when another of the dog's admirers (doubtless a backer who had won money by the brute's indomitable pluck) wishing to do greater honour to these obsequies, exclaimed, "Wait a while! I'll run and fetch a Bible (*sic*) and read the Burial Service over him! It's sure no Christian ever deserved a-more than he did!"

In Lancashire and Yorkshire the practice of Dog-fighting was so prevalent at the commencement of the eighteenth century that we find complaints of it in the printed chronicles of the time. The biographer of the Rev. John Lees (1700), a worthy divine and eminent schoolmaster at Saddleworth, relates how his subject was unremitting in his efforts to suppress the evil—the good man was not content to warn his youthful pupils, but we are told he constantly used his persuasive powers on the adults of his flock, to induce them to give up a practice which was then the disgrace of the County Palatine and the district of the West Riding adjacent.

Of all the old-time but now forbidden sports, Dog-fighting seems to die the hardest.

Within recent years a case of permitting premises at Darlaston to be used for a dog-fight was tried at Wednesbury Police Court. About twenty men were present in a club-room while two dogs were "played" at each other by two men who held them by their hind legs. The police found a bucket of water, two sponges, a rag, and all the other paraphernalia. One of the bulldogs had its muzzle almost torn away; and the case was one of such unmitigated barbarity that the defendant was sentenced to two months' imprisonment with hard labour.

In another case tried in London, the scene of the encounter was a "pit" formed of strong boarding and fitted up in a room within the roof of a public-house. This pit was two feet deep and six feet square; it was lighted by two conveniently fixed oil lamps. In this case it proved that the defendants "handled" the two bull-terriers, during the progress of the struggle, blew in their faces to revive them, and at intervals dragged them apart to let them recover their breath. They were then set-to again. When one of the canine combatants was severely injured, the hat was handed round to make a collection on his behalf—or his master's. A collection was also made at the outset in lieu of a charge being made for admission. There were the usual officials, as time-keepers, stake-holders, and setters-on. In fact, every formality was complied with, and the circumstances fully warranted the imposition of the heavy penalty with which the offence was visited.

The dogs used in other cases which have been brought into court under the Act forbidding cruelty to animals have been bulldogs, bull-terriers, and cross-breeds, all formidable creatures in a fight. Not a few of such encounters resulted in the death of one or both antagonists.

Although Dog-fighting has long been illegal in the mother country, it is still practised in the Transvaal; bulldogs and bull-terriers are specially bred in and around Birmingham to be sent out to Johannesburg, Kimberley, and other large centres at the Cape, for the avowed purpose of fighting.

Wednesbury, or "Wedgbury" as it was once commonly called, was noted for the breeding of these dogs. "Bulldog tenacity" has become acknowledged as one of the national characteristics of an Englishman—a fact which accounts for the high admiration in which this breed has invariably been held.

It was the tenacity of these animals in "holding on" to the bull or the bear that first brought the breed into prominence in the realms of Sport. No better illustration of this characteristic propensity can be found than in the episode of a terrific fight between an English bulldog and the half-wild wolfdog, "White Fang," so vividly described in Mr. Jack London's new novel of that name.

Many tales have been told of their prowess, but none so full of all-round interest for the true dog-lover as one related in the "Recollections of Sir Horace Rumbold":—

> "Among the most faithful of his friends, this young diplomatist, while at the Court of Wurtemburg, regarded a bull-terrier, 'the flower of his species.' Ben, as he was named, was 'as much above the common level of dog-kind in pluck, sagacity, and devotion, as a Shakespeare or a Bayard above men.' He was of Staffordshire breed, speckless white, all but two lovely black patches over the eyes, so evenly traced as to seem painted. He had 'the chest of a bull, the sinews of a tiger, the heart of a lion, the gentleness of a lamb, and the most exquisite tapering tail.' Endowed with remarkable, original, and independent traits of character, his particular passion was for fighting with other dogs and exterminating wretched tabbies. His adventures were as extraordinary as those of his master. One day he nearly worried to death the plethoric Blenheim spaniel of Analia Stubenrauch, the actress, whose influence over his Wurtemberg Majesty was as salutary as that of Lola Montes was pernicious over his Royal neighbour at Bavaria. Unlike most bull-terriers, Ben was a great swimmer, and great was the adventure he had one day with a shark. At another time on board a ship he watched the man dropping the lead for a long time, and eventually could not resist the temptation of jumping in after the lead."

A Dudley variety of the fighting terrier had its organ

of smell of a flesh colour, and not of the normal black hue; hence any dog with this light-coloured kind of snout is now spoken of as being "Dudley nosed."

There was a Birmingham champion dog named "Madman" some sixty years ago, which became celebrated for the scientific way in which he vanquished every antagonist placed in front of him. He was a long-faced bull-terrier, and on one occasion fought for ten minutes inside a screen in front of a roaring fire, which was considered the most trying ordeal to which any fighting dog could be submitted.

This celebrated dog, and another noble brute of equal merit, named Old Victor, were the property of Mr. James Hinks, of Birmingham, who did more to improve the bull-terrier than any other breeder; in fact, all the good dogs of this breed at the present day derive their pedigree, either from Madman or from Old Victor—the latter strain being at the moment the more "fashionable."

While the tail of the fighting bull-terrier was allowed to grow to its natural length, its ears were generally cut to stand erect in two sharp points. This was supposed not only to smarten the appearance of the dog, but it was also a useful precaution for minimising the risk of its opponent's seizing and holding it by the ear.

It was a matter of reproach that till a very few years ago, notwithstanding the illegality of dog-fighting, the ear-cropping of these animals was not tabooed by the Bull-terrier Club, or the yet more powerful Kennel Club.

Hear the evidence of a writer in the *Pall Mall Gazette* who witnessed the agonising operations a bull-terrier had to undergo in preparation for the ordeal of the judging bench :—

"The terrier is eight months old, and practically full grown. Not by accident, but by design, have its ears been left uncut so long. Your real expert among bull-terrier professionals takes care never to clip his dog until the ears are properly formed and fully grown. Of course, the longer they are left the greater the agony; but what of that? That is not the fault of the cropper, or of the owner or breeder, is it? Blame nature, if anyone. Teething should also be well over before the scissors are applied, for it has a tendency to draw the ear out of shape.

"Usually there are half a dozen croppers and assistants in the croppers' room, who have come to take part in the operation or to enjoy the spectacle, but though between them they could, no doubt, hold down a couple of mastiffs, the victim will none the less have to be nicely bound. Observe how handy these fellows are in the work of seizing the terrier and binding him head and foot. They do it as easily as the young men at the stores tie up a parcel. First the muzzle is bound round and round with tape, then the front legs are pulled back against the sides and as much over the back as they will go, and bound; finally, the hind legs are stretched out and also tied together. Every possible precaution is taken against the animal writhing over much, under the shears which are immediately to be applied, because movement militates against a perfectly successful operation. The great object is to get the ears cut perfectly level, and to a fashionable shape. The jags and irregularities which may often be seen on the rims of terriers' ears show that the cropper has begun his work too soon, or that the victim has writhed considerably under the shears. The dog is laid on his back, held by one or two of the men, and out come the shears. These are very sharp, and, from their shape, evidently made for the express purpose of ear-cropping. Clip, clip, clip! They first cut down from the tip of the ears, and then upwards, in order that no ragged bits of flesh may be left. As the work proceeds—it will take the best part of an hour—the victim quivers incessantly, but, being so securely bound and held down, not sufficiently to interfere with the neat cropping of the ear; even more pathetic than these slight movements is the low moan, which is all the sound it can utter.

"One ear finished, the second is attacked. The cropper, being hideously proficient in his work, fits the cut-off portion of the ear to the second as a guide for the shears. In this way does he insure both being cut exactly in the same shape. While the shears open and close the chief cropper and his assistants and admirers chat sociably about things canine, and are apparently quite unconscious of the awful agony which the victim is going through; nor are they in the least inconvenienced by the flow of blood. They are no more affected by trifles of this character than those who lay low the ox at the shambles. Utterly degraded by the work which 'the fancy,' in

*G. Morland, Pinx.* *W. Nicholl, Sculp.*

EVENING, OR THE SPORTSMAN'S RETURN.

*To face page* 341

its imperious demand for terriers with cropped ears, sets them to accomplish, how can one expect any glimmering of humanity from these men who have sunk so much lower than the brutes on which they operate?

"Cropping is, of course, illegal, but the malefactors who are paid by the bull-terrier 'fancy' to do it, in probably nine hundred and ninety-nine cases out of a thousand are quite secure from all punishment. They take, of course, certain precautions: do not ply their horrid trade in the light of day, and as a rule see to it that no outsider shall witness the operation. It is rather a lucrative business, as much as a couple of guineas being sometimes paid for a really well-performed job. The cropper as a rule belongs to the lowest class among dog fanciers. He is a kind of hanger-on at dog-breeding establishments, ready to do any dirty work required to be done for a consideration."

The writer's words bear the impress of truth; but it must be confessed that many dog owners manage to perform the operation of cropping by a few dexterous cuts with an ordinary pair of scissors, and all is over in a very short time.

As the dog enters into the sports and pleasure pursuits of man more than any other creature, it may be permitted here to offer a few remarks on man's arbitrary treatment of him. Other breeds of dogs were cropped for no possible reason beyond the mere whim of fashion. Happily the practice is beginning to die out. Black-and-tan Terriers till quite recently were cropped for show purposes; and it is still thought that nature may be improved upon in this direction in the case of several other breeds.

Pointers and Fox Terriers were often subjected to another form of mutilation, though in this case with some show of reason. The removal of the "denx claw" is said to be necessitated to prevent the entanglement of this, most prominent of a dog's hooked nails, in brambles when in pursuit of game. The brindled bulldog often had a fifth claw to the hind foot—this was the old Wednesbury variety, so famous for its ferocity and obstinacy in retaining its grip. The colliers who bred these dogs always drew the incisor teeth to enable the dog to bite deeper.

While the brave fighting terrier was subjected to the horrible cruelty of "cropping," he was more fortunate than many of his cousins in escaping the cutting of his tail, or "docking," as it is called.

Fashion long decreed that unassisted Nature was quite incompetent to produce certain animal forms which could satisfy the ideals of the dog-fancier; hence the practice of docking the tails of certain breeds of dogs, for show and other purposes. Those most commonly docked are Fox Terriers, Irish Terriers, Airedale Terriers, and Spaniels. Two other kinds have been so regularly and persistently docked that fanciers have persuaded the public they are born tailless—these are the Dutch Schipperkes and the English Bobtail Sheepdogs. But both these breeds come into the world with the usual caudal appendages, which have to be removed artificially before it is possible to gull the public with the description "natural bobtails."

The docking of a dog's tail can never be necessary except in the case of that member being injured or diseased. The removal of the tail is impossible without the infliction of pain, the amount of suffering varying according to the age of the creature operated upon. If a pup is to be docked the operation should be performed at least before the dog is nine days old; while the vertebræ are cartilaginous the end joints may be removed with the infliction of very little pain, and so easily that a pinch of the finger and thumb will effect it. Old-fashioned fanciers were in the habit of biting off puppy dogs' tails with their teeth; it is more professional nowadays to remove the superfluous length of tail with the aid of special surgical instruments. However the operation may be performed there can be no doubt whatever that a cruelty is perpetrated if the pup has advanced towards maturity sufficiently for the cartilage to become ossified and the joints knitted together.

The Kennel Club and other societies for improving the breeds of dogs have at last decided to discourage all these forms of mutilation; though the Old English Sheepdog and the Schipperke, if born with tails, as they nearly always are, must still be docked for show purposes. Fox Terriers, Spaniels, and the others mentioned, are always docked; the argument in defence of the practice being that, they are such persistent tail-waggers, they would be likely to startle the game by doing this with long tails.

But no ear-cropping is now allowed; the Kennel Club rules—it is said, at the request of His Majesty Edward VII.—have made this a disqualification.

To the popularity of Dog-fighting as a sport eighty or a hundred years ago, numerous pertinent allusions will be found in Borrows' notable work, "Lavengro."

# XXI

## BEAR AND BADGER-BAITING, RAT-KILLING, ETC.

Bear-baiting requires a bear-pit—Antiquity of the sport—The great baiting by ban-dogs at Kenilworth in 1575—Whipping the Blind Bear—The Bear Garden at Southwark—Popularity of the Sunday baitings there—Under royal and noble patronage—Eighteenth-century popularity—Diversions at Hockley-in-the-Hole—The bear usually the victor—Impromptu baitings—Bear-baiting at Madeley Wakes (Salop) in 1825—Terms derived from the sport—Badger-baiting—The badger becoming rare—Sawing away the animal's jaw—A prosecution for badger-drawing—Long-faced bull-terriers bred for the sport—Rat-killing as a sport—Small terriers employed—A human worrier of rats—Rabbit Coursing—Objections to it as a spurious sport—Coursing interpreted to be "hunting" and not "baiting."

DOG-FIGHTING and Bull-baiting naturally led to the pitting of dogs against other beasts of fighting propensities. Hone's "Every-day Book" (vol. i. p. 492) records in 1825 the baiting of a lion at Warwick by six mastiffs, in which the handling of the animals was performed by one Samuel Wedgbury, who is described as a London breeder of dogs.

Bear-baiting differed from Bull-baiting inasmuch as the latter was practised in the open, the victim being merely tethered to a stake; but for the baiting of a bear it was necessary to provide a large sunken pit from which the animal could not possibly break loose.

As far back as the twelfth century the baiting of bulls and bears was a favourite holiday pastime in England, and it continued to be popular for many a day.

When Queen Mary visited her sister during her confinement at Hatfield House, the royal ladies were entertained with a grand baiting of bulls and bears, with which they declared themselves "right well contented."

Elizabeth took especial delight in seeing the courage of her English mastiffs pitted against the cunning of Ursa and the strength of Taurus. On May 25, 1559, the French "ambassadors were brought to court with music to dinner, and after a splendid dinner were entertained with the baiting of bears and bulls with English dogs. The queen's grace herself and the ambassadors stood in the gallery looking on the pastime till six at night."

The diplomatists were so gratified that her Majesty never failed to provide a similar show for any foreign visitors she wished to honour.

If Queen Elizabeth could take a womanly pleasure in the Bear-baiting provided for her in those famous festivities at Kenilworth, when on the sixth day there were turned loose no less than thirteen bears to fight indiscriminately a number of "ban dogs" (a kind of mastiff), we surely should feel no surprise in learning that such entertainments were often brought to a close by another inhuman diversion.

This was known as "Whipping the Blind Bear"; and as described it was "performed by five or six men standing circularly with whips, which they exercise upon him without mercy, as he cannot escape because of his chain. He defends himself with all his force and skill, throwing down all who come within the reach, and are not active enough to get out of it; on which occasions he frequently tears the whips out of their hands and breaks them."

The earliest theatres in London for the exhibition of dramatic performances were preceded by the old Bear

Gardens, round or octagonal buildings, the appearance of which has been made familiar to us by pictures of the Globe Theatre of Shakespeare's time, which was actually an adaptation of one of these gardens. Pictures of the Old Bear Garden at Bankside, Southwark, as it appeared in 1574, and again as it was in 1648, are given in Hone's "Table Book." They are mentioned at an earlier date by Cowley, who flourished in the reign of Henry VIII.:—

"What follie is this to keep with danger
A great mastive dog and fowle ouglie bear;
And to this end—to see them two fight
With terrible tearings, a ful ouglie sight.
And methinks those men are most fools of al
Whose store of money is but very smal,
And yet every Sunday they wil surely spend
One penny or two, the bearward's living to mend."

Stowe tells us that on the west bank there were "two bear gardens, the old and the new; places wherein were kept beares, bulls, and other beasts to be bayted; as also mastives in several kennels, nourished to bayt them. These bears and other beasts are kept in plots of ground, scaffolded about for the spectators to stand safe."

The buildings were circular and unroofed, evidently in humble imitation of the ancient Roman amphitheatre, the most popular exhibitions taking place on Sundays, when the price of admission was usually one halfpenny. Sometimes the grounds included a pond, which always adjoined the cage, to enable the bear to indulge in his propensity for bathing and washing.

This Old English pastime was patronised by the nobility for centuries, was long one of the delights of the vulgar, and almost as a matter of course it formed part of the entertainment provided for Queen Elizabeth at Kenilworth in 1575, as we have just seen. In the reign of James I. the Bear Garden was under Royal protection, and the Mastership of it made a patent place. One celebrated actor held the position, and the annual profits on the Garden were very large. James did not discourage the sport beyond forbidding it on Sunday.

Evelyn in his Diary, alluding to the Games and Diversions which characterised the Court of Charles II., records that on June 16, 1670, he visited the Bear Garden "where was Cock-fighting, with Dog-fighting, Bear and Bull-baiting, it being a famous day for butcherly sports."

In the times of the Commonwealth, however, it was a forbidden amusement. With the Restoration it revived, and Burton speaks of Bull and Bear-baiting as a pastime "in which our countrymen and citizens greatly delight and frequently use."

Bear-baiting rose into high favour again after the Restoration, though it had been so sternly checked by Parliament in 1642, and the practice did not wholly discontinue in London till 1750.

Any attempt on the part of the present writer to describe the kind of amusement provided two centuries ago at places of popular resort in the Metropolis would pale into utter insignificance before the glaring terms of a newspaper advertisement which is dated 1710. Here is the contemporary testimony as to the state of national morality in Christian England at that period :—

"AT THE BEAR GARDENS, HOCKLEY-IN-THE-HOLE.

"This is to give notice to all Gentlemen Gamesters and others, that on this present Monday is a match to be fought by two dogs, one from Newgate Market against one from Hony Lane Market, at a bull, for a guinea, to be spent. Five let-goes out of hand; which goes fairest and farthest in, wins all.

"Likewise a Green bull to be baited which was never baited before, and a bull to be turned loose, with fire-works all over him, also a mad ass to be baited.

"With a variety of bull-baiting and bear-baiting, and a dog to be drawn up with fire-works.

"To begin exactly at three of the clock."

Could the most insatiable human brute in the world wish for a greater variety of "sport" to his taste than was offered to him here? This was the place where crosses of ribbon were stuck on the foreheads of favourite bulldogs, and when these were removed and stuck on the bull's forehead the dog was cheered on till he had recovered the treasured decoration. In 1716 a "wild bull" was baited with fireworks, and the bears were baited to the death at this same delectable resort.

The poet Gay, in his "Trivia," says:—

"Experienced men, inured to city ways,
Need not the calendar to count their days.
When through the town, with slow and solemn air,
Led by the nostril walks the muzzled bear;
Behind him moves, majestically dull,
The pride of Hockley Hole, the surly bull.
Learn hence the periods of the week to name—
Mondays and Thursdays are the days of game."

Though the encounter between the bear and the mastiffs was always a ferocious attempt to "settle their ancient grudge *per duellum*," in the results the balance was usually in favour of the former. The bear had the advantage of size, superior strength, and the protection of a thickly furred skin which practically amounted to invulnerability. The contest was one of teeth against claws; there was an immense amount of "fending and prooving, with plucking and tugging, skratting and byting, by plain tooth and nayl"; in all of which, while it was possible for a dog to be torn, lacerated, and mangled, the bear seldom got a wound which "a month's licking would not recover." Of course the bear could

Drawn & Etched by .

THE COUNTRY SQUIRE *taking a peep at* CHARLEY'S THEATRE WEST *where the performers are of the Old School.*

London Published by Jones & Co May 22. 1821

ell as "pynch," and he could "wynde" while the battle raged with much "clawyng, torsing, and tumbling."

The noise and tumult, both in the pit and amongst the excited spectators, which accompanied these encounters, has given us that common and frequently used phrase, "As noisy as a bear-garden."

Besides the exhibitions which regularly took place in olden times in specially erected buildings, such as has been described as existing in the Metropolis, occasional Bear-baitings of an *al fresco* character were got up in many places till well into the nineteenth century. The main difficulty always to overcome was the provision of the bear. In a few of the larger towns a bear was kept on purpose; in other places the sport was dependent on the arrival of a travelling bear. Even a dancing bear, led about to the music of pipe and tabor, would sometimes be submitted to the trial of a baiting—if a sufficient amount of consideration money were forthcoming.

Illustrative of the state of feeling with regard to these practices, here is an extract from a collection of old Salopian lore, entitled "Spring in a Shropshire Abbey," by Lady Milnes Gaskell; it is a little shrivelled old man named Timothy Theobald who thus relates his Loppington experiences:—

"It war a royal do. For they had not only bulls, but bears. 'I mind me,' he continued, after a minute's hesitation, 'as it war in 1825. There were great rejoicin's. Folks druv and came in from all parts, and it war a grand celebration, and all given because the parson's daughter war marryin' a squire. But then parsons were parsons in those days. They rode, shot, and wrestled, besides preachin'. 'Tis true as there war a few what objected. Now at Madeley Wakes they had grand games on too. All the colliers, I've heard grandam say, used to come down and bet free and easy, like gentlemen born. Many was the time, I've heard 'em say, folks used to see the collier folk ranged down to make a lane like for the bull or bear to pass along. My word! as old Matt. Sykes used to say. It war a mighty question which looked best, beast or dog, for when 'twas a bull they only slipt one to a time. "One dog one bull," that war what they used to say to Madeley. Oakengates, I've heard say, war the last place where they baited the bull in Shropshire. And I allus say,' said old Timothy, with a spark of enthusiasm, 'that 'tis a mighty fine feather in the cap of that place, as it war the last as kept up the good old English sport.'"

One of the last known remnants of a Bear Cage in the Midlands disappeared at the demolition of Birchfield House, Handsworth, only a year or two ago.

To the literature of the sport we are indebted for several well-known words besides the term "bear-garden."

In Tudor times all great nobles had their "Bear-wards," and kept their herds of bears, which were regularly trained for the arena.

An old song entitled "The Jovial Bear Ward," goes in this strain:—

"Tho' it may seem rude
For me to intrude
With these my Bears by chance-a;
'T were sport for a king
If they could sing
As well as they can dance-a."

Also one who tended, or led the brute about, was called a bear-ward, or sometimes a bear-tender. Hone, in his "Table Book" (p. 596), tries to explain the term "Bear-tender." He opines that a children's game known as "Bear and Tenter," in which a boy crawls on the ground as a bear, and is protected from the buffets of all the other boys by one who acts as his tenter, had its origin, not in imitation of Bear-baiting, but from the practice of the scions of English noble families being always sent on the grand tour of Europe under the care of tutors, or "bear leaders." This is altogether an unsatisfactory explanation, and far less feasible than the one given on p. 312.

In the Black Country and the surrounding Midlands there was in common use, till about 1825, the word "berrod," a corruption of "bear-ward, just as one who regularly got up bull-baitings was termed a "bullot."

BADGER-BAITING could only be a popular sport when badgers were more abundant in the land than they are now. With the great increase of the population and the encroachments of humanity upon those solitudes which once formed the domain of the larger English beasts, the badger has become comparatively rare. It may surprise many to learn that the supply of badgers for the Birmingham baitings was regularly kept up as late as 1830 from Sutton Wood, not more than seven miles away from that populous city. One old sportsman recounts that on the night George IV. died he was engaged in Sutton Woods catching badgers; he remembers the occasion so well because of the terrific thunderstorm which marked the date, and which the folk afterward said was the manifestation of the imps below making merry at having captured the redoubtable George at last. Storm notwithstanding, a fine thirty-six pound badger was caught that night and exhibited next day at the Boar's Head Tavern, Perry Barr.

If the repeated employment of a captive badger necessitated the cutting away of a portion of its lower jaw, as has been asserted, it is perhaps as well there are now fewer badgers to maltreat.

One of the last reported cases of Badger-baiting occurred at Preston in 1897, when a prosecution took place for the offence.

The badger was kept in a box in a loft. When the dog was introduced, a lamp was fixed in such a manner that both the dog and the badger would be enabled to see each other in their encounter.

The box was about two feet square, covered at the top with wire netting. Attached to the box was a tunnel two or three yards long. When the dog was brought in, it made straight for the tunnel, and got into the cage where the badger was. Then began a desperate fight, the dog yelping, and the badger giving mouth too. Presently the dog succeeded in drawing the badger about half the length of the tunnel, when another severe tussle ensued. This resulted in the badger's getting a better hold, and dragging the dog back into the square box. Here the contest was resumed with redoubled fury, the dog yelping and the badger screaming. At last the owner of the dog, afraid for the life of his animal, opened the lid of the box, and lifted it out by the tail. The dog, however, would not loosen his hold of the badger till its mouth had been prised open with a poker. Both animals were shockingly bitten.

Other cases brought into court have disclosed the fact that some dogs are really quite expert in their badger-drawing. And it also appears to be not an uncommon thing for surreptitious Badger-baiting to be carried on under cover of ostensibly "trying dogs on a few rats."

Towards the end of the period in which Badger-drawing and Bull-baiting were looked upon as quite legitimate sports, a special breed of long-faced bull-terriers was developed for these purposes by a Birmingham fancier named Hinks. Among some of the champions of this class was the celebrated dog named "Madman," to which allusion has been made previously, which was ultimately sent abroad to provide sport for the officers of a certain British regiment on foreign service.

RAT-KILLING as a sport—not the rough-and-ready *al fresco* worryings enjoyed by taking a sharp little terrier along a brookside, or on a purposeful visit to a rick-yard —but as a set entertainment round a rat-pit, still lingers in some parts of the Birmingham and Black Country district. Very recently the following notice was exhibited in a tavern window :—

"At the —— Inn, Oldbury, a rat-killing Leger will take place on Saturday, November 1, when the proprietor will give £1 10s. if there are ten dogs at 2s. 6d. each. If over ten dogs all money added. Heats, the best of three ; final, the best of five."

The smaller the dog that can kill the greatest number of rats in the shortest time, the more highly prized is the canine conqueror ; a tiny terrier may be worth more than its weight in gold.

The conditions of a match are generally "rats for pounds" (as it is expressed) ; that is to say, a dog weighing nine pounds is taken as the standard, and set the task of killing three rats within one minute. This is the time limit usually in vogue, and the dog accomplishing the task in the shortest time is adjudged the winner.

Any competitor weighing only so little as one ounce above that standard gets an extra rat to finish off ; for in matching the accepted scale runs in this wise : A dog any weight up to nine pounds must have three rats to kill ; one over nine and up to twelve pounds, four rats ; one over twelve and up to fifteen pounds, five rats ; and so on, the allowance being one rat for every three pounds weight of the dog.

The contests take place in a rat-pit, which is a kind of circular cage without top or bottom, some three or four feet in diameter, and nearly the same in height. The pit is constructed of thin iron bars, placed vertically about an inch apart ; it can be placed on the floor of any apartment in which a match is to be brought off, the spectators generally sitting or standing around, as in a circus or cock-pit.

The breed of dog most commonly employed is a cross between a Fox Terrier and a Bull Terrier—a combination which gives the alertness of the one and the determination of the other, in an animal possessing a wide mouth with strong jaws.

Some famous dogs have been pitted with as many as thirty, forty, or even a hundred rats, and matched against time to kill the lot. It is seldom that a dog escapes without a nasty bite or two from the vicious rodents. Should any of the caged victims try to escape from their furious assailant, the official in charge who "plays" the animals, is armed with a short stick with which to knock them back again as they climb the bars.

Even Rat-killing, like every other pastime into which an element of bloodthirstiness enters, and the fascination of which is contained in the spirit of the invitation "to go out and kill something," has proved itself susceptible of degradation. Some brutalised specimens of humanity have not disdained to put themselves on the level of snapping, snarling dogs, in emulation of their inbred rat-killing propensities. Among "men" of this type was a Birmingham character called "Blewey," who frequently backed himself to kill rats faster than a terrier dog. The rats were tied to stakes on a table, and this worthy gained great fame for himself by seizing them with his teeth and breaking their backs. The hostelry which acquired distinction in this particular line was The Jim Crow Inn, Hill Street.

Little objection can be taken to Coursing where a strong hare has a free run for his life in the open. The speed and dexterity of the greyhound are pitted against the swiftness and doubling of the hare. And when the quarry is at last overtaken the *coup de grace* is quickly and mercifully given; poor puss is caught across the back in the long and powerful jaws of the hound, the leverage of them being sufficient to give a crushing "snap" that stops the heart action almost instantaneously.

There are at least two objections to RABBIT COURSING, both of them weighty and amply sufficient. First, little Bunny is by far too weak to stand the strain of a prolonged chase—for does he ever, in his native warren, stray too far away from his bolting-hole? And secondly, this modern form of sport is almost invariably conducted within closed areas, under such conditions that the doomed rabbit is always denied the fair play of "a race for life." Often, too, the hounds used in these cheaper coursing matches are inferior, both in strength of jaw and dexterity of "kill," to the pure-bred greyhound.

However, if the rabbits coursed are of a "wild" nature, no offence against the law (12 & 13 Vic. cap. 92) is committed; it is not "baiting" within the meaning of the Act. At the present time hope runs high that legislation will soon make Rabbit Coursing as obsolete as Bull-baiting.

The R.S.P.C.A. has always allowed that Coursing is "hunting" and not "baiting." Baiting implies some kind of antagonism, or resistance, or retaliation. If the animal baited be not combative enough to return the menace or attack of the animal with which it is baited, close with it, and fight, there is no inducement to engage in the sport of baiting.

A spiritless, frightened animal, which runs away on the approach of an enemy is not "baited," but pursued, or "hunted."

The same views are adopted with regard to Ratting. The rats killed in a Rat-pit by terriers nearly always fly from their antagonist. They are most certainly in a "wild" state. And further, they are vermin, therefore attainted as being destructive of human property.

Rat-killing matches, being usually promoted by "sportsmen" who have lost their sense of fair play, are conducted amidst surroundings that must, almost of necessity, be of a debasing character; for their concomitants are invariably cruelty, gambling, and vile language; so that taken altogether they cannot but be regarded as an insult to our morality.

The truest sportsman is the tenderest lover of animals; he may kill them, but he never hurts them. Also he is of a fibre too straightforward and too honourable to take a mean advantage, either of man or of animal. Often enough the degradation of sport begins when the mere lust for blood is allowed to supersede the healthy pursuit of game; as, when it artificialises the hunting instincts of primitive man—a heritage of itself by no means derogatory to our primeval ancestors—and produces such bastard forms of it as the wholesale butchery of hand-reared pheasants, or the worrying to death of timorous little conies, and the other effete developments of modern so-called "Sport."

It has been well said by an Eastern poet, Omar Khayyam, that Sport tends to bring the nations together, and in the cosmopolitan brotherhood thus cemented every English sportsman may turn to another great man of the East and find his prototype, his worthiest model, in one whose manly prowess in the field is not lightly commended—in Nimrod of old, of whom it is said in those sonorous words of our English Bible: "He was a mighty hunter before the Lord."

# Index

www.ingramcontent.com/pod-product-compliance
Lightning Source LLC
LaVergne TN
LVHW050914080826
845145LV00001B/85

* 9 7 8 1 8 4 3 4 2 8 5 3 4 *